MUCH ADO About KEANU

A CRITICAL REEVES THEORY

SEZIN DEVI KOEHLER

CHICAGO
REVIEW
PRESS

Published by Chicago Review Press Incorporated
814 North Franklin Street
Chicago, Illinois 60610
ISBN 978-0-913705-22-3

Library of Congress Control Number: 2025930286

Portions of this book have previously appeared in articles published by the author in *Black Girl Nerds*.

Interior design: Nord Compo

Printed in the United States of America
5 4 3 2 1

For River Phoenix

CONTENTS

ACKNOWLEDGMENTS

As Keanu Reeves's Batman says in *DC League of Super-Pets*, I work alone. Except for . . .

My GoFundMe superhero major donors who helped keep me insured and cover my many medical bills, from botched carpal tunnel surgery to elbow reconstruction surgery, all while I worked to finish this book: *Candice Dayoan. *Erin Archuleta. *Fester MacKrell, Liam Newman, and Ripley Newman. *Fedora Saraos Schooler. *Elspeth Stewart. *Christina Brzustoski and Sofya Stonger. *Lisa Tegethoff. *Marian Allen. *Susan Vollenweider. *Elizabeth Frederick. *Sarah Groshell. *Joe Silber. *Bryan Jury. Nicole Drake. Nadra Kareem. Seema Patel. Rebecca Brown. Angela Kang. Tracey Thorpe. Sara Devens. Missy. Veera Lapinkoski. Laura Kampmeyer Jaeggi. Kerry Ruby. Azline Robinson. David Alford. Kirsten Westby. Tim Sell. Anonymous times five. The *s are for repeat contributors whose generosity saved my left arm.

And more GoFundMe donors who pitched in multiple times during the course of getting this book to press: Victoria Moreno-Jackson. Kaylea Smith. Scarlett Harris. Rachel Price. KJ Harrad. Angela Tupper. Katie Dutch. Rae Recher-Deslich. Aimie Billon. Anonymous times four.

And the PEN America U.S. Writers Aid Initiative for their medical emergency writer's grant assistance. And the financial support of Alan "Buddy" Koehler, who was so excited about my first traditionally published book and would have been thrilled to see his family name in bookstores and around the world.

And Alicia Sparrow, the intrepid editor who originally acquired this book and helped me develop the proposal and concept. And the team at Chicago Review Press who took a chance on publishing my nerdy opus—especially my editor Devon Freeny, whose attention to detail is unparalleled and whose insights made this book so much more awesome.

And my best Florida friend and neighbor Ginny Sitar, and her husband Gary, whose home (and puppies) were my sanctuary over the first three years it took to bring this book to life.

And my best sister-friend Rebecca Castle and my nephew Diego, for their unconditional love and kindness that kept me going through way too many obstacles, in whose delightful Bay Area Victorian I finally finished this tribute to Keanu Reeves.

And my mentor Abeer Hoque, who never stopped encouraging and believing in me, and whose faith helped me manifest the work you're about to read. And Tania De Rozario, whose virtual write-in group was where I developed chapters and wrote the first drafts in community. And Kelly Glass, Liv Monahan, and Jonita Davis from the Pitch Party chat group where I shared my early outlines and brainstorms.

And my healers, who helped with body and soul crises over the course of writing: Tamara Jefferies. Dr. Wolfson and Hernan. My occupational and physiotherapists Cindy, Jennie, Sedrina, Cameron, Yasmin, Darlene, Mark, Brianna, Carly, Danielle, and Sheilla. Jamila Nichole. And Lojo Washington and Sarah from Queen of Sheeba, West Palm Beach, for nourishing me with the best Ethiopian food in the world as I celebrated every step of this book's journey.

And my brilliant research helpers: Emily Sedaka. Brennan Moline. David Jon Fuller. Ben Raphael Sher. Karin Louise Espejo Hermes. Simon Bacon. Allison Moon. Janet Brennan Croft. Erin Giannini. Josh Samuels. Rodney Turner. Alyssa Barton. Madeline Potter. Sisheng Chris Zhang. Samuel Paulson. Emily Lanigan.

And the folks I haven't mentioned already who were indispensable to creating this book: My nephews Elijah and TJ Moten. Paula Ashe. Danielle Haspel. Hilda Muñoz. Cornelia Almásy-Biedermann. Nina Kessler. Heidi Rini Armstrong. Sarah Astarte. Beth Winegarner. Kirsten Kempfer. Agnes

Barton-Sabo. Jessika Bolton. Shawna Sunrise. Miles Blanton. Nina Asay. Rose Margaret Deniz. Meredith Lenore. Jhilya Mayas. Karen Singer. Kay Wilde. Sheila O'Daniel and John Schonder. Monica Bell Sloan.

And the folks who played the soundtrack of my post-writing hours: Bret Domrose, Rob Mailhouse, and Keanu himself of Dogstar. RuPaul Charles. The 1st Wave DJs on SiriusXM, including Marky Ramone, Richard Blade, Swedish Egil, Matt Sebastian, Belinda Carlisle, Billy Idol, and more.

And in memoriam of the people I and my community wish were still here: Wendy Soltero. Buddy Koehler. Molly and Dixie Sitar. Grampa Tony and Valerie Black Feather. Shari Kessler. Brenda and Reid Scott. Jon Stonger. Bob "Roberto" Frey. Lola Thompson. Chris Stander. Sarah May. Alyson Mead. Valerie Thomas. Garvard Good Plume. Clifford White Eyes. Allison Dewart. Thorfeld MacKrell. Dottie Rapp. Galen Stagner. Bruce H. Kunert. Merv Singer. Mark Stewart. Mariposa Ramos Fronhofer. Peter Hamilton Stewart. Tony Oakley. Aftab Hasnain. Goulet Billon.

And finally, you for reading this book. Thank *you*.

INTRODUCTION

Always Be My Keanu

IN THE SUMMER OF 2021, as I sat miserable in my house with both hands in braces, wondering whether I'd ever be able to write pain-free again, this book came to me like an emissary of joy. Earlier that year my left hand had been accidentally smashed in a door, and I spent the rest of 2021 with my orthopedist trying to figure out if a microfracture in my wrist was the source of the unbearable pain. Turns out, it was nerve damage from a year's worth of undiagnosed carpal tunnel syndrome along with intersection syndrome. Doctor's orders were no computer time. I had to find other ways to keep my mind and spirit occupied. Keanu Reeves is a performer whose work I've loved since I first laid eyes on him in *The Brotherhood of Justice*, back in 1987 when I was just eight years old. At forty-two, I found myself taking new comfort in watching Keanu movies on loops as my shredded hands slowly mended. Keanu has the power to bring a smile to my soul no matter how bad I'm feeling, and during the course of my six-month convalescence I often asked my friends to send Keanu pics and memes to cheer me up.

As I meditated on what I would want to write when I recovered, I discovered nobody had published an in-depth exploration of Keanu's artistic output. And I might be the first multiracial, nomadic Asian American woman, whose upbringing mirrored Keanu's in many ways, to deep-dive into Reeves's work. I wrote the first drafts of this book's outline with just two fingers on my phone. As I endured months of physiotherapy and steroid injections into my wrists, this project became my motivation for healing. And with every Keanu film I rewatched, another chapter was born. My now-chronic hand injuries mean I can only write fifteen hundred words at the computer at a time, and that's how I eventually created this book: slowly, thoughtfully, and always with love and respect for the incomparable Keanu Reeves.

I have broken this book into three parts, each centered on a significant card of the tarot, an archetypal language of human personality and behavior. On one hand these cards symbolize the archetypal nature of recurring motifs in Keanu Reeves's own work. But they are also references to the cards employed by a psychic Cate Blanchett in Reeves's southern gothic film *The Gift*, and the deck used to set terms for John's duel with the High Table in *John Wick: Chapter 4*. We begin our hero's journey with "The Emperor," a major arcana tarot card symbolizing a great public figure who many admire and respect, as I deep dive into *Point Break, John Wick*, and analyses of race and gender in Reeves's films and television appearances. In "The Devil," I'll guide you through the darker corners of Reeves's film catalog, discussing issues of gender-based violence, the myth of the American Dream, the perils of technology, and even a discussion of on- and off-screen smoking. By "The World," we emerge from the darkness of the underworld into the broader sociocultural reaches of Reeves's work, discussing queer theory, history, comedy, philosophy, and even a reconsideration of Keanu's critics' worst-of picks.

Our phone booth has just arrived, so let's hop on in. Ready, dudes? Away we go.

PART I

THE EMPEROR

IN THE TAROT, the Emperor represents power and control through the image of a man in a position of leadership or authority, either inherited or earned. When a reader pulls tarot cards, they usually appear face up—in their positive aspect. The Emperor revealed in an upright position is a benevolent ruler who is beloved and respected. He is an equal to his Empress, and their union brings balance and order. However, the Emperor reversed—or in an upside-down position—is a despot who puts himself first and will stop at nothing to get what he, and he alone, wants at the cost of anyone who gets in his way. From Johnny Utah to John Wick, Keanu Reeves's work embodies the best—and sometimes worst—of the Emperor.

1

WHAT'S SO GREAT ABOUT KEANU?

Reeves in the Collective Consciousness

IN *ALWAYS BE MY MAYBE* (2019), Sasha Tran (Ali Wong) stumbles over the question posed by her jealous friend Marcus (Randall Park) about her unexpected celebrity love interest: *What is so great about Keanu Reeves?* Her desperate response is "He was the greatest North American box office draw of the '90s and early 2000s!" This might be true, but Keanu is far more than that.

According to one scientific study, everyone likes Keanu Reeves.[1] To establish a baseline for a 2020 thesis on exhaustivity—"the meaning of 'all-ness'"—University of Groningen Faculty of Science and Engineering student Robin Heiminge used the statement "All people like Keanu Reeves." Heiminge explains, "In this interpretation the entire set of people, exhaustively (all, without exception) like Keanu Reeves. That is to say, there exists no such person that does not like Keanu Reeves." While this might not be 100 percent true, there are very few other actors so universally well liked that they could safely set this baseline.

Thanks to his prolific movie career (seventy-eight movies at last count) and endearing real-life persona, Keanu Reeves has become the

3

universal screen saver of pop culture. Even if you aren't following a Keanu fan account on Twitter/X or Instagram or a Keanu-related group on Facebook, nobody can go a few days without some reference to Keanu or his movies popping up. He is the Emperor, Keanu Reeves ruling as both actor and person.

As a known Keanu devotee in all my various personal and professional circles, I have weeks when I'll be getting tagged hourly across social media with the newest Keanu meme or news story making the rounds. Friends in my DMs send me old Keanu photos as they surface again online, my favorite being the ones I've never seen before. Sometimes a colleague e-mails me a snapshot from behind the scenes of one of Keanu's many upcoming projects or a note about a TV show or movie they watched with a Keanu reference they suspect I'll appreciate. They are never wrong.

Because Keanu Reeves is more than just cultural wallpaper. He's the opposite of the old Gertrude Stein quote: there is *a lot* of there there. And for the longest time, I seemed to be the only person I knew who was critically engaging with all of Keanu's fundamental *thereness*. I was often met with ridicule when I'd make the claim that Keanu Reeves is a fucking fantastic actor. Or white folks would argue with me about Keanu being a person of color. People in general would reduce Keanu to his most basic on-screen form: to them he's Ted "Theodore" Logan of *Bill & Ted's Excellent Adventure* fame, a vacuous himbo surfer dude who speaks only in monosyllables.

There were others who saw past the facade. Since as early as 1994, college courses have been taught about aspects of Reeves's on- and off-screen personas.[2] In 2008, fringe website Whoa Is (Not) Me was founded for the specific purpose of "defending Keanu and his acting against those who would besmirch his fine name."[3] And Keanu's *Neon Demon* director Nicolas Winding Refn praised him to *Vulture* in 2015: "The thing about him which is so unique is that he's the only movie star I can think of that actually transcends generations. Every ten years, a new generation rediscovers him in their own way. I don't know anyone else who has done that."[4] (Here's something that's about to blow your mind when it comes to Keanu Reeves's reputation as the poster boy—often literally—for Generation X: Reeves was born in 1964, one year shy of being a member of this cohort. Which means? Yup. Keanu Reeves is a tail-end boomer. I'll give y'all a sec to process this paradigm-shifting information.)

Then in 2016 came the extraordinary love letter "The Grace of Keanu Reeves," in which culture critic Angelica Jade Bastién legitimized Reeves as a good actor, actually, helping remove the mainstream media's invisibility cloak around Keanu's genre-spanning talent.[5] As a result, many other Keanu devotees who also happened to be writers and film critics started emerging from the woodwork to explore their own nuanced perspectives on and deep love and respect for the performer. Like the *Observer*'s Film Crit Hulk, whose 2018 think piece laid out new evidence that Keanu Reeves is a talented actor.[6]

By 2019, the first crop of books about Keanu Reeves began hitting the shelves, including Marisa Polansky's hybrid comic *If Keanu Were Your Boyfriend: The Man, the Myth, the Whoa!*; Larissa Zageris and Kitty Curran's tongue-in-cheek essay collection *For Your Consideration: Keanu Reeves*; James King's 2020 comedic philosophy text *Be More Keanu*; and Chris Barsanti's *What Would Keanu Do? Personal Philosophy and Awe-Inspiring Advice from the Patron Saint of Whoa*. August 2020 saw the release of the first straightforward bio of the actor, *Keanu Reeves' Excellent Adventure: An Unauthorized Biography*, which was unauthorized for a reason: the book is filled with typos, factual inaccuracies, and poor sourcing. It also whitewashes Keanu's identity—something that, in fact, almost all of these new titles are guilty of (more on this in chapters 5 and 6).

Today, there are a collective sixty-four hundred results and counting for Reeves through academic search engines Sage, JSTOR, and Google Scholar. *The Journal of Celebrity Studies* has entire pages of their catalog dedicated to him.[7] Their offerings includes a piece by Renée Middlemost published in 2022, "The Incredible, Ageless Reeves: Aging Celebrity, Aging Fans, and Nostalgia," that strangely reads like an obituary when I can easily argue Keanu Reeves is as much in his prime right now as he was back in the 1980s.[8] Maybe even more so, as Keanu's often inscrutable interviews reveal just enough of him to fuel the zeitgeist while maintaining his privacy. Because of this, there seems to be a kind of quantum physics of Keanu. He is everywhere, all around us, in human and character form. But do we really know him?

It doesn't seem to matter. The *Journal of Celebrity Studies* even titled the introduction to their Keanu-themed special issue "Keanu Reeves as Palimpsest"—a palimpsest being a reused item of which the original remains in trace form. Reeves himself is an object being reinscribed and reinterpreted by all who happily look upon him.[9]

Amid all this renewed attention to Keanu as an icon and interest in him as a person, his cachet as pop culture's universal screen saver has continued to grow, steady as an oak tree in the background of all our lives. The Emperor of our hearts. References to his many movies, his laid-back real-life persona, and his meme-able public statements continue to proliferate. Keanu was first dubbed the internet's boyfriend, and then a god of cyberspace.[10] The world's parasocial relationship with the man has taken on a life of its own.[11]

And the multitude of Keanu references in other media are as plentiful as the army of Mr. Smiths in *The Matrix Revolutions*. When I began researching this book, I asked my extensive network for mentions of Keanu in general pop culture, and while everyone knew there must be many, nobody could think of any off the top of their head other than the obvious examples I'd already offered (for instance, his off-screen presence in 2003's *Lost In Translation* as Anna Faris's costar in an imaginary kung fu movie filming in Japan). I had to use targeted keywords to find the many examples that follow, which is rather weird: mentions of Keanu are ubiquitous, yet people blank at recalling specific examples. Keanu is oxygen—always present and easy to take for granted, but undeniably essential. He is so omnipresent that there is an entire website dedicated to the question of whether Keanu might be an immortal.[12] You'd be hard pressed to find another movie actor for whom references to their life and work across the pop culture spectrum are as expansive—or, more importantly, loving—as Keanu Reeves.

"Wake Up, Neo"

Let's start with Keanu's most quoted and referenced work: *The Matrix*. I would argue that just about every "Whoa" uttered on-screen since 1999 has come across like a reference to Reeves's Neo in the original *Matrix* watching Morpheus (Laurence Fishburne) make his impossible jump across two building roofs. That's how thoroughly Keanu left his mark with just one perfectly uttered word.

Reeves's work in this film resonates across generations and around the world. In 2019's *Good Boys*, then twelve-year-old actor Jacob Tremblay said he was inspired by the scene "when Neo is shooting the guns and doing the slow-motion flips" for his character's paintball fight sequence.[13] *The Matrix* was nearly than twice the kid's age and he was using it for acting reference, speaking to the movie's huge and continuous draw all these years later. And on *The Matrix*'s twentieth birthday, India's News18 collected five Bollywood moments borrowed from the film, including a scene where a character dodges spit the way Neo dodged bullets, and an homage to Neo's other monosyllable moment, when he whispers "No" and freezes a hail of gunfire from Mr. Smith (Hugo Weaving) and his fellow agents in midair.[14] These are just a couple examples of the wide and enduring reach of the franchise. *Total Film* is one of many pop culture websites that collects the best of pop culture's *Matrix* homages, a list that just keeps growing.[15]

If you thought *The Matrix* was referenced extensively in visual media and the arts, I could write an entire book on the references that proliferate within the work of academics and public intellectuals. Slovenian philosopher and cultural commentator Slavoj Žižek penned the book *Welcome to the Desert of the Real*, taking its title from Morpheus's quote as he shows Neo the true postapocalyptic state of the world—which was itself a reference to a concept explored in French philosopher Jean Baudrillard's book *Simulacra and Simulation*.* Žižek's book, in turn, applies "Baudrillard's ideas to the World Trade Center attacks via the 1999 science-fiction film The Matrix."[16]

And several works have been written exploring *The Matrix*'s philosophical underpinnings, such as a 2009 Cambridge University thesis on how the work of René Descartes shapes the franchise, and *The Matrix and Philosophy*, edited by professor William Irwin, which explores all the various philosophies that feed into the narratives of the first three films.[17] "Whoa" doesn't even begin to cover the thousands of academic pages exploring Keanu's Neo and company through a variety of lenses.

---

* Baudrillard's work is also referenced visually in the *Matrix* films: In the original *Matrix*, *Simulacra and Simulation* is the hollowed-out book where Neo hides the pirated discs he sells for cash. And the coffee shop featured in *The Matrix Resurrections* is called Simulatte.

"Party On, Dudes."

While not as highbrow as *The Matrix* and its philosophical references, Keanu's sci-fi comedies *Bill & Ted's Excellent Adventure* (1989) and *Bill & Ted's Bogus Journey* (1991) have secured similar pop culture immortality for time-traveling dudes Ted "Theodore" Logan (Reeves) and Bill S. Preston, Esq. (Alex Winter). Ever-growing pages on the Internet Movie Database (IMDb) collect the dozens of references to these lovable doofuses in other films and TV programs over the past three decades.[18] They include the many episode titles promising a character or characters' "Excellent Adventure," including *Cheers*, *Melrose Place*, *The Simpsons*, *Agents of S.H.I.E.L.D.*, and so many more. And like Keanu's "Whoa" in *The Matrix*, Bill and Ted's enthusiastic descriptor "Most excellent" echoes through pop culture, adding an unexpected pop of humor in films like *Practical Magic* (1998), when Aunt Jet (Dianne Wiest) and Aunt Frances (Stockard Channing) exclaim "Most excellent!" after their love spell starts working on their niece Sally (Sandra Bullock) and the man she will marry.

More than thirty years later, the homages keep coming. In *Avengers: Endgame* (2019), James "Rhodey" Rhodes (Don Cheadle) uses *Bill & Ted's Excellent Adventure* as a point of reference when discussing the theoretics of time travel. And in 2022, season 4 of the '80s-set series *Stranger Things* included the Extreme song "Play with Me" from *Bogus Journey* on its own soundtrack, an homage that ends up foreshadowing that the *Stranger Things* plot will also involve time travel. (Nerdist notes that this song is anachronistic in the show, since it wasn't released until 1989 and season 4 is set in 1986—a metatextual bit of time travel.)[19]

More Homages

Another Reeves film that hasn't stopped making the pop culture rounds is his 1991 surfing action thriller *Point Break*. In Marvel's *The Avengers* (2012), Tony Stark (Robert Downey Jr.) calls long-haired Patrick Swayze look-alike Thor (Chris Hemsworth) "Point Break." Simon Pegg's comedic ode to action movies, *Hot Fuzz* (2007), references *Point Break* extensively, even down to mimicking the famous moment when Keanu's undercover FBI agent Johnny Utah shoots into the air in frustration as Swayze's bank-robbing antagonist Bodhi gets away. And E! News has pointed out the debt owed to *Point Break* by one of the twenty-first century's biggest action franchises: not only are the *Fast and the Furious* movies centered on similar plots involving heists by crooks with sort-of hearts of gold, but the first film seems to nod directly to the connection, setting a scene in the real-life fast food joint Neptune's Net in Malibu, the same one where Tyler (Lori Petty) works in *Point Break*.[20]

Speed (1994) is another influential Keanu vehicle, with its quotable one-liners like "Pop quiz, hotshot" and "Shoot the hostage." In Todd Phillips's raunchy comedy *Road Trip* (2000), a group of friends decide to jump a small broken bridge in their car, failing spectacularly where Keanu and company succeed in *Speed*, jumping their bus across a huge gap in the freeway. In fact, like "Whoa" and "Most excellent," most impossible vehicular jumps across broken roadways in pop culture feel like implicit nods to *Speed* director Jan de Bont's bonkers action set piece. Oscar-winning director Christopher Nolan even included *Speed* in a list of classic films that inspired his World War II epic *Dunkirk* (2017), crediting its "ticking-clock nail-biter" pacing—to which we fans of this film can all attest. To this day my own heart begins racing whenever I see a car's speedometer reach fifty miles per hour.[21]

Recognition of Keanu's Asian and Indigenous Heritage

In a key set of Keanu homages on television, Dr. Max Bergman (Masi Oka) on the 2010s reboot of *Hawaii Five-0* dresses as a Keanu character every season for Halloween: first Neo from *The Matrix*, then Ted "Theodore" Logan, Siddhartha from *Little Buddha* (1993), Johnny Utah, Chevalier Raphael Danceny from *Dangerous Liaisons* (1988), and finally John Wick. Max's cosplays are particularly meaningful since he's an Asian man in Hawaiʻi, reminding audiences of Keanu's own Asian and Indigenous Hawaiian identity—something that doesn't happen nearly as often as it should.

But one film is doing its part to make up for pop culture's lack of attention to Keanu's Hawaiian roots: Netflix's 2021 adventure comedy *Finding ʻOhana*. A veritable love letter to Keanu, it follows a

Brooklyn-based Hawaiian family led by single mother Leilani (Kelly Hu), who returns to her ancestral home of O'ahu after news that her father Kimo (Branscombe Richmond) needs help. In tow are Leilani's precocious geocacher daughter Pili (Kea Peahu) and girl-obsessed son Ioane (Alex Aiono), both of whom resent leaving the city for the summer. This *Goonies*-inspired tale includes the possible discovery of rich stuff that would allow Kimo to hold on to their family land, but with many Hawaiian twists along the way.

References to Keanu overflow in *Finding 'Ohana*, starting with neighborhood kid Casper (Owen Vaccaro) noting that Pili's physical prowess is "Some John Wick fancy business." Pili's room has a poster of Keanu, and when she looks at it she smiles and says "Breathtaking"—a nod to Keanu's much-memed speech at the E3 gaming convention announcing his participation in the video game *Cyberpunk 2077*. ("You're breathtaking!" a man in the E3 audience had shouted; "*You're* breathtaking! You're all breathtaking!" Keanu replied without skipping a beat.) Later, we find out Casper has named his walking stick Keanu, and the Keanu stick saves the day on multiple occasions. There is a requisite bullet-dodging *Matrix* homage once the action really gets revving. And Ioane and his new friend Hana (Lindsay Watson) have a long conversation about Keanu, in which Hana names him a Hawaiian treasure and Ioane counters by calling him a "sad Canadian," jealous of how much Hana seems to love Mr. Reeves.

Keanu might be Canadian, but he is also a member of the Indigenous Hawaiian 'ohana, or family, by way of his grandmother, a well-known matriarch named Momilani Sarah Victor Abrahams, whose ancestry also includes Chinese and Irish heritage. *Finding 'Ohana*'s most meaningful nods to Keanu are intertwined with the movie's central themes: the importance of reconnecting with family, in particular Hawaiian Indigenous traditions as they are passed down through bloodlines.

Key and Peele's *Keanu*

While *Finding 'Ohana* delves into Reeves's racial and ethnic heritage, the comedy heist movie *Keanu* (2016) captures his enormous impact on the aesthetics of popular culture. Online memes are ruled by two things—cats and Keanu Reeves—and in *Keanu* comedy duo Key and Peele meld them in the most absurd way with a story about two mild-mannered cousins, one of whom adopts an adorable kitten he names Keanu, only for them to discover that it's the missing pet of a violent gangster. "Everybody here seems to like Keanu," Jordan Peele's Rell Williams says about the kitten— which is also the subtext behind the mountain of oblique and obvious Keanu Reeves references throughout the film. Reeves even makes a cameo as himself, speaking through his namesake kitten in a dream sequence.[22]

But first there's an opening gun battle that directly references the Neo/Trinity shoot-out in *The Matrix*, and Rell's plans for a photo calendar featuring his new pet that has Keanu the cat skydiving like in *Point Break*. There's major Bill and Ted energy between Rell and his cousin Clarence Goobril (Keegan-Michael Key), which doubles when Key and Peele also show up as brutal villains Oil and Smoke Dresden, like the Evil Bill and Ted robots in *Bogus Journey*. The drug dealer Hulka (Will Forte) notes that his dream is actually to build motorcycles and be a stuntman in his spare time; Reeves has his own bespoke motorcycle company and does most of his own stunts. Reeves's dialogue as Keanu the cat also echoes his past roles: "I'm your spirit teacher. People can't be excellent to you unless you're being excellent to yourself. . . . Clarence, it's time to wake up. Where you go from there is a choice I leave to you."

And of course there are multiple parallels to *John Wick* (2014). Like John, Rell is grieving the end of a relationship (a breakup instead of the death of his wife) when an adorable animal (a kitten instead of a dog) appears on his doorstep, giving him new reason to live but then pulling him into a whirlwind of violence when the cat is kidnapped (instead of killed) by gangsters. But Key and Peele insist that these parallels are coincidental, as they had already developed the story when the original *John Wick* came out. In fact, at first Reeves passed on a cameo in the film because of its (unintentional) *John Wick* vibe—until his sister saw the trailer and showed Keanu. He found it charming enough that he changed his mind and recorded his Keanu Kitten voice-over via Skype for the movie's final cut.[23]

Cameos as Himself

Keanu isn't the only film where Reeves has most thoughtfully cameoed as a version of himself, and as with *Keanu*, a lot of care goes into these choices. As Ted "Theodore" Logan says in *Bill & Ted Face the Music* (2020), "In case you're wondering, I'm essentially an infinite me."

In Ali Wong and Randall Park's *Always Be My Maybe*, he plays a Keanu who gives unsolicited life advice to his adoring fans, cries over the animal that gave its life for his gourmet meal, humblebrags his accomplishments, name-drops celebrity connections, and demonstrates his fearlessness by smashing a vase over his own head. Reeves pokes fun at influencer culture and his own celebrity with such over-the-top perfection, embodying a sort of Keanu Squared, that his fifteen minutes of screen time steal the entire movie. Phil Yu, the film critic also known as Angry Asian Man, wondered on Twitter which was better: the moment when Randall Park's Marcus punches Keanu, or the song Park wrote about it, "I Punched Keanu Reeves," which plays over the end credits.[24] And Keanu's greeting of his in-film love interest, Wong's Sasha Tran, by blowing her exaggerated kisses has been memed to Venus and back again but somehow never gets old.*

Reeves contributed a smaller cameo to another send-up of celebrity and Hollywood culture, *Ellie Parker* (2005), appearing on-screen with his band Dogstar. The cameo reflects Keanu's real-life experience as we see people handing him scripts as he performs with the band and after the show—everyone is trying to connect with Keanu while fully ignoring his bandmates. (Dogstar also made a brief appearance in 1999's *Me and Will*, a moving female friendship drama about motorcycles and drug addiction.) Keanu made brief solo appearances as himself in two other showbiz satires, Jay Mohr's short-lived sitcom *Action* (1999) and the 2009 miniseries *Bollywood Hero*, where he also pokes fun at celebrity entitlement.

In 2017, Keanu made a cameo in Netflix's teen romantic comedy *SPF-18*, in which he offers his Malibu beach house for the son of an old surfing buddy to enjoy with his friends the summer after their high

---

* I also like to think that Sasha's comment "You're so good with your thumbs" is a reference to Keanu's *Even Cowgirls Get the Blues* (1993), a story about a woman with oversized thumbs who uses them for both hitchhiking and sexing.

school graduation. While a mostly cringe movie, *SPF-18* actually falls in line with Keanu's other cameo roles in its commentary on Los Angeles and its celebrity culture, with subtle embedded critiques of Hollywood mythmaking even as the film celebrates Tinseltown. Keanu's presence in all these L.A. movies is interesting considering the myriad ways Keanu fails to meet the stereotypes of "Hollywood actor." His indifference to coming across as the typical celebrity may even explain why he feels free to criticize Hollywood with these cameos, compared to other stars who feel greater pressure to toe the industry status quo for the sake of their reputation in the industry.

Another telling Keanu Reeves cameo occurs in Zach Galifianakis's odd, metatextual talk show spoof *Between Two Ferns: The Movie* (2019). As one of Galifianakis's "guests," Keanu essentially embodies the "Sad Keanu" meme while withstanding his host's verbal abuse.* "Is it frustrating to have people think of you as a complete bozo? When the truth is that you're just a man with below-average intelligence?" Galifianakis asks, and Keanu looks legitimately hurt by the questions. "Do you research your roles?" Galifianakis asks. "Yeah," Keanu replies, to which Galifianakis responds, "Have you ever considered researching a character that has taken acting classes?" Keanu claps back with "Right now I'm acting like this is fun. How am I doing?" Galifianakis's questions intentionally reflect the way the general public thinks and speaks about Keanu and his many roles.

But the real Keanu is far from stupid. Because as much as he's part of the Hollywood machine, he's savvy enough to cultivate a down-to-earth persona that assures us—his audience—that he's very much one of us. And part of how he maintains this image as a normal guy who happens to be famous is through his self-deprecating cameos, in which he punches up not only at himself but at his own industry too. With so many examples in his filmography, this can't be an accident; these are deliberate choices Keanu Reeves has made.

---

* For more on Sad Keanu, a meme that started spreading in 2010 after the internet discovered a paparazzi photo of Keanu sitting alone on a bench looking gloomy, see the write-up on the website Know Your Meme: https://knowyourmeme.com/memes/sad-keanu.

Fake Quotes

But there's a flip side to Reeves's underappreciated intentionality, a significant aspect of his fame over which he has no control. And that's the entire industry that has popped up online to promote fake quotes Keanu never said and deepfake his face onto staged acts of heroism for clicks. The hoaxers have even gone so far as to deepfake a Dogstar song with Keanu Reeves on lead vocals; it spread so widely that that the band's real lead vocalist, Bret Domrose, saw a need to call it out as a fake in interviews.[25] (Keanu is actually the band's bassist and doesn't provide vocals at all.)

A fake quote that is constantly making the rounds is "If you have been brutally broken but still have the courage to be gentle to other living beings, then you're a badass with a heart of an angel." Though there is no evidence that Keanu actually said this, it has been cited by hundreds of websites online. It's even made it into books published about Keanu, including *What Would Keanu Do?* and *Be More Keanu*. And because this quote has circulated so widely and for so long, no journalist has asked him to confirm it either. It's just become a part of a cultural tapestry around Keanu that has no known basis in reality. And it's not the only quote that has.*

Like a certain American president, randos on the internet love to spread fake news and alternative facts, to the point where very few of the meme quotes attributed to Keanu are things he actually said. This is an important reminder to always check your sources when sharing information online. Just because something sounds like Keanu said it doesn't mean he did. And in a dangerous era of misinformation, even little things like faked Keanu quotes do a lot to undermine collective knowledge bases. In fact, this phenomenon of molding Keanu to one's own personal designs fits neatly into the thesis of Shenja van der Graaf's chapter in *The Ashgate Research Companion to Fan Cultures*. In "Much Ado About Keanu Reeves: The Drama of Ageing in Online Fandom," Van der Graaf exposes and explores the toxic nature and quiet violence of many Keanu fan groups, both on- and offline, from the 1990s through to the early 2010s.[26] Way to *not* be excellent, dudes.

Almost worse are the instances where hoaxers deepfaked Keanu's face, including an infamous video in which he allegedly stopped a robbery in

---

* For more on this, see "Deepfakes and Fake Keanu Quotes" in chapter 12.

real life. Nope, he didn't, and the creators have come forward with another video documenting how they managed to fool so many people.[27] It's wild that they even saw a need for it, because Keanu Reeves is well known for *real* kind deeds, like organizing a bus ride for fellow air travelers after their plane made an emergency landing.[28] There is no need to fake Mr. Reeves being a hero when he already is one in so many ways.

But it seems that because Keanu is such a huge part of our collective consciousness, people feel they have a right to further extend his renown and to insert themselves, even if anonymously, into his overarching legacy. These deepfaked videos and concocted quotes feed into fundamental and wide-reaching misunderstandings of Keanu Reeves as a human being— and a performer—that continue to be perpetuated through a variety of media.

Disconnect Between Persona and Reality

"I'm Mickey Mouse. They don't know who's in the suit," the real Reeves told *Vanity Fair* in 1995, and that couldn't be truer.[29] Fans see him as a Zen master spouting (often made-up) bons mots of wisdom and enlightenment, but he's also known for being a workhorse who films intense action scenes with a 103-degree fever and begins stunt training directly after neck surgery.[30] There have been years where Reeves has released six, seven, even (in 2016) nine projects in a row. What exactly is Zen about being a workaholic? And how do you explain his very un-Zen cigarette habit, which he's never been able to break after all these years? It's wild how these conflicting conceptualizations of Keanu Reeves are packaged and disseminated together as if there's no contradiction at all.

This unacknowledged disconnect between Keanu's super-chill Buddha persona and his workaholic reputation runs throughout Larissa Zageris and Kitty Curran's essays in *For Your Consideration: Keanu Reeves*. One of the most egregious examples is in the chapter titled "Keanu and Race, or Why Keanu Reeves Is the Goth Audrey Hepburn," in which they note:

> Both Keanu Reeves and Audrey Hepburn's down-to-earth enig-
> matic appeal has been put to good use by filmmakers. Both actors
> have a knack for emoting through silent expression and artless

gesture. Even without laying everything bare, they give us a main-
line straight into their emotions. As a result, both are the ideal
audience ciphers. You might go to a George Clooney movie to
watch him be George Clooney, or a Will Smith movie to watch
him be Will Smith, but with a Keanu Reeves movie, you go to
see *yourself* be Keanu.[31]

Putting aside the backhanded compliment to both Reeves and Hepburn in calling their performances "artless," the focus on the supposed
blank-slate quality of Keanu's acting obscures the vintage star with whom
Keanu has far more in common: Marilyn Monroe. Keanu and Marilyn
both have on- and offstage personas that they can flip the switch on at
will. Both are well-studied actors who lean toward Stanislavski's Method
acting techniques: if they appear as blank slates it is a conscious choice, not
the result of a lack of talent or a phoned-in performance. They are both
autodidacts with an intense love for learning, reading, Shakespeare, and
live theater. They both have reputations for not being smart when they
are in fact highly intelligent and creative. Both had exceedingly troubled
childhoods with absentee biological fathers, leading to a lifelong search
for surrogates. (Thankfully Reeves survived his own childhood ordeals,
whereas Monroe's life was cut short.) Both are consistently regarded as two
of the most physically beautiful people who ever existed. And even now,
decades after they proved themselves as gifted performers, they still have to
deal with people calling them mediocre or even bad actors. Yet these same
people who denigrate Marilyn and Keanu are also obsessed with them.

Like I mentioned earlier: The quantum physics of Keanu Reeves is
real. And weird.

Which leads me to how Keanu Reeves's racial and ethnic heritage
plays into all the above, in particular the ongoing whitewashing—or "ethnic ambiguity," as the euphemism goes—of Keanu's identity by white
audiences and critics who feel more comfortable ignoring his status as
a visible person of color in the Hollywood machine. Keanu is magically
coded as both white and "exotic" in his appearance; he's the universal
Everyman and simultaneously the Other.

To Curran and Zageris's credit, at least they attempt to explore Keanu's
ethnic heritage in *For Your Consideration*, even if they rather randomly

connect it to Audrey Hepburn—who is decidedly not Asian. The authors' reasoning for the link has to do with the grotesque and forever offensive yellowface featured by Mickey Rooney in Hepburn's *Breakfast at Tiffany's*, which they connect to Reeves through Hollywood's mistreatment of Asian actors. This perfunctory analysis is still more than one sees from many other authors and film critics, who pen entire books about Reeves while entirely overlooking these important details about his identity—often as they continue disseminating fake quotes.

To many Asians of varied backgrounds, Keanu has never passed as white, even if he's been claimed by white people. As a multiracial Sri Lankan American woman myself, seeing our extended communities diminished in this way is exactly why representation matters so much, why Reeves is so important to us specifically, and why the white writers examining the work of artists of color need to work a whole lot harder to engage with the nuances of their subjects. Or better yet, leave it to a person of color to explore how a nonwhite actor's identity informs how their work is created and received.

Keanu Reeves is an indelible part of our collective consciousness, but for some he exists in a manufactured and doctored version of himself that they created—a mythical raceless figure who is more comfortable for them to engage with than the totality of his complicated, Asian, Indigenous Hawaiian humanness who also happens to be a world-renowned movie star. This book will dive deep into the waters where many white critics, academics, and audiences are afraid to tread when it comes to beloved Keanu Reeves. Because someone so crucial to our consciousness deserves more than surface skimming, and the depths of his art only become clear when we approach Keanu in his totality, including the context of his identity and ethnic background.

Angelica Jade Bastién writes, "Keanu is more powerful than actors who rely on physical transformation as shorthand for depth, because he taps into something much more primal and elusive: the truth."[32] There are also fundamental truths about Keanu Reeves himself that shape how his performances have been groundbreaking, in particular—but not limited to—when it comes to representation for Asian and Indigenous Hawaiian people. Where others have made an entire industry of compartmentaliz-ing Keanu's fundamental truth as a multiracial human being, it's long past time to acknowledge and explore the groundbreaking fact that an Asian/Indigenous Hawaiian is now part of the core code in our personal imaginations, as well as a vital cog in our shared transnational collective consciousness.

Once upon a time an actor named Keanu Reeves played a character named Neo who reshaped the world for everyone's benefit. Decades later, Keanu Reeves has become that character in real life, and I've only just begun exploring the hows and whys of this important transformation.

2

I SAVED YOUR LIFE, BRO

Johnny Utah as Shape-Shifter and Code-Switcher

THERE ARE TWO TYPES OF PEOPLE IN THIS WORLD: those who make the rules and those who break them. In *Point Break* (1991), rookie FBI agent Johnny Utah (Keanu Reeves) is the third kind—someone who must learn how to break the rules to enforce them. You'd think if one day you showed up at work and found out your new investigation into a gang of surfing bank robbers entailed hanging out at the beach while learning how to surf full time, you'd be stoked at the lucky turn of fortune. But not "blue flamer" Johnny Utah. He wants to work. The real work. With guns drawn and uncomfortable stakeouts to ID and nail the bad guys. A role where he's taken seriously, despite his young age and lack of experience. He has something to prove within the codified system of law enforcement itself, and he knows posing as a surfer undercover isn't the path to any of what he really wants. Even if he ends up solving the case, this isn't the way he wants to win.

Utah's profound disdain for his surf compadres is palpable in one particular moment, as Utah and his partner Angelo Pappas (Gary Busey) collect hair samples from the young surfer dudes populating Los Angeles's various shorelines to identify the break where the prolific bank robbers known as the Ex-Presidents might surf. While Pappas flashes his badge and cuts beachgoers' hair with scissors in totally illegal seizures of evidence, Johnny leans into his undercover surfer persona, with an exaggerated Valley boy accent reminiscent of his turn as hapless Ted "Theodore" Logan in *Bill & Ted's Excellent Adventure* (1989). Utah coerces a surfer into holding really still, claiming there's a gnarly insect about to crawl into his ear, and pulls out a huge chunk of blond hair as he pretends to catch and kill the insect. "I saved your life, bro," Johnny says to the bewildered stoner in his most vocal of frys. "Close one!" As Johnny walks away, his dudebro veneer instantly drops, and underneath is contempt personified. Even after spending all this time on the beach posing as a surfer, Johnny Utah still sees himself as above the beach bums who flout the rules of organized society. This quietly spectacular moment of Johnny Utah's shape-shifting comes courtesy not just of Reeves's performance but also of director Kathryn Bigelow's vision.

Unlike others who have worked with Reeves, Bigelow knew exactly what to do with Keanu to create an entire film of these nuanced moments in which the multiple layers of Utah's character development are perfectly visible on-screen. *Point Break* remains one of Keanu's most extraordinary performances of his career because of it. The humanizing potential of the female gaze has never been so obvious as it is in *Point Break*, with Bigelow taking a story that could have coasted on surfer machismo and objectification of women and transforming it into a love story on multiple fronts: There's the platonic love that Ex-Presidents leader Bodhi (Patrick Swayze) and his surf compadres have for the ocean and for each other, a love that Johnny Utah eventually gives himself over to, despite his best efforts to remain detached. There's Utah's workaholic devotion to conventional notions of law and order—duty as a form of love—which sparks his initial disdain for surfing and surfers. And of course, there's the romantic love story that develops between Johnny and his reluctant surfing teacher Tyler (Lori Petty), though at first under false pretenses. The two-hour runtime of the film allows plenty of room for this sort of emotional action amid the kinetic action, something sorely lacking in so many other action films. And at the center of it all is Keanu Reeves's multilayered performance as Johnny Utah.

But we almost didn't get this version of *Point Break*, as the film passed from Ridley Scott to James Cameron before ultimately landing with Kathryn Bigelow. Those other directors were interested in more established stars for the role of wounded football star turned FBI agent Johnny Utah, like Matthew Broderick, Val Kilmer, Charlie Sheen, and even Willem Dafoe. But when Bigelow caught the *Point Break* wave, she "fixated" on Reeves for the role, even though he had already been typecast as a doofus himbo after his role in *Bill & Ted's Excellent Adventure*.[1] And her gamble paid off big-time. Watching the film now, it's hard to believe that none of the three main stars knew how to surf until they were cast, and Lori Petty had never even swum in the ocean before.[2] Patrick Swayze ended up the daredevil of the bunch, taking skydiving lessons and scaring the film's insurance men by wanting to do his own aerial stunts—which he performed beautifully on-screen.[3] And *Point Break* is where Reeves himself established his preference for doing many of his own stunts, learning how to shoot, surf, and engage in hand-to-hand combat in the making of the movie.

Yet despite everyone's hard work and attention to detail, *Point Break*'s initial reception was lukewarm at best. Roger Ebert gave the film 3.5 stars but a mixed-bag review, writing, "The plot of 'Point Blank,' [*sic*] summarized, invites parody (rookie agent goes undercover as surfer to catch bank robbers). The result is surprisingly effective."[4] *Time* minced no words, panning the movie with "So how do you rate a stunningly made film whose plot buys so blithely into macho mysticism that it threatens to turn into an endless bummer? Looks 10, Brains 3."[5] *Entertainment Weekly* called Keanu "too placid to play a driven young federal agent."[6] The *Washington Post* called it "gorgeous but dumb as a post," and about Keanu's work they snarked:

> Reeves is a perfect choice for the youthfully malleable Utah; as an actor, he seems perpetually on the verge of a thought that can't quite work its way to the surface. He's charismatically puppy-brained and, watching him, we get caught up in the slow-motion meshing of his mental gears.[7]

Ouch.

Back in 1991, *Rolling Stone*'s Peter Travers was also no big fan of the film, noting, "Bigelow can't keep the film from drowning in a sea of surf-speak. But without her, *Point Break* would be no more than an excuse to ogle pretty boys in wet suits."[8] By 2018, though, *Rolling Stone* made an entire about-face, with April Wolfe claiming, "*Point Break* is the greatest female-gaze action movie ever."[9] Clearly it's taken some time for critics to catch up with the nuances of Bigelow's film—though they still underrate Reeves's stellar performance. In 2015 Thrillist noted that the movie is "still an action masterpiece," but about Keanu they wrote, "Despite Reeves' reputation for vacant stares and lunk-headed line readings, his calming blankness brings a stabilizing force to *Point Break*."[10] A backhanded compliment if there ever was one. There was even a play adaptation, *Point Break Live!*, that cast the role of Johnny Utah each night from a member of the audience who read from cue cards, noting, "This method manages to capture the rawness of a Keanu Reeves performance even from those who generally think themselves incapable of acting."[11]

Wipeout.

One of the few critics who seems to have understood Keanu in *Point Break* from the get-go is the *New York Times*' Janet Maslin, who said in her 1991 review, "A lot of the snap comes, surprisingly, from Mr. Reeves, who displays considerable discipline and range. He moves easily between the buttoned-down demeanor that suits a police procedural story and the loose-jointed manner of his comic roles."[12] And of course Keanu's other modern-day defender Angelica Jade Bastién writes, "The opening of *Point Break* illustrates how Keanu's relationship with the camera informs his onscreen masculinity. He carries himself with a supple vulnerability, at times even a passivity, that seems at odds with the expectations for an action star."[13] Bastién goes on to say, and this is our only point of disagreement, that "Keanu tends to let his scene partners take the lead, becoming almost a tabula rasa on which they (and we) can project our ideas of what it means to be a hero, a man, a modern action star."

The idea that Keanu is a blank slate on which audiences project themselves is an all-too-frequent assessment of the actor's performances.[14] It's reductive, and *Point Break* alone is evidence to the contrary. Johnny Utah doesn't just passively reflect the expectations of the viewers or the other characters, he jumps between different versions of himself, a conscious shape-shifter and code-switcher.

In order to set off Johnny Utah's shape-shifting and code-switching, you need solid constants for him to work against. Bigelow gives him plenty, beginning with the opening scene, in which we first meet Johnny Utah at a stationary gun range during an FBI shooting test. Johnny is scary focused, his forehead in that scowl of deep concentration that Tyler will comment on much later. As heavy rain pours around him, Johnny doesn't miss a single target, getting a perfect score that we find out helped him graduate at the top of his class at Quantico. In another context, we might read Johnny as a cold-blooded, psychopathic killer who dispatches targets without qualm or hesitation. But at the news of his 100 percent on the marksmanship test, Johnny's face breaks into a childlike grin and he flashes a thumbs-up to his instructor, the response of someone eager to please but also hungry to get ahead.

Utah's next shift occurs when he meets Supervising Agent Harp (John C. McGinley), a cliché of a law enforcement dragon boss if there ever was one. Utah says everything the boss man wants to hear, with an open expression of attention and interest as his supervisor Harp lobs insult upon insult, trying to crack Johnny's eager demeanor. Johnny plays along with Harp's tirade, agreeing with everything he says, including his rant about the importance of eating healthy: "Sir, I take the skin off chicken." But Johnny isn't a pushover, which he demonstrates by grabbing a dough-nut and taking a huge bite out of it, telling Harp, "I love these things." It's here that Harp realizes there's more to Johnny then just a blue flame, and the kid might end up being trouble. "We must have an asshole shortage," Harp rages at Johnny Utah. And it's only when the chief is gone that the annoyance hiding under Johnny's veneer of civility becomes visible and he spits the words "Not so far."

And then comes Pappas, Utah's abrasive new partner in crime-solving, and the unit's resident fuckup who's holding on to his job by ever-fraying threads. As Utah approaches him for the first time, Pappas is blindfolded for a swimming test and starts unknowingly talking shit about his green-horn partner right to his face. The respect-your-elders gaze Utah recently bestowed on Harp drops as he quietly seethes that Pappas has clearly been complaining about him all day. He hedges his anger only slightly with a smile when Pappas realizes he's stepped in it, Utah clearly enjoying the shift in the balance of power.

It's through Pappas that we start to learn of Johnny Utah's master manipulation skills, as Johnny coerces him into sharing his theory about the bank robbers being surfers. Johnny is so hungry for a win of any kind, he doesn't even care that nobody else in the precinct considers Pappas's theory anything but an ongoing joke—and that the joke might be on him too if it's wrong. As the one tasked with going undercover, Johnny reminds Pappas again and again that learning to surf was never his idea and he hates having to do it. But once again Johnny clearly gets a kick out of the shift in power dynamics, the fact that his involvement means Pappas must relinquish his solo hold on the surfer theory. Watching Johnny pretend he doesn't enjoy leveraging his situational malleability to his own ends is part of the subtle and clever shading Reeves and Bigelow bring to the character.

While most of the banter between Johnny and Pappas is of the comedic variety, they share one particularly poignant moment during the botched raid in which they bust the wrong group of surfers. Pappas kills a man, and Johnny almost has his face turned to dog food by a lawn-mower. "It's been paper targets up until today, huh?" Pappas says as a visibly shaken Johnny washes his face. This is not the face of a cipher. The figure of Johnny Utah in the cracked mirror is openly rattled, hands shaking, on the verge of a panic attack, and not just because they raided the wrong bad guys. The reality of Johnny's chosen line of work is finally sinking in, and that eager blue flame is dimming right before our eyes. By one of Pappas and Utah's last scenes together, after the Ex-Presidents' final robbery and with multiple people dead in a shoot-out, including an off-duty cop, Johnny no longer bothers with his company-man mask. He is seething with rage, from hair tips to toes, and the list of things he's furious about is long and detailed, one of the main sources being his own role in the mayhem abounding.

Utah's relationship with love interest Tyler is just as complex. As befits a film so grounded in the female gaze, Tyler's three-dimensionality does an incredible amount of heavy lifting, and not just when she saves Johnny Utah from drowning by dragging him out of the water herself. One scene in particular floats to the top, reflecting the subversive genius of Kathryn Bigelow's filmmaking: After Tyler's daring rescue, we watch her change out of her swimming clothes at her car. This is a woman who is accustomed to occupying male spaces like surfing, so she has learned how to avert the male gaze by carefully moving her towel over and around her body as she strips from wetsuit to bikini to shorts and shirt without showing anything but calf and arms. A male director in this genre absolutely would have had her flash a boob or her butt or more. But Bigelow gives Tyler agency and autonomy over her body—which only makes Johnny's eventual betrayal cut even deeper.

And it cuts deeper still considering Tyler sees through Johnny Utah right from the start, even with that charming smile that he thinks hides so much. When he asks her to help him learn how to surf, she asks, "This is a line, right?" Johnny's manipulation skills go into overdrive to convince her to go against her gut feeling; he even leans over onto the counter to put himself at her eye level and not show even the slightest indication he's lying about every single thing he's saying. It's in this moment that we see Johnny Utah not as a hero figure but rather as an opportunistic borderline sociopath who will say and do anything to further his career, placing it above all else, including human decency. Earlier, Johnny coldly calculated how to leverage the intimate details of her life, saying, "I gotta find an approach. A way in. Here we go. Both parents deceased. Airplane crash, San Diego, '84. Yeah. Definitely," plotting to use Tyler's traumatic loss of her parents to manipulate her into the nonconsensual scenario that will eventually risk her life.

Tyler continues to see through Johnny's variety of masks, in particular noticing the scowl of concentration that comes and goes from his brow over the course of the film. It's Utah's lawman tell, and it contrasts with his other facades so dramatically it's strange almost nobody else notices it, both in the movie and in the audience. Tyler even outright says how his level of focus is "like you're doing all this for a school project or something," a 100 percent accurate description of Utah's ongoing motivation in and out of his surfer character.

For Tyler herself, the seeds of Johnny's lies have bloomed into very real love, which causes her to begin to misread Johnny's cues as we approach the climax of the film. Johnny finally tries to come clean about his identity to Tyler, but she misinterprets his hesitations and bumbling as the signs of an emotions talk, quipping, "Men are so bad at this," and giving him a pass on coming clean. Yes, the men in *Point Break* indeed are bad at this. At honesty. At all of it. Through the female gaze, the only hero of this story is Tyler—a fact often overlooked due to the overwhelming combination of Keanu Reeves's and Patrick Swayze's on-screen chemistry and charisma.

As the narrator puts it in the similarly bromantic action movie *Fight Club*, a "changeover" is a narrative moment in the third act of a movie when the plot has twisted but the audiences won't realize it until later. In *Point Break*, the first evidence of the changeover is when crack shot Johnny Utah, with his perfect marksmanship in the rain, who once wanted nothing more than to be the hero who gets the bad guys, misses wounding Bodhi and company even though he has them dead in his sights in their getaway car. This is followed up by Johnny having Bodhi in his crosshairs after their epic foot chase through Los Angeles and not being able to take the shot. But the real kicker of the changeover comes when we realize that what Johnny has represented as an agent of the capitalist state has rubbed off on Bodhi as much as Bodhi's Zen outlook has infiltrated Johnny's ability to compartmentalize right and wrong: Bodhi breaks with the Ex-Presidents' tradition and goes for all the cash in the bank vault, leading to three deaths and counting. Until this point, Bodhi has served as a contrast to Johnny Utah's lawman persona, the counterculture voice who insists there are other ways to live a fulfilled life than within the confines of mainstream society. So, what really throws Johnny now is finding out that underneath it all Bodhi is actually as opportunistic as Utah himself and has sacrificed his supposed family for money he'll barely have the chance to spend. Then, just as Johnny is beginning to internalize that he himself might be the bad guy in the narrative, Bodhi flips the script again by kidnapping Tyler, having a sadistic enforcer on call to murder her if necessary, and leaving a trail of dead comrades in his wake.

For most of *Point Break*, we believe Bodhi is this enlightened being who has found personal freedom through surfing and living outside the bounds of conventional society—the Hermit tarot card in motion. "This was never about money for us," he lies. "It was about us against the system. That system that kills the human spirit." He talks such a good game that unlike Johnny, who is visibly code-switching throughout the film, we don't realize Bodhi is an even more convincing shape-shifter until almost the end. "I hate violence," Bodhi says. But in practically the next breath he lectures as he hands out guns, "You project strength to avoid conflict." For Bodhi, bank robbery is a game of power, and he uses everyone around him as pawns and discards them when they no longer give him leverage. Where many read Bodhi as a stabilizing force for Utah in *Point Break*, he becomes the opposite.

And it's through this shift that Utah is forced to grapple with his own identity. He's no longer a straightforward foil to Bodhi but instead a far more complicated hybrid. By the end of *Point Break*, Johnny Utah has transformed into a lost boy, someone who has left behind the culture of law he once represented but hasn't necessarily fully embraced the subculture he infiltrated either. We close with Johnny Utah in a liminal space that was shaped by many of Bodhi's lies, but where everything Utah learned from surfing remains true.

Surfing is the opposite side of the coin from law enforcement. It's community, not hierarchy. It's flowing, not forcing. Being at one with, instead of being in opposition. Surrendering, not overpowering. As the Wire Train song that plays over Johnny's early surfing lesson goes, "To rise and fall, without the hands of gravity." Law enforcement is the very definition of gravity, and Johnny Utah starts the film as the embodiment of this weight, the sort of overeager recruit that is infamous for burning out quickly. By the end of the film, however, Johnny's voice and gait have changed, and his shape-shifting seems to be settling into a final form that is developing its own code of what's right and wrong. He knows he can't just let Bodhi get away with all the terrible things he's done, but he also cannot deny his brother-in-surfing the opportunity to leave life on his own terms. Johnny might have begun *Point Break* joking, "I saved your life, bro." But by the end he does, in a way, save a bro's life, freeing Bodhi to surf his once-in-a-lifetime wave and embrace his crushing fate. When Utah throws his badge into the ocean, he finally sheds his law enforcement identity and opens himself to something entirely new.

And in the end, it's not just Johnny Utah who changes forms in *Point Break*. Keanu Reeves's own racial and ethnic identity adds another level to the various layers of code-switching we witness throughout the film. Due to Keanu's multiracial Chinese and Indigenous Hawaiian background, the role of Johnny Utah becomes a vital moment of representation for both communities, in particular when it comes to the character's background as a former football star.

Through the lens of Reeves's Indigenous Hawaiian ancestry, Johnny Utah would be one of just a handful of Indigenous Americans to reach legendary status in the world of football, and he offers a tribute to their trailblazing legacies. *Point Break* came out in 1991, but it wasn't until 2019 that the first Indigenous Hawaiian football player, Kevin Mawae, was inducted into the Pro Football Hall of Fame.[15] And this is in spite of the fact that Indigenous Hawaiians had been represented in the sport since 1892, when John Henry Wise on the Oberlin College football team made history as the first Indigenous player.[16] Despite this long history in the sport, Indigenous Hawaiian players appear only sporadically on the list of the greatest football players, with huge gaps in representation over the years.[17] In that context, Johnny Utah's legacy becomes even more important.

But it's Keanu's Asian heritage that makes Johnny Utah especially memorable and unique when it comes to representation. I mean, are there *any* Asian football players who are household names?[18] Nope. Why aren't there more Asian players? There's no good answer that doesn't rely on racist assumptions about size and strength.[19] So if we view *Point Break* as the story of a well-known and beloved college football star of Asian descent whose career ended before its time, Johnny Utah becomes a truly groundbreaking character. Even decades later, when have we ever seen Asian football heroes in American movies? The only other example is another Keanu film, *The Replacements* (2000), in which he once again represents as an Asian/Indigenous star quarterback with a twist. This means that without Keanu Reeves, we would have no Asian representation in American football on-screen, making *Point Break* an historic moment as well as an exceptional action movie.

And thanks to Keanu, we can also link Johnny Utah's code-switching to the behavioral gymnastics that multiracial people, or the "ethnically ambiguous," must perform regularly just to go about their lives. As a star quarterback from a background that's wildly underrepresented in American football, Johnny would have had to learn how to deal with the same sorts of microaggressions that people like Supervising Agent Harp send his way—how to maintain a cheerful facade, vent his frustrations quietly, and carefully manage circumstances to overcome an imbalance of power all while swallowing any valid discomfort or anger. By the time Johnny Utah grows his hair long and tosses his badge into the ocean, he's not just rejecting the myth of law and order he was tasked with upholding; he's rejecting code-switching entirely.

Portraying Johnny Utah as a code-switcher is not just an active creative choice that Keanu Reeves made; it also reflects the daily experiences of Keanu himself, a multiracial individual who lives and works primarily among white folks. Like Johnny Utah, in both college football and the FBI. Keanu's social and cultural importance in *Point Break* isn't just because of his performance—but his phenomenal and controlled take on a character in search of himself is legendary in its own right.

3

BABA YAGA OR A MAN

A Queer Reading of *John Wick*

WHEN *JOHN WICK* HIT THE SCENE IN 2014, it broke the mold of action movies. Thanks to its dark fusion of film genres, unique fight choreography, and fresh world-building with Keanu Reeves at the center of it all, *John Wick* unexpectedly stole the hearts of audiences—and critics. The *National Post* called it the best action movie of all time, praising its refusal to compromise on its action, characters, or storytelling, or its use of both practical and digital effects.[1] With each sequel, also helmed by director Chad Stahelski and writer Derek Kolstad, its thrilling world-building has expanded in colorful vision and immensity.

Drawing from inspirations that run the gamut from classic Bruce Lee movies to Sergio Leone's spaghetti westerns to the Wachowskis' cyberpunk epic *The Matrix* (1999), *John Wick* is a feast for the studied cinephile. The series pays tribute to virtually every kind of cinema that exists: martial arts, film noir, grindhouse, horror, and even the old-fashioned kind of romance in which a sensitive gangster with a heart of gold finds love to mend his wicked ways. Outside the world of cinema, it draws from global history, feudal traditions, politics, economics, art, and the athletic visual poetry of ballet to create a criminal underworld that feels real even as it transcends all the bounds of acceptable society.[2] (I'm looking at you, gun chase on horseback over the Brooklyn Bridge.) Long before its conclusion in *John Wick: Chapter 4* (2023), *Rolling Stone* had already called it "the last great American action-movie franchise" thanks to its "cinematic carnage choreographed with panache, screen violence treated with a comprehensive yet bespoke sense of style."[3]

Of course, its surprise success also owes a lot to Keanu Reeves's turn as the sensitive, heartbroken, and complicated super-assassin forced out of retirement. *John Wick* prompted *Vulture*'s Angelica Jade Bastién to boldly claim that Keanu is in fact Hollywood's greatest action star.[4] But there's something else that makes John Wick extraordinary even beyond the action genre: John Wick's assassin moniker of "Baba Yaga"—which opens the franchise up to a queer reading that can code John Wick as transgender, making it the first action series of its kind in an entirely new way.

For all its careful placement of real-life inspirations throughout the series,[5] this one external reference was confusing from the get-go. I lived in Prague for four years and knew from my time consuming Eastern European art and culture that the mythological figure of Baba Yaga is a woman, one of the most powerful and feared witches in Eastern European and Russian folklore. The word *baba* in that region even directly translates to "woman"—or, more specifically, "grandmother."* Baba Yaga usually appears either as a wizened, deformed old lady or, when she's being tricksy, a beautiful young woman with luscious hair. I've never heard of her being identified as a man. So, what would Baba Yaga, the woman witch, have to do with John Wick, the man assassin?

Stahelski, Kolstad, and Reeves have all been almost comically tight-lipped about the origins and background of the character, aside from doling out tiny snippets about John's background in the films themselves. Could the first film's reference to Baba Yaga as "the boogeyman" have been a translation or research error spotted too late to correct, and now they're just going with it? Sure. Maybe the creators meant to use the term *babayka*, another monstrous Russian folk figure that more directly translates to "boogeyman."[6] In a huge undertaking like *John Wick*, even

---

* Interestingly from a South Asian perspective, *baba* in my part of the world translates to "father."

the most painstaking creative efforts will inevitably feature a mistake or two, and online discourse continues to point to Wick's nickname as a singular supposed error in an otherwise perfect narrative.[7]

Then again, the name *babayka* doesn't have the same fearsome reputation as Baba Yaga outside of Eastern Europe and Russia. And giving Wick that nickname instead wouldn't have packed the same punch.

So maybe it's not an error at all.

What if Stahelski and Kolstad chose this nickname on purpose? Meaning, when the mobsters of *John Wick* refer to the title character as Baba Yaga, they *do* mean *that* Baba Yaga, the folkloric nightmare figure who appears in the guise of an old woman witch. What if Jonathan Wick is transgender? And what if the Baba Yaga nickname also functions as a transphobic slur born out of jealousy at a trans man's almost supernatural abilities as an assassin?

Let's break this down methodically, like John cleaning his weapons. In the original folklore, Baba Yaga lives alone in the woods in a tall house on chicken legs. Baba Yaga will not bother you unless you provoke her. Or call on her. She hates to be called on, so you'd better make sure invoking her name is well thought out, because there's no going back once she's at your doorstep. And if you bother her for her powerful services and don't pay her exact price, you forfeit your life to her, and possibly the lives of other people connected to you. One such story is included in the book of Russian fairy tales by Alexander Afanasyev that John Wick uses to keep a secret stash of gold markers and a photograph of his late wife Helen (Bridget Moynahan). In "Vasilisa the Beautiful," the Russian version of Cinderella, young Vasilisa travels to Baba Yaga's cottage for help with her abusive stepmother and stepsisters. With the help of Baba Yaga and an enchanted doll that requires regular feeding, Vasilisa's tormentors are vanquished. Vasilisa goes on to marry the czar.

When we first meet John Wick, he has retired from the international organization of mobsters, assassins, and other nefarious sorts whose illicit activities drive a criminal underworld lurking under the surface of normal life for everyone else. Like Baba Yaga at her most reclusive, Wick lives in a remote house in the woods of upstate New York, a home he previously shared with his wife, who recently died of a terminal illness. Deep in his grief, John has withdrawn further and further into himself. That is, until the arrival of Daisy, a beagle pup sent by dearest Helen to be delivered to John's doorstep after her death. In another parallel to Baba Yaga, John is minding his own damn business until brash mob boss's son Iosef Tarasov (Alfie Allen) breaks into his house to steal John's vintage Boss 429 Mustang, badly beating John and killing Daisy. This kicks off a series of events that by the end of *Chapter 4* has a death count of 439, as an ocean of corpses still haven't finished paying the price for this initial breach of privacy.

As John gets deeper back into the underworld's terrible games, being used as a pawn by people like crime boss Santino D'Antonio (Riccardo Scamarcio) and Winston (Ian McShane), manager of the assassin-friendly hotel the New York Continental, more and more is revealed about John's former world and the sinister council that controls it, the High Table. John Wick's own background remains ambiguous until *Chapter 3* (2019), when we find out he's Jardani Jovonovich, an orphan adopted by the Ruska Roma, portrayed in the films as a crime family of Romani heritage. But was Jardani Roma, or adopted from outside? This remains unclear until *Chapter 4*, when Katia (Natalia Tena) confirms his Romani heritage.

A leader of the Ruska Roma in New York City known only as the Director (Anjelica Huston) uses the front of a ballet academy to train assassins from childhood and beyond, and we get a quick tour of her institute, where John was both raised and trained. Training is gendered, as Romani culture can be in general,[8] with all the girls learning ballet and all the boys wrestling. But something strange caught my eye: All the ballerinas have similar tattoos to John, including the large cross on their left shoulder. Even extremely young ballerinas are already sporting at least the left shoulder cross, if not the difficult-to-read Latin phrase FORTIS FORTUNA ADIUVAT across their backs.* However, the boy wrestlers' tattoos

---

* The tattoo across John's back reads FORTIS FORTUNA ADIUVAT, "Fortune favors the bold," which is a slogan of the US Marines. Some have claimed that this means John was in the military, but this theory doesn't hold water in the context of the High Table. By *Chapter 3* we learn John was trained by them from childhood to be an assassin. A military stint makes no sense. Also, in a deleted scene in *Chapter 2* (2017), when John meets with a Catholic cardinal, they exchange the words "Fortis fortuna adiuvat" as if it indicates the subgroup of the underworld they are both members of, much like how the phrase "I have served, I will be of service" is used throughout the trilogy. GraceEvie, "John Wick 2 Deleted Scenes, John Wick Meet the Pope [sic]," Reddit, July 13, 2018, https://www.reddit.com/r/movies/comments/8yl2qn/john_wick_2_deleted_scenes_john_wick_meet_the_pope/.

aren't front and center in the same way as the ballerinas', and the boys
do not have the dramatic shoulder cross. It's a small detail that suggests
Stahelski wants us to associate John's own tattoos with the women of the
institute, not the men.

But while the on-screen Romani in *John Wick* are in some ways far
from traditional—they are covered in tattoos and piercings, for one—
would they sanction a gender transition? Roma expert Dr. Lucie Fremlova notes throughout her groundbreaking book *Queer Roma* that the
LGBTQ+ members of the community are not necessarily socially ostra-
cized or stratified in the way suggested by stereotypes about the Roma as
bound by tradition and strictly policing gender and sexuality.[9] Certainly,
John Wick is problematic for not featuring any actual Roma actors on-
screen—Romani scholar Madeline Potter told me over Twitter/X, "I find
the complete lack of Roma across cast in Roma roles (usually whitewashing) extremely harmful and actively creating erasure and confusion as to
who the Roma are."[10] But the possibility of queer Roma on-screen is a step
forward for envisioning a more inclusive community, even if it requires
a lot of reading between the lines.

Could the Director and her colleagues have decided Jardani Jovonovich would be a more effective assassin as a boy—hence the girl's nickname of Baba Yaga that follows him as a destabilizing tactic to downplay
his power as John Wick? It's certainly possible. It's essentially illegal to
be queer in Russia and has been for a long time. Did Jardani's biological
parents allow him to transition, hence their deaths and his secret trafficking to the USA, where the Director harnessed his strengths as a boy?
Also possible. Or is he simply a cis man? Possible, too. But what's wild
is, thanks to the Baba Yaga moniker, we can fully entertain the theory
that John Wick, the titular character of now one of the biggest action
franchises in the world, is trans.

It's also notable that most everyone refers to John Wick as Baba Yaga
behind his back, furthering the idea that it's meant to be disparaging. The
few people who use the nickname to his face include villains Viggo Tarasov (Michael Nyqvist) in the first movie and Killa Harkan (Scott Adkins)
in the fourth, who spit it mockingly, and Wick's longtime ally Winston,
who throws it in his face to remind him of what the underworld did to
him and how they disrespect him daily. As Winston puts it, "The real

question is: Who do you wish to die as? The Baba Yaga? The last thing many men ever see? Or as a *man*, who loved and was loved by his wife? Who do you wish to die as, Jonathan?" You can see John's face tighten at the mention of Baba Yaga. It's a subtle example of Keanu's exceptional silent acting technique, his expressiveness resulting in a sad flicker of a shadow over John's face that signals a kind of defeat. Winston hopes his words will manipulate John into shifting allegiances from the High Table back to him, and the loaded Baba Yaga nickname is his trump card. It works. John disobeys the High Table once again, and Winston turns on him anyway. In the context of a trans John Wick, this transphobic moment is one of the biggest betrayals John has suffered yet, hitting even harder coming from his supposed friend.

In researching John's hidey-hole library book of Russian fairy tales by Alexander Afanasyev, I discovered that in the years since *John Wick* first came out, the figure of Baba Yaga has gone through a feminist renaissance of her own. As with Medusa from Greek myth, modern interpretations of Baba Yaga posit her not just as an evil monster but as a powerful figure of female independence in all spheres of life— personal, economic, and even spiritual. From 2013 to 2015 the *Hairpin* even featured an advice column written from Baba Yaga's perspective that encouraged people to lean into their grumpy, solitary, forest-witch selves.[11] And according to Andreas Johns, author of *Baba Yaga: The Ambiguous Mother and Witch of the Russian Folklore*, Baba Yaga's connections to the cycles of life and death have created in her a kind of Earth Mother status. Like the Earth, Baba Yaga can be helpful and life affirming on a good day or a destructive force with a taste for human flesh on a bad one, sometimes running this entire gamut in her interactions with a visitor to her chicken-legged hut.[12] Baba Yaga refuses to be constrained, and tales about her run rife with chase scenes as she pursues people who have wronged her, who owe her, or who just got too close to her hidden cottage and pissed her off. Sound like anyone else we know?

As I meditated on this fresh context about Baba Yaga, a line by mob kingpin Viggo Tarasov in the original *John Wick* began to echo in my brain: "Well, John wasn't exactly the boogeyman. He was the one you sent to *kill* the fucking boogeyman." This presents another possible explanation

for Wick's Baba Yaga nickname: What if it was chosen simply because
Baba Yaga was the most terrifying figure the underworld could think of
from the wide scope of Russian culture to instill global fear of a human
man known as Jonathan Wick? What if it doesn't matter that Baba Yaga's
and John's genders don't match when they share the ability to inspire
horror, panic, and an existential dread in anyone who draws their attention? This interpretation provides a feminist bent to the franchise that
only deepens a queer reading of *John Wick*.

Because even if we put aside the idea that John Wick might be
trans, there is still another queer reading to consider: that John Wick
is bisexual. Over the course of the series, we meet a number of John's
former colleagues who seem to have nonspecific grudges against him
that can easily be interpreted as those of lovers scorned. That's the case
with three female associates: Ms. Perkins (Adrianne Palicki) from the
original *John Wick*, Gianna D'Antonio (Claudia Gerini) in *Chapter 2*,
and Sofia Al-Azwar (Halle Berry) in *Chapter 3*. Ms. Perkins is in such a
jealous rage she veritably assures her own death by conducting business
on Continental grounds so she and John can die together. Gianna's calculated, burlesque undressing in front of John before she kills herself, as
well as the melancholy way John returns her burning gaze, are next-level
unspoken indicators of past sexual intimacy. And Sofia shoots John in
the chest as a greeting, even though he helped her save her daughter,
a pissed-off assassin ex-girlfriend move if there ever was one. But in
Chapter 2, bathed in the pink, purple, and blue of so-called bisexual
lighting,[13] we also have a male assassin from John's past, Cassian (Common), whose lingering glances at John are tinged with the melancholy
longing of a broken heart that hasn't healed yet. Cassian is the only foe
of John's who seems genuinely upset at having to fight him. But he's
also a consummate professional with a job to do to the death, per his
contract with the High Table. His and John's conversation at the bar
of the Continental is loaded with queer subtext; though they are only
talking about work, both actors' faces demonstrate a much deeper connection than just colleagues. The fact that Cassian is one of the few nem-
eses John doesn't kill outright adds weight to their special relationship
before John abandoned everyone to make a new life with Helen. John
wounded Cassian long before he leaves him with a knife in his chest on

a New York subway car, and only one of those grievous injuries was a professional courtesy.

A queer reading of *John Wick* doesn't stop with John himself. *Chapter 2* features the mercenary Ares, whose name is that of the male Greek god of war, played by lesbian actress Ruby Rose. In *Chapter 3*, the character of the Adjudicator is played by Asia Kate Dillon; when Reeves found out that Dillon is nonbinary in real life, he agreed that the character be portrayed as openly enby too.[14] And *Chapter 4* offers a huge array of queer-coded characters—the most out of all the films. There's butch Katia of the Ruska Roma, purple-suited villain Killa Harkan, the Marquis (Bill Skarsgård) with his sparkle three-piece suits, and Klaus (Sven Marquardt) as the quintessential leather daddy. Akira actress Rina Sawayama has come out as pansexual in real life, so we can possibly read her *Chapter 4* character as pan too.[15]

And because *Chapter 4* really leans into the fairy tale aspects of the franchise's fictional universe, like the Berlin rave where the partygoers seem completely oblivious to the violence around them—faerie-like behavior if I've ever seen it—it only deepens a queer reading of the series as a whole. Faeries are frequently portrayed in folklore as androgynous, pansexual, polyamorous, and many other queer qualities we can easily transpose onto *John Wick* and its characters. The larger mythic context to *John Wick* is central to Ann C. Hall's paper "John Wick: Keanu Reeves's Epic Adventure." Hall goes into great detail analyzing the series as a modern example of the heroic epics of ancient literature like *The Odyssey* and *The Iliad*, and proposes that as a classic epic adventure, the franchise should actually be read not as a straightforward action movie but as a complicated, multilayered work of art.[16]

A queer reading of the text is also supported by Simon Bacon's reading of *John Wick* as an example of a gothic text in "'But Now, Yeah, I'm Thinking I'm Back': The All-Consuming Gothic Nostalgia in the John Wick Franchise," since queerness was also often hidden in the nuances of gothic texts, often by closeted authors for whom it was unsafe to come out.[17] As Laura Westengard puts it in "Queer Gothic Literature and Culture," "Since the first Gothic novel, Horace Walpole's *The Castle of Otranto* (1764), the Gothic has included themes of transgressive sexuality." She goes on to note, "The broad understanding of queer as both odd and as indicating non-normative genders and sexualities helps us understand the way the term is conceptualized in relation to the Gothic," further explaining:

> Queerness in this sense functions as a placeholder for non-normative genders and/or sexualities and serves as a refusal to be neatly defined, pinned down or contained by any single or unchanging meaning, making it a flexible term but also potentially confusing and disturbing to those who expect tidy and predictable behaviours, identities and meanings. This refusal to remain strictly moored to the status quo reflects the disruptions of early Gothic narratives in which the inciting incidents mark a departure from "normal" life and takes readers into the realm of the irrational, perverse and supernatural.[18]

All of which describes the events of the *John Wick* franchise deliciously. *John Wick*'s abundant queer subtext is one way that the series adds new layers of meaning to the traditionally hypermasculine action genre. Most other action films happily promote an institutionalized version of toxic masculinity that reproduces archaic notions of how to be a man, embodied in some hugely muscled, emotionless killing machine who receives a woman as a prize in the end. *John Wick* upends these action genre expectations, avoiding gratuitous sex and nudity and giving its action scenes a physical and emotional weight by staying away from the frenetic editing and overreliance on CGI that fill most modern action films. And while there might be occasional homoerotic subtext in other franchises like *The Fast and the Furious*, *Mission: Impossible*, and the Jason Bourne films, the gender identity and even the heterosexuality of those series' main stars can't be called into question the way they can with *John Wick*.

Ultimately, it doesn't matter if any of these queer interpretations are ever proven correct. Just the fact that these possibilities exist at all elevates the entire genre, and blazes a trail for different kinds of representation in action filmmaking. Keanu himself has broken the mold of the traditional action movie star during his four-decade career (more on this in the next chapter). Now an entire blockbuster action franchise follows suit, giving us not only creative action scenes but also nuanced world-building that can be interpreted through an intersectional, queer, and feminist lens, and in other nontraditional ways.

A queer reading of *John Wick* becomes an extension of Brennan Moline's thesis in "Keanu Reeves' Body as Battleground," which argues that Keanu embodies an inclusive kind of masculinity that can be both read and experienced as an alternative to traditional masculine action movie figures.[19] As it turns out, in John Wick's world you can be Baba Yaga *and* a man. You don't need to choose.

4

POP QUIZ, HOTSHOT

Re(eves)imagining the Action Hero

Is it a bird? A plane? No, it's Keanu Reeves smashing (almost) every action hero trope in the genre's wheelhouse. In the history of action movie stars, has anyone ever been knocked out, beaten down, and even killed in the end as often as Keanu Reeves? By my calculations, not one. He displays a consistent vulnerability on-screen that often finds him with his women costars as equals or even betters.

It starts in *Point Break* (1991), when Keanu's Johnny Utah almost drowns while attempting to surf for the first time and has to be rescued by a peeved Tyler (Lori Petty), who later agrees to teach him surfing. In *The Matrix* (1999), Reeves's Neo is saved by Trinity (Carrie-Anne Moss), and he dies at the end of *The Matrix Revolutions* (2003). Yes, he's brought back in *The Matrix Resurrections* (2021), but that film also reveals that Neo is no longer "the One"—there's a chosen two and Trinity is the other. And in dystopian action horror *The Bad Batch* (2016), Reeves's character the Dream is protected by a cadre of machine-gun-wielding pregnant young women.

These moments are only the start of how Keanu's films redefine what it means to be an action hero. And like so much in his career, this tendency is no accident. In the *John Wick* oral history *They Shouldn't*

Have Killed His Dog, series screenwriter Derek Kolstad tells an anecdote about going over to Reeves's house and seeing his office stacked with hundreds of screenplays. He's not being typecast or cherry-picked for certain types of scripts; he has access to every project on offer. And "he reads them all," Kolstad says—which means that Keanu personally chooses each project he stars in.[1] From the choices he ends up making, it's clear that Reeves is drawn to unique narratives that challenge the action movie status quo.

The Emperor of Losing Fights

When Reeves allows his action heroes to be constantly humbled by the greater strength of his foes, he shatters traditional, toxic notions of impenetrable masculinity. By the end of *John Wick: Chapter 3—Parabellum* (2019), John has cut off his own ring finger in service to the High Table council that controls the international criminal underworld. Not long after, he is shot and falls over a balcony, plummeting three stories and bouncing across awnings before thudding to the ground, where he is taken to safety by another assassin, the Tick Tock Man (Jason Mantzoukas). *John Wick: Chapter 4* (2023) is a montage of many more John Wick beatdowns, including John's death at the end.

While in these vulnerable states, Reeves often ceases to be the protector figure we expect from an action movie's leading man. Instead, in a welcome reversal, he's being watched over by others. All four *Matrix* movies feature scenes of Keanu strapped to a table or chair, while he's sent from the real world into the cybersphere, as does the cyber action thriller *Johnny Mnemonic* (1995), when his high-tech courier is receiving and downloading his data packages. Not only does the titular Johnny end up writhing in agony from the overloaded wet-wired data port in his brain, but this weakened state sets the stage for several clobberings that leave him unconscious and in the care of a bounty hunter named Jane (Dina Meyer)—another example of a Reeves action hero being saved by a woman. The title character in the supernatural actioner *Constantine* (2005) dies twice on-screen, both times brought back by supernatural forces. And while Reeves's Kai in the samurai action fantasy *47 Ronin* (2013) is a savior figure in many regards, he's also pummeled to hell and back, and he himself is not ultimately saved, dying with his ronin brethren by the end.

Even in animated form, as the first Batman of color in *DC League of Super-Pets* (2022), Keanu's Dark Knight is slapped into a coma by a guinea pig. Sure, it's an evil, mutated, superpowered guinea pig. But still, Batman doesn't tend to get knocked all the way out that often, so in the context of Keanu Reeves's creative choices, it makes sense why this version of the character would be the one he plays.

And my favorite: when Johnny Utah in *Point Break* gets his butt whupped by a naked woman named Freight Train, played by the fierce Julie Michaels. It's probably the best example of how, from the start of his career, Keanu Reeves has flouted the rules of action movies, forging his own path that often involves updated and more three-dimensional ideas of masculinity. Because despite all of these beatdowns, Reeves's characters remain heroic and even aspirational. They don't need to be completely indestructible to be iconic leading men.

The Lean

But it's more than just allowing himself to appear human on-screen. Keanu's action heroes have a most excellent habit of getting down to the eyeline of the women whose help he needs. In *Point Break*, as he attempts to woo Tyler and convince her to become his surfing instructor, he leans over and rests his elbows on the counter between them so he can look straight into her eyes. For much of the duration of *Speed* (1994), once bus passenger Annie (Sandra Bullock) is forced to take the wheel of the booby-trapped vehicle, Reeves's SWAT officer Jack Traven is bent over so he can look in her eyes, not only to offer moral support but to ask for her opinion when he's at a loss. He's not like other action stars who insist on maintaining the impression they know everything. Or those who utilize camera angles (and ditches) to make sure they always appear taller than their women costars (**cough* Tom Cruise *cough**).

Throughout his long career, Keanu has tended toward roles that play with presentations of masculinity, always managing to bring out a sensitive and thoughtful side to these badass characters. We just spent chapter 3 going through a queer reading of the *John Wick* franchise, something that would be virtually impossible in other action franchises featuring more traditional action stars. And who can forget how Jack Traven in *Speed* replaces action hero braggadocio with extreme politeness? This aspect was brought to the character by Reeves himself, according to the film's screenwriter, and is a huge part in the film's continuing success.[2] Though other action heroes might occasionally display hints of homoeroticism or moments of vulnerability, they're drowned out by the sorts of toxic masculinity that Keanu's films are careful to avoid: misogyny, violence against women, and completely gratuitous scenes set in strip clubs for no reason other than to have the camera zoom on glittery tits and thong-clad asses, if the women are clothed at all. While Keanu's action heroes might have familiar motivations—saving the world (*The Matrix, Johnny Mnemonic, Chain Reaction*), saving a group of people (*Speed, 47 Ronin*), saving someone they love (*Point Break, Replicas*), or that old standby of revenge (*John Wick*)—Keanu Reeves brings them to life in a way that changes the accompanying social and cultural paradigms.

Keanu's sensitive version of an action hero has received a great deal of academic attention, making him one of the few action stars whose work in this genre is regularly analyzed by writers and thinkers at the university level. In "'There Is No Spoon': Transnationalism and the Coding of Race/Ethnicity in the Science-Fiction/Fantasy Cinema of Keanu Reeves," Julian Cha discusses at length Keanu's on-screen vulnerability as an example of the neutered, desexualized Asian man trope.[3] Marianne Kac-Vergne in *Masculinity in Contemporary Science Fiction Cinema* also discusses Keanu's passivity as an action star as if it's a bad thing.[4] I see their point, but in light of everything else I will discuss in the book—including more on the intersection of race with Reeves's work in chapters 5 and 6—I take a more positive view. So does Jeanne Hamming, who writes about a new masculinity evident in roles such as Keanu's Neo in *The Matrix* that encourages connection, particularly with nature and the environment.[5] And sociologist Brian Brutlag's extraordinary "Bodies in Pods: Masculine Domination, Sexuality, and Love in *The Matrix* Franchise" discusses how the notion of love as presented in *The Matrix Resurrections* socially, culturally, and thematically ties the entire franchise together.[6] These are not the kinds of works that are usually written about other action stars.

Muscles Not Included, or Needed

As the heightened version of himself in 2019's *Always Be My Maybe*, Keanu Squared declares, "I never cower in the face of danger." And this has long been true both on-screen and behind the scenes, as Reeves has done most of his own stunts since his breakout action vehicle *Point Break* in 1991.

But the fearless Keanu Reeves has never bulked up his physique the way other action stars have. The most muscular he's ever been in his career was during the filming of *Speed*, and even then he was downright petite compared to contemporaries such as Tom Cruise, Vin Diesel, Jason Statham, and Dwayne Johnson. And his luscious mane of shaggy, chin-length hair certainly helps take that ubermasculine edge off. Keanu's action heroes also rely on his expressive face to do as much heavy lifting as his deceptively strong body.

The only modern action star with both a physique and a vibe similar to Keanu's is the iconic martial artist Jet Li, who similarly finds himself in unique action films that offer more than just epic fight scenes: they also offer emotion, humanity, and deep pathos. Reeves's and Li's slim builds help the sensitivity and vulnerability of their characters rise to the surface in a way that larger and more muscular action stars can't match.

In fact, in *Chain Reaction* (1996), Keanu's character Eddie, a motorcycle-riding machinist, finds himself in hand-to-hand combat with a henchman who is easily twice his size. Knowing he is outmuscled, Keanu breaks the sacrosanct rule of action movie heroes and kicks the bigger guy straight in the crotch. There was no way Eddie would have won that fight otherwise. Similarly, by *John Wick: Chapter 4*, Wick's battle with the High Table has him so exhausted and fed up he's punching, kicking, and even shooting men in the balls. And this is in a series where Halle Berry's dogs were already going for nuts in *Chapter 2*, and in *Chapter 4* the canine companion of Mr. Nobody also follows suit. The entire franchise rejects the macho sanctity of *no hitting men below the belt*. I'm here for it. Penises are not sacred, no matter what the patriarchy tells us.

A similar moment of tactical thinking over brute force occurs in *Speed*, when Keanu's Jack Traven realizes he cannot stop a bomber with a hostage, so he goes ahead and shoots the hostage nonlethally to deprive the bomber of that advantage—again, the only way he was going to win the fight. Slovenian philosopher Slavoj Žižek has dubbed moments such as this an "ethical heroism," as they eschew the notion that the hero must immediately defeat the villain and instead allow the hero to settle for a small loss that allows regrouping with only minor casualties.[7]

It's also more of a mental than a physical struggle for one of the intrepid action heroes of *Toy Story 4* (2019), "Canada's greatest stuntman" Duke Caboom. As the voice of Duke, Keanu portrays his struggle with an anxiety-based identity crisis that has him choking when he should be hitting the gas pedal. His spiritual battle culminates in a statement that could have been written by Keanu himself: "Be who I am right now." And then Duke proceeds to help save the day. As with Reeves's Batman, even his animated avatars tend to reflect a nontoxic masculinity.

But because he's Keanu Reeves and never fails to push an envelope when it's offered, we get a glimpse of a massively beefed-up Keanu in *Bill & Ted Face the Music* (2020), witnessed in one of the timelines gone awry as the hapless duo attempt once again to save the universe. In this particular scene, we find the alternate Bill and Ted in a maximum-security prison after their attempts to steal the song to save the universe from their future selves land them in jail. Usually lanky Ted is almost as wide as he is tall, all veins and bulging muscles and a neck that could break boards all on its own. I took a moment to imagine if Reeves looked like that all the time, the way many action stars have sculpted their bodies. He would have had an entirely different career—and I probably wouldn't have enough material to write this book about him. As that musclehead in *Face the Music*, Keanu reminded me of John Cena, the wrestler turned actor who also does his best to bring a softer side to his roles, but who doesn't have the same kind of range simply because of his heavyweight physique. Could Cena have believably portrayed everyman Thomas Anderson at the start of *The Matrix*? Would he have needed to shoot the hostage in *Speed* when he looks like he can pulverize Howard Payne with his bare hands? Could Cena pull off Johnny Utah infiltrating the Dead Presidents bank robber gang with that build? Or heartbroken ex-assassin *John Wick*? Not without changing the entire nature of the character and film.

In Brennan Moline's essay "Keanu Reeves' Body as Battleground," he explores how Keanu's physicality transcends the screen—in particular, how the huge scar on his abdomen from a real-life near-fatal motorcycle accident in 1988 is often featured in Keanu's movies instead of being covered up.[8] This ascribes an inherent Keanu-ness to each of his characters, as they all have gone through some gnarly event in their past that similarly scarred them, even if that event is not discussed within the narrative itself. The scar becomes a symbol of the humanity and vulnerability of not just Keanu's characters but also Keanu himself, an on-screen fusion of fiction and reality that every other action star takes great pains to avoid as they plastic-surgery away their scars.

The World's Only Ambidextrous Action Hero

Another distinctive aspect of Keanu's physicality shows his flexibility as an action star: although he's left-handed in real life, over the course of his career he's become ambidextrous, and he's now able to wield just about every weapon known to humans with either his left or his right hand—and sometimes both simultaneously. If we played a drinking game where we took a swig every time Keanu changes his handedness in a given action movie, we'd more likely than not be drunk before the film even hits its third act. In fact, the only thing Reeves does consistently with his left hand on-screen is smoke cigarettes.

For example, in *Point Break* Johnny Utah shoots right-handed but plays football and surfs left-handed. For fight scenes in *Dangerous Liaisons* (1988) he appears to be right-handed until he fences, which he does with his left hand, while in *47 Ronin* he leads his swordplay with his right hand but signs his blood oath with his left. Similarly, in the police corruption exposé *Street Kings* (2008) he shoots righty but writes lefty. In the *John Wick* films we see Wick wielding swords, throwing knives, and more with both his left and right hands, depending on which side he needs for leverage.

The first (and so far only) overt acknowledgment of Keanu's ambidexterity is in *John Wick 4*, when the Bowery King (Laurence Fishburne) gives him a gun with an ambidextrous safety. But behind the scenes, the filmmakers were actively developing his ambidexterity far beyond that one small reference. Director Chad Stahelski said his biggest beef with the studio on *Chapter 3* was over the CGI effects needed to paint out John's missing finger as he continues to fire guns and fight with his left hand as well as his right.[9] And Keanu took it upon himself to train for months on how to swing nunchucks with both hands for *Chapter 4*, apparently spending those months knocking himself out in the process.[10] Never say this man isn't wholeheartedly committed to his art. These details add so much to fresh viewings of the *John Wick* films.

Keanu's handedness is a small detail. But tracked across his entire career, it becomes an impressive feat of physical prowess that has no comparison elsewhere, singlehandedly (pun intended) making Reeves one of the most unique action stars in the history of the genre.

Lack of Copaganda

Another striking feature of Keanu Reeves's action movies that sets him apart from his peers is the distinct lack of copaganda, which most other action stars have been guilty of promoting. *Copaganda* is the handy portmanteau for narratives that glorify law enforcement and portray the police state, its policies, and its violent actions as heroic, when in reality cops are more often than not agents of white supremacy who disproportionately target men and women of color and queer folks across the board.[11]

Point Break begins with Johnny Utah as a gung-ho lawman whose entire ethical framework revolves around the authoritarian ideology of the FBI. But by the end, Reeves's character has abandoned the job that was his identity, growing his hair long in a rejection of his former self. He even allows Bodhi (Patrick Swayze) to swim out to his suicide rather than arresting him, throwing his badge into the ocean as he rejects the rule of law altogether.

In the *Matrix* franchise, the main villains are the body-jumping digital "agents" like Mr. Smith (Hugo Weaving), who are charged with hunting down anyone trying to break free of the virtual world where the machines have enslaved humanity. Mr. Smith and his colleagues are suited up like federal law enforcement agents, and as they chase down Neo and his crew they often take over the bodies of police officers, making it very clear who the bad guys are meant to represent.

One of Reeves's most scathing indictments of law enforcement is *Street Kings*, a movie without one redeeming character in its 109-minute runtime. Cowritten by lifelong critic of the LAPD James Ellroy (who also penned the novels *L.A. Confidential* and *The Black Dahlia*), it stars Reeves as Detective Tom Ludlow, an undercover cop whose brutality and no-holds-barred violence is infamous in the LAPD and beyond. This violence is sanctioned by his superiors and peers, because it gets the results they want. When Ludlow is accused of murdering a fellow officer, he becomes the scapegoat for an entire shit show of corruption that turns out to be a fundamental part of the LAPD system—a system that they would like to maintain indefinitely. What's particularly notable here is that Reeves is playing white despite his multiracial Asian and Indigenous Hawaiian heritage, an example of whitewashing that serves to highlight the inter-nalized racism of many police officers of color as they align themselves with structural white supremacy. "What happened to just locking up bad people?" Ludlow asks Captain Wander (Forest Whitaker). "We're all bad," Wander responds, and real-life law enforcement tends to agree.

Keanu's directorial debut, the martial arts action movie *Man of Tai Chi* (2013), takes place in Hong Kong, and even across the planet the story does not lean into copaganda, exploring underground murder fight clubs and their intersection with police violence. A woman cop, Inspector Suen Jing Si (Karen Mok) is ultimately the figure who exposes the long-standing criminal conspiracy, herself a marginalized figure on the police force due to her gender.

The *John Wick* franchise explores an entire criminal underworld that appears to work in tandem with law enforcement. We even meet Jimmy (Thomas Sadoski), John's police contact who assists in covering up John's and others' mob-related violence. The cops in the Wickiverse have been bought and paid for by the High Table—*that's* who they protect and serve, not your average American citizens.

One Reeves actioner that seems like straightforward copaganda is *Speed*—until we examine the bomber's motivation. Howard Payne (Dennis Hopper) is a former bomb squad cop, disgruntled because after a lifetime of service to the thin blue line, his surrogate family rejected him after he was disabled on the job. Payne even uses the cheap gold-plated retire-ment watch to build his bomb; it was all he was given after everything he sacrificed. There would be no *Speed* without the police treating one of its own like he's as disposable as the citizens of color who they regularly harass and murder.

In chapter 11, as I explore the relationship between Keanu Reeves movies and the myth of the American Dream, the list of anti-copaganda narratives will expand dramatically to include films outside the action genre, including *The Brotherhood of Justice*, the *Bill & Ted* franchise, *A Scanner Darkly*, *The Gift*, and even the comedy caper series *Swedish Dicks* (2016–2018). Is it just happenstance that so many of Keanu's films defy Hollywood's culture of copaganda? Given the sheer numbers, the lack of a similar trend in other action stars' filmographies, and Reeves's reputation for choosing his roles personally from the many hundreds available at any given time, it seems like far more than a coincidence. His choices suggest that he's interested not just in telling unique stories and shaking up the status quo, but also in the social and cultural significance of these stories.

Normalizing Gun Violence

"Sitting on a bullet, thinking of power," Hans (Udo Kier) sings to Keanu and River Phoenix's characters in *My Own Private Idaho* (1991). The lyric reflects the one way that Keanu is in troubling lockstep with his action film peers across generations: how much his films normalize gun violence. This aspect of his work hits me particularly hard as a gun crime survivor myself.

The casual access to an abundance of firearms becomes a running gag in the *John Wick* series, and *Chapter 3* has Keanu repeating Neo's famous request from *The Matrix*: "Guns. Lots of guns." There's even a cutesy name for the stylized gunplay in Keanu films: "gun fu," which is now used colloquially to describe shoot-'em-up movies.

Normalizing gun violence is a problem when on average there is more than one mass shooting every day in the USA.[12] Keanu and company can experience guns as a fictional threat, but the rest of us in the US have to deal with the violent reality of mass shootings and other gun violence. Roxane Dunbar-Ortiz's *Loaded* is a vital reading on the history of gun violence in the USA, revealing how the Second Amendment has been literally weaponized against communities of color, starting with Black and Indigenous people.[13] It's normal now as well that white male shooters are called "lone wolves" and mentally ill, rather than the products of a culture that seems to really enjoy killing innocents.[14]

It's in an unlikely place that we find one of the few direct references in Reeves's career to the long-term traumatic impact of gun violence and war: the romantic drama *A Walk in the Clouds* (1995). Reeves plays Paul Sutton, a former soldier suffering from severe post-traumatic stress after his experiences in World War II. Paul says, "Once the shooting starts you just go blank," a sign of pure disassociation from the horror that raged around him.

Since Keanu Reeves did so much heavy lifting, sometimes literally, to remake the action genre in his image, it's notable that the one area where he "failed" is the one where he didn't even attempt to defy Hollywood conventions, for the simple reason that he enjoys the challenge of undertaking fight training and performing action scenes—which happen to include gunplay.

5

I (STILL) KNOW KUNG FU

Claiming an Asian Identity

As a beloved Hollywood celebrity with few controversies to his name, Keanu Reeves does seem to regularly elicit one strange debate: the veracity of his Asian heritage. In 2013 Twitter was ablaze with outrage at the supposed whitewashing of Keanu's role in the samurai fantasy *47 Ronin*, comparing the film with Tom Cruise's white savior vehicle *The Last Samurai* (2003), until folks in the know reminded everyone that Keanu is, in fact, Asian himself. This same uproar reignited in 2019 when Ali Wong said it was important for her romantic comedy *Always Be My Maybe* to include all Asian love interests—why then, the outraged commentators demanded, was one of them being played by Keanu Reeves as a heightened version of himself?[1] Once again, a whole lot of white people lost their minds at the reminder that Keanu is, in fact, Asian.

One of the most troubling aspects of Keanu Reeves's celebrity is how his Asian identity is often whitewashed by audiences and critics alike. (His Indigenous heritage, meanwhile, is often entirely ignored—other than by Hawaiian academics.)[2] It's also a telling sign of unconscious biases and racism that Keanu's movies centering his Asianness, such as *47 Ronin* and his 2013 directorial debut *Man of Tai Chi*, end up on his worst-of lists even though these films are fabulous in their own ways.

Unfortunately, Reeves himself has clouded the discourse with some of his own choices about his appearance. Marianne Kac-Vergne's *Masculinity in Contemporary Science Fiction Cinema* discusses in detail how Keanu's skin pales on camera from *Point Break* (1991) to *The Matrix* (1999).[3] By now, it's almost as if Keanu hasn't seen the sun since the 1990s, when his Asian and Indigenous features were accentuated by his deep tan. This is a concerning example of colorism, the phenomenon by which virtually every nonwhite culture favors lighter skin and Anglo features—a terrible consequence of white supremacy's insidious global influence. Because of this aspect of Keanu's appearance, the myriad discussions about his white-washed characters and general white-passing are not entirely unfounded, even for those of us similarly multiracial people of color who have always recognized Reeves's complicated racial and ethnic heritage.

Of the thousands of manuscripts that discuss Keanu Reeves in the academic databases Google Scholar, JSTOR, and Sage, a huge majority of them center around debates about Keanu's Asianness and often about where he aligns with perceived whiteness on-screen. In particular, his role in the *Matrix* franchise[4] and his wildly problematic turn as Siddhartha Gautama in *Little Buddha* (1993)[5] have received an overwhelming amount of academic attention, much of which focuses on themes of Orientalism—a white supremacist framework that exoticizes Asian people and cultures while simultaneously whitewashing them for Western consumption.

In Chrishandra Sebastiampillai's article "Crazy Rich Eurasians: White Enough to Be Acceptable, Asian Enough to Be an Asset," she writes about Keanu in relation to another multiracial white/Asian actor, Henry Golding, but the argument she makes about Golding also applies to Reeves: "Golding is an asset precisely because he fulfills Western conventions of beauty in his British heritage *and* supplies an Asian heritage that is simultaneously authentic and exotic."[6] In *Undercover Asian: Multiracial Asian Americans in Visual Culture*, LeiLani Nishime says of the man himself, "Keanu Reeves [is] a symbol par excellence of the flexibility of Asian racialization in visual culture, a flexibility that enables mainstream media narratives to represent racial categories as irrelevant while still punishing those who would not adhere to racial hierarchies."[7] In other words, enough people have coded Reeves as white that his actual multiracial background can conveniently be overlooked.

But in the following sections, I'll push back against that tendency, and explore the problems and complexities of Keanu's Asian identity on-screen.

Model Minority Tropes and Other Spotlights on Asian Identity

As much as certain segments of the population ignore or downplay Keanu Reeves's Asian identity, it's fascinating to note how often the actor plays a character with a stereotypically Asian American profession, in some ways contributing to the "model minority" myth that continues to plague Asian communities.* Examples include when Reeves plays a doctor (*Something's Gotta Give, Thumbsucker, To the Bone*), a scientist (*Chain Reaction, The Day the Earth Stood Still, Replicas*), a lawyer (*Bram Stoker's Dracula, The Devil's Advocate, The Whole Truth*), a businessman (*Sweet November*), and a techie (*Johnny Mnemonic*, the *Matrix* series). What's particularly wild about the sheer number of white-collar professionals Reeves plays is how often these portrayals are met with disbelief, since Reeves is better known for his himbo comedic roles like Ted "Theodore" Logan in *Bill & Ted*. It's fascinating how much the public expects Keanu to play a lovable doofus when roles like that are in the firm minority of Keanu's extensive catalog.

In *The Subject of Film and Race: Retheorizing Politics, Ideology, and Cinema*, Gerald Sim offers a groundbreaking "critical race film theory" that explores how film criticism/theory codes racial bias (sometimes unconsciously) in a variety of ways that have often gone uninterrogated due to a lack of film critics of color. Sim hypothesizes that many of the negative reviews of Reeves's work stem from a conflation of Keanu Reeves the laconic-presenting person and his turn as Ted "Theodore" Logan in *Bill & Ted*, a mash-up that is then used as the lens through which all other Keanu Reeves roles are analyzed.[8] I wholeheartedly agree with Sim's contention, and I connect it to the tension described by Nishime and Kac-Vergne: (white) audiences and critics will only allow Keanu to

---

* It's important to note that the model minority myth exists at the intersection of race and capitalism: it's a capitalist fabrication that pits marginalized groups against each other to prop up white supremacy.

be a certain amount of Asian, thereby rejecting him in roles that explicitly code him as Asian through his on-screen occupation.

We should be similarly skeptical of the negative response when a role highlights Keanu's Asianness in ways other than his character's occupation. Take *47 Ronin*, which features Keanu as Kai, a half-white, half-Japanese man who was orphaned and raised by forest demons called the Tengu. My few criticisms of the film include that it might have been even more effective in Japanese rather than English, and it was an odd choice to feature white actor Ron Bottitta as the narrator. But with an all-Asian cast of incredible martial artists, fantastic creatures from Japanese folklore, and even dragons, *47 Ronin* should have been a hit with critics and audiences. Instead, the movie was widely panned and crashed at the box office.

The same goes for *Man of Tai Chi*, which is set in Hong Kong with an Asian cast. Keanu's fantastic directorial debut not only has a *Fight Club* meets *Unleashed* vibe but also includes some of the most thrilling fight scenes put to screen. As Tiger Chen, martial arts star Hu Chen goes up against foes who are sometimes two or three times his size, including Reeves himself as the shark-eyed ubervillain Donaka Mark. Yet *Man of Tai Chi* has also been unceremoniously panned by critics and was a big enough commercial failure that Keanu hasn't returned to the director's chair since. A shame indeed.

Always Be My Maybe is the only film to openly highlight Keanu's Asian identity that has been both a critical and an audience success. Part of that is a credit to the exceptional writing and the extraordinary chemistry Reeves shares with every costar, which renders his over-the-top version of himself fully lovable despite being an absolute dickhead. Yet, as mentioned earlier, even this film couldn't escape a brief online backlash as white audiences questioned why Keanu Reeves was cast as an Asian love interest, which confirms just how much resistance there is to perceiving Keanu as overtly nonwhite.

It's time to recognize that the Keanu-as-Ted notion of what his on-screen roles "should" be like is unfair, negating the artistry Reeves brings to each of his roles to instead view him as simultaneously exotic and a mirror to white audiences. It's not Keanu Reeves's multiracial heritage but this reductive perspective that deserves to be disregarded.

Asians as the Other

Things become even more complicated, and not always in a good way, when we consider Keanu's Asian (and Indigenous) identity in relation to the movies where he plays social outcasts and outsiders. In *The Day the Earth Stood Still* (2008), Reeves plays Klaatu, an alien sent to destroy humans after we have climate-changed the planet to the brink of oblivion. Klaatu's alien contact, who has been embedded on Earth for seventy years, is Mr. Wu, played by Hollywood legend James Hong. Klaatu speaks Mandarin to Wu, who defends humans even though he recognizes that they are a scourge. What's troubling here is that by portraying two Asian American actors as aliens masquerading as humans, the film furthers the notion of Asian Americans as the Other. *Othering* is a phenomenon by which particular groups of people are treated as if they're inherently different or foreign—in this case, nonwhite people are seen as not "real" Americans. Worse, the film specifically portrays Klaatu and Wu as spies working for a hostile foreign power, especially troubling since Asian Americans are often accused of not being real Americans and of plotting to infiltrate and dismantle Western culture. This dynamic is the reason why during World War II Japanese Americans were herded into concentration camps as potential spies, even those who had never been to Japan or even spoken Japanese.[9]

In Kenneth Branagh's 1993 adaptation of Shakespeare's *Much Ado About Nothing*, Keanu's Don John is effectively the leader of the outsiders, and an illegitimate half brother to the prince. He's the son of his father's other woman and also an Other in his nonwhiteness, as Julian Cha notes in "'There Is No Spoon'": "Don John also interacts almost entirely homosocially with his companions Borachio and Conrade and has no love interest in the film. Alienated by the nucleus of the men and by all the women of the estate, Don John/Reeves is the outsider and the ethnic Other who is excluded from the group of close-knit brothers-in-arms." Cha details how this particular kind of Othering has resulted in a stereotype of the desexualized or asexual Asian man, whose "nonthreatening sexuality" is often commented on as a positive without interrogating the racist connotations behind the sentiment.[10] But I would argue that the way Keanu's Don John smolders his way across the screen—in a performance laden with queer subtext, as I will unpack in chapter 14—takes some steam out of this particular example.

While there's so much I appreciate about Cha's analysis, his reading of *Much Ado* gets further complicated by the fact that Don John's half brother Don Pedro is played by Denzel Washington, a Black man who—in the context of this version of *Much Ado About Nothing*—is not Othered in the least. We have here an interesting moment in which class hierarchy displaces a race reading, whereby Don Pedro's mother was the legitimate wife of the king and Don John's a mere mistress. So ultimately Don John's Otherness stems from his social status and antisocial behavior, not his racial identity.

Internalized Racism and Asian Alignment with White Supremacy

Street Kings (2008) explores another common but polar opposite phenomenon: the rejection of an Asian identity for the sake of assimilation, as Reeves plays someone who is actively trying to pass as white. Detective Tom Ludlow is referred to as white multiple times in the film's dialogue, but in light of Keanu's real-life identity, this can be read as a reflection of the many mixed-race folks in real life who discover that they moderately pass and then go on to align themselves with white supremacy. Ludlow even has a stunning Tarantino-esque monologue in which he strings together every racial slur that exists in the span of a couple minutes. This also happens in real life, as internalized racism causes certain folks of color to embrace the worst of whiteness to prove themselves to white people and distance themselves from any other ethnicity. Similarly, in *Exposed* (2016) Reeves plays Detective Galban, a cop who covers up the evil deeds of his white partner. As I watch *Street Kings* and *Exposed* in a post–George Floyd world, I cannot help but link Reeves's Ludlow and Galban with Tou Thao, the Asian cop who stood by as Officer Derek Chauvin murdered Floyd.

Though Keanu's Asian identity adds complexity to roles such as these, there are other movies in which Keanu has to be read as actually playing white. In *The Devil's Advocate* (1997), Kevin Lomax's parents are both played by white actors, which erases Reeves's heritage altogether. (Though it's rather amusing to note that in one of the key roles where Keanu is unambiguously white, his father is the actual devil, played by an outrageous Al Pacino—more on the concept of white devilry in chapter 9.) In *The Brotherhood of Justice* (1986), Keanu's parents don't appear, but his younger brother (Danny Nucci) blames a crime spree on "ethnic minorities" only to be chastised by their Latina housekeeper: "White boys don't steal?" So it seems that Reeves is playing white for purposes of the narrative. Similarly, *Under the Influence, The Night Before, The Prince of Pennsylvania, Tune in Tomorrow, Feeling Minnesota*, and *The Lake House* all have Reeves cosplaying as a white dude. As much as each of these movies has something unique to offer, from performance to plot to music and more, it is disturbing that they whitewash Reeves's own identity without any real interrogation.

But it's important to note that many of these examples of whitewashing are from rather early in Keanu's career. This may reflect both the social norms of the late twentieth century and the growing efforts to promote racial literacy in Hollywood in the decades since then. But we might also see in it a shift in the power dynamic of Reeves's own career: the brighter his star shone, the more he was able to choose roles that fit his actual racial and ethnic identity (with a few exceptions like *John Wick*, where he plays a Romani man).

Asians and Other Marginalized Communities as Interchangeable

But potentially one of the worst issues with Keanu Reeves's casting is that his "ethnic ambiguity" is frequently leveraged on roles that don't reflect his actual Chinese/Indigenous and white mixed-race heritage. It's a problem because it plays into the "they all look the same" stereotype regarding Asian appearances. It's a stereotype that rears its ugly head even in dialogue in Keanu's underdog sports film *The Replacements* (2000), when Jamal (Faizon Love) calls his teammate Fumiko (Ace Yonamine) Chinese. When Fumiko reminds him he's Japanese, his response is "Same difference."

The closest Keanu has come to explicitly playing his own race is in *47 Ronin*, but he plays a character who's half *Japanese* and half white. And the only time he's played an Indigenous character is as a "full-blooded Indian" in *Even Cowgirls Get the Blues* (1993), even though Indigenous Hawaiians wouldn't be referred to as Indians or Native Americans.

In *Little Buddha* Keanu wears brownface to play Nepalese prince Siddhartha Gautama. While it's great that an Asian man plays an Asian man here, there's an enormous difference between Chinese, Nepali, and other South Asian peoples. It's also deeply offensive that *Little Buddha*'s central characters end up being a white family, but I'll discuss that more in chapter 15.

Sometimes Reeves's "ambiguity" has him representing marginalized groups that are completely unrelated to his own racial and ethnic identity. *Freaked* (1993) finds him playing a dog-man hybrid who seems to be of Cuban descent, styled after revolutionary Che Guevara. In *John Wick: Chapter 3—Parabellum* (2019) we find out Reeves's title character is a Romani man. Again, it's great that the writers brought a marginalized identity into a franchise that's become a mainstream phenomenon, but as I mention in chapter 3, Madeline Potter suggests that this is a fetishized and unrepresentative version of the Roma considering there isn't one Romani actor in the franchise.

And then there are times when his character's cultural identity seems deliberately unclear. While *Man of Tai Chi*'s Donaka Mark has a Japanese American–sounding name, "Donaka" is actually not a Japanese given name, a fact Reeves himself confirmed when discussing the character's development: "We made it up as a name so I didn't take it from anywhere. It has a Japanese aspect to it. If you see Donaka's set, there's a cave-y aspect to it, the stone. His office has a stone [material]. I wanted him to be a darkly, earth element."[11] Interestingly, though, Donaka phonetically pronounced corresponds to the Gaelic name Donnchadh, which translates to "dark warrior." The meaning is certainly well suited to Keanu's character in this movie, and it also serves as an apparently subconscious nod to Reeves's Irish heritage on his mother's side, bringing an unintentional poetry to this villain's backstory even as the cultural nonspecificity is mildly problematic.

Asian and Indigenous Representation in Unlikely Places

On the positive side, thanks to Reeves's background we end up with Asian and Indigenous Hawaiian representation in surprising places. In early films like *River's Edge* (1986) and the first two *Bill & Ted* movies,

Keanu plays a young man with an absent parent, so it's easy to imagine the unseen mom or dad is Asian, Indigenous, or both. And a huge number of Keanu's movies leave out any discussion of his character's family, often for the drama of making him an orphan figure with no blood ties to call on. But ironically, this dynamic ends up leaving the most room for us to insert Reeves's actual racial identity into his role—to interpret him as an Asian/Indigenous character without the movie having to explicitly say it.

The juiciest such moments come in Reeves's period pieces. *Dangerous Liaisons* (1988) and *Much Ado About Nothing* remind audiences that yes indeed there were Asian nobles in Europe during the 1600s and 1700s. *Bram Stoker's Dracula* (1992) reflects the fact that an Asian legal clerk like Jonathan Harker was wholly within the realm of possibility in Victorian England. And *A Walk in the Clouds* (1995) represents for the many Asian American and Indigenous servicemen who fought in the front lines during World War II, even as Japanese Americans were being interned in concentration camps. I dive much further into Keanu's period pieces in chapter 15.

And in films like *The Gift* (2000) and *The Whole Truth* (2016), set in Georgia and Louisiana, respectively, Keanu Reeves's presence serves as yet another important reminder: there are Asian people who live in the American South. Very few on-screen narratives acknowledge this fact of American life, and with the notable exception of Mira Nair's *Mississippi Masala* (1991), the short list is mostly of film and TV projects from the past decade, including *The Walking Dead* during Steven Yeun's years on the show (2010–2016), *Claws* (2017–2022), *Minari* (2020), *Mona Lisa and the Blood Moon* (2021), *Blue Bayou* (2021), and *Unseen* (2023).

Keanu's multiracial presence also adds nuance to films that could otherwise come across as offensive white savior narratives. In *Hardball* (2001), for instance, Keanu plays Conor O'Neill, a gambling addict who gets saddled coaching an inner-city baseball league of adorable Black youths to help pay off his debts. Reading Keanu's character as a person of color makes this a rare and beautiful moment of Asian/Indigenous and Black solidarity on-screen in what might otherwise be a generic underdog sports film.

And even though Keanu rarely plays an explicitly Asian character, his films are filled with imagery from Asian cultures. In particular, Buddhist sculpture and art make regular appearances. The *John Wick* franchise is positively brimming with Asian influences, but my personal favorite is the photo print of Sri Lankan pole fishermen by John and Helen's bed. It's something that I'm one of the few people to notice because I'm Sri Lankan myself. It's rare to see any mention of Sri Lanka anywhere in Western visual media, so this is a special moment of representation indeed.

A Reluctant Asian Figurehead

In a frank discussion with *Essence* about his race and heritage, Keanu Reeves notes his connection to his Chinese heritage through his grandmother. But he also says that he doesn't want to be "a spokesperson" for people of color.[12] And in an interview with NBC News about being characterized as a person of color he says, "I don't know if I agree with that statement. But I don't not agree." In the same interview he also admits, "My relationship to my Asian identity, it's always been good and healthy. And I love it. . . . We've been growing up together."[13]

I do understand his reticence to go all in on these discussions about race and ethnicity, especially since—as I've outlined in this chapter—some of his roles have entailed whitewashing his identity, playing racial identities that are not his own, and generally passing as white in the eyes of many (white) critics and fans.[14] But with seventy-eight movies under his belt at the time of this writing, the majority of which we can read from a racially literate lens that incorporates his Asian and Indigenous identities, at this point Keanu can't avoid how other multiracial Asians recognize him as not just one of us but one of our most visible community members.

There is no denying that Keanu Reeves is a multiracial person of color, and on more occasions than not, his identity adds beautiful nuance to films that wouldn't otherwise be there. And he's been doing this work around Asian (and Indigenous) inclusion since the early 1980s, amassing a catalog of mostly positive and important representation that's unsurpassed by any other actor of his cohort. While there have been some unfortunate missteps along the way, Keanu Reeves's consistent presence on-screen as a multiracial individual has been a vital step for the growing number of examples of active Asian representation that have been remaking Hollywood and cinema in general into a more inclusive and equitable place for our communities.

6

HE IS THE ONE

Keanu Reeves as the Multiracial Messiah

Multiracial People as Bridges

Considering Keanu Reeves's Asian or Indigenous background individually, as we did in chapter 5, only gets at a part of what makes him such a crucial figure at the intersection of race and celebrity. Just as important is his identity as a multiracial individual, considering the fraught role mixed-race people have been called on to play in society's collective imagination.

For as long as I can remember in my lived experience as a multiracial American woman with Sri Lankan (both Tamil and Sinhalese), Lithuanian, and Portuguese heritage, I am often on the receiving end of the utopian notion that mixed-race individuals like me are the future of a racially equitable world. *If everyone is multiracial, how can there be discrimination?* I was told over and over again, even as my daily encounters with racial microaggressions told an entirely different story about how I was perceived, especially by white and other monoracial people.[1] Like, if I got a dollar every time someone asked me "Where are you from?" two dollars for the inevitable follow-up "No, where are you *really* from?" and three dollars for the kicker "But where are your *parents* from?" and then ten bucks for every increasingly intrusive question after that, I'd be living well like Keanu on the residuals from his hit movie *Speed*. I am confusion personified: none of my explanations satisfy the questioners. Like my actual physical body is the "scramble suit" featured in Keanu's dystopian sci-fi movie *A Scanner Darkly*, that makes me everyone and no one simultaneously.

A study in *Psychological Science* found that white folks living in homogenous areas have a growing prejudice against mixed-race individuals, as our so-called ethnic ambiguity is unsettling to them.[2] The study's lead author, Jonathan Freeman, told New York University, "The results suggest that this bias arises in individuals with lower interracial exposure because they visually process racially ambiguous faces in a more difficult and unpredictable fashion, and this unstable experience translates into negative biases against mixed-race people."[3]

But the utopian notion isn't just inaccurate, it's also unfair, putting the burden of creating a nonracial future on the children of interracial partnerships. It's not our responsibility to function as human bridges across cultures, especially when many of us are forced to choose one side of our heritage over the other, often depending on how society defines us based on our physical features.[4] When your body is forced to become a bridge, it's not long before it becomes painful, with people constantly treading over you from one side to the other.[5] That is, unless you're one of the "chosen" mixed people who pass as either white or monoracial, or who gets claimed by whites and thus receives the privileges afforded by this proximity to whiteness.

Keanu Reeves belongs in this latter category, having become so much of a chosen one that social theorist Tanya Horeck has dubbed him "God of the Internet."[6] And when examined through the lens of Keanu's multiracial identity, his roles often embody the multiracial messiah figure that is the supposed future of a postracial society.

Reeves in Messiah Roles

"He is the One," Morpheus says in *The Matrix* (1999). And while *The Matrix Resurrections* (2021) will eventually complicate this simple formulation, the first three *Matrix* films operate under the premise that everything hinges on and centers around Keanu Reeves's Neo—even after his death in *The Matrix Revolutions* (2003). He's a "cinematic Christ-figure,"

as Anton Karl Kozlovic calls it, a character who, over the course of a narrative, transcends the bounds not just of the physical but also of the spiritual,
the metaphysical, and even the supernatural.[7] I mean, right at the start of
The Matrix, Thomas Anderson/Neo's client Choi (Marc Aden Gray) says,
"You're my savior, man. My own personal Jesus Christ." The messianic
reading is not even subtext, it's just *text*. Other examples in Kozlovic's
discussion include the main characters in *Superman: The Movie*, *K-PAX*,
E.T. the Extra Terrestrial, *12 Monkeys*, and the 1951 version of *The Day
the Earth Stood Still*—analysis that could now extend to the 2008 version
of *Day*, in which Keanu plays the Christlike Klaatu, which hadn't been
released yet at the time of Kozlovic's analysis.

As Kozlovic's examples indicate, such messiah roles aren't unique to
Reeves. But he's played a *lot* of them in his career, from Ted "Theodore"
Logan in the *Bill & Ted* franchise, one of the chosen two responsible for
saving the entire universe, in the process dying not once but twice in order
to be reborn again, to a live-action cameo in *The SpongeBob Movie: Sponge
on the Run* (2020) as a sage named Sage with such a familiar look that
it inspired a photographic meme claiming, "A grandma had this picture
on her mantel because she thought it was Jesus."[8]

This messiah complex takes a dark turn from time to time. For example, in *The Bad Batch* (2016), Keanu's cult leader the Dream has appointed
himself not just savior of the harsh desert world of those expelled from the
USA but also the personified God figure who impregnates young women
to build a new world in his own image. The film features another antihero
multiracial messiah in Miami Man, played by Jason Momoa; like Reeves,
Momoa's background includes Indigenous Hawaiian and Irish heritage, as
well as Samoan, German, and Pawnee. Such narratives are the dark side
of the messiah complex Reeves often finds himself in on-screen.

Especially noteworthy are the occasions when the savior role connects
directly to Keanu's multiracial identity—not always in a positive way.
As mentioned in the previous chapter, *Little Buddha* (1993) has Reeves
playing Nepalese prince Siddhartha Gautama in brownface. According to
director Bernardo Bertolucci, he looked for an Indian actor who could
play the role but "couldn't find anybody," and "then I read somewhere
that Keanu is half-Chinese-Hawaiian." Praising his performance in *My
Own Private Idaho* (1991), Bertolucci added, "I noticed a lot of innocence

in Keanu's face."⁹ In *The Subject of Film and Race*, Gerald Sim writes that the director cast Reeves because to him, "the multiracial face held a universal aesthetic: an innocence that made him look like he walked on air. In essence, he equated racial ambiguity with social dislocation and spiritual detachment"—two key thematic notions of the Buddha himself.¹⁰ Partly because of his turn as Siddhartha, Keanu himself in real life is often perceived as a Zen master in word and deed, even though his workaholism contradicts this characterization.¹¹

Keanu's "hybrid" background is also reflected in the character of Ortiz the Dawg Boy in *Freaked* (1993), the fantastic social satire codirected by Reeves's *Bill & Ted* costar Alex Winter. Ortiz is part man and part dog, straddling not just cultures but an interspecies bridge as de facto leader of Elijah C. Skugg's Freek Land. And in *My Own Private Idaho*, which features a number of references to colonization and Indigenous genocide in Portland and the Pacific Northwest, Reeves's Scott Favor could be read as half Indigenous, since we never properly meet his mother on-screen. And he's certainly a messiah figure of sorts, to the ragtag collective of unhoused sex workers who are all waiting for Scott to return to his mansion on the hill and raise them out of poverty once he inherits the kingdom of his father, the (white) mayor of Portland.

Even the graphic novel written by Keanu himself, *BRZRKR*, features a mixed-race messiah, an eighty-thousand-year-old god-human hybrid turned weapon, who will be played by Reeves in the planned film adaptation. The mother whose magic spell willed the main character Unute, a.k.a. B, into being is Black, and his father is a white man with ginger hair. In B's backstory, his father is a colonizer figure who exploits him, and his father ends up killing his mother when she objects to the resulting greed from having access to such power.

Given these connections, it's no surprise that when Will Harris wrote *Mixed-Race Superman: Keanu, Obama, and Multiracial Experience*, he would associate Keanu Reeves with another multiracial messiah figure: President Barack Obama.¹² Obama was the charismatic leader who was supposed to usher in a postracial political landscape where racial discrimination was fading in the rearview mirror. And Keanu, as Julian Cha notes in "'There Is No Spoon,'" "has secured a position as a hybrid and transnational entity in the cultural imaginary and has had the preternatural power to have mass appeal and to navigate along and across racial/ethnic borders."[13]

The *Matrix* Quadrilogy

But the ultimate example of Reeves as a multiracial messiah, and the one that has received the most academic attention, remains *The Matrix*, in which Keanu's interracial body serves as both burden and panacea for visions of a postracial society. For instance, Lisa Nakamura's "Race in the Construct, or the Construction of Race: New Media and Old Identities in 'The Matrix'" is a fantastic exploration of multiculturality as it is expressed through the original trilogy. Nakamura writes, "This future-world is emphatically multiracial; rather than depicting a world in which race has been 'transcended,' or represented solely by white actors (who command more money at the box office), we are shown a world in which race is not only visible but necessary for human liberation."[14] Nakamura discusses Keanu Reeves's casting in relation to the racial designation of "Other" that was added to the US Census in 1999, the same year the original *Matrix* came out:

> This official recognition that people who don't fit into one racial "box" do exist in demographically significant numbers represents a significant paradigm shift in our national conceptions of race, one which this film recognizes by making a character of mixed race its hero, literally "the One," humanity's only hope against oppressive whiteness and the enslavement and eventual eradication of humanity which it represents in the film.

Nakamura points out that virtually all of the villainous agents who keep humanity enslaved within the Matrix are represented by similar-looking white men and cops, while Zion, the civilization of humans who have escaped the Matrix, is a blended community whose leaders are predominantly Black; one of them is even played by real-life Black activist-intellectual Cornel West. She connects this to the fact that "non-whites and women are the ones who would *want* to wake up from this particular dream," the dream being the actual nightmare of the Matrix for marginalized people.

Though sociopolitical analysis such as this dominates academic writing about the franchise, some academics focus on other cultural and religious aspects of its messianic main character. To Brian Brutlag, Neo's power stems from his embrace of genuine love, freed from the authoritarian structures that work to repress and control it.[15] This hammers home Neo's Christlike nature, since the old-school readings of Jesus are as a figure of love and compassion for all—a message that has been grossly distorted in most actual Christian practices. On the other hand, Amjad Hussain's "Religion, Film and Postmodernism: The Matrix, a Case Study" characterizes the religious symbolism of the films as postmodern, in that they incorporate both Judeo-Christian and Eastern religious ideas in a pluralistic way that denies the possibility of arriving at any objective truth.[16] This falls in line with the sort of multicultural rupture that folks like Keanu are thought to represent on-screen.

One example of Eastern influence in the films is the character of Rama-Kandra, a rogue program within the Matrix who speaks of his belief in karma. Though he appears only in the second and third films, he's mentioned in the fourth installment as the creator of the resurrection pods that bring Neo and Trinity back into the Matrix. Rama-Kandra and his wife created their daughter out of love, which is the subversive act that got them labeled rogue programs within the Matrix in the first place. Thus the character echoes both Brutlag's analysis, emphasizing the power of love in defiance of authoritarianism, and Amjad Hussain's ideas about the series' postmodern religious fusion, as an Eastern-coded character who empowers Neo's Christlike resurrection. Adding even greater resonance is the fact that Rama-Kandra is played by Bernard White, a Sri Lankan American actor—one of the few diasporic Lankan actors who've carved out careers in Western cinema. *Revolutions* is also one of the only films in Western cinema that actually features Sri Lankan people, a big deal especially for multiracial Sri Lankans like me who rarely see folks sharing my heritage represented on-screen at all, let alone in narratives taking place hundreds of years in the future. It's nice to know that as difficult the world of *The Matrix* might be, we still survived centuries from now.

LeiLani Nishime gets the same thrill I do by kindly informing people that yes, indeed, Keanu Reeves is a multiracial Asian/Indigenous man and watching their brains melt. But she also explores the tacit fact that race—like the Matrix itself—is a construct. "Race only appears when we go looking for it," Nishime writes in "Guilty Pleasures: Keanu Reeves, Superman, and Racial Outing."[17] The notion of "whiteness" often subsumes certain groups or individuals to suit its ultimate goal of maintaining white supremacy. Through this lens, what it means to acknowledge Neo as a multiracial messiah depends on whose gaze is identifying him as such. This complicating factor is reflected in the series itself, when we find out at the end of *The Matrix Reloaded* (2003) that the machines have been using the concept of the One embodied by Neo as a kind of opiate of the masses, to give people hope in a world outside of their system, essentially weaponizing people's faith to keep them enslaved. We discover there have been many Ones before Neo, and their function was to *seek* freedom without ever achieving it. The One is a Christ figure who is crucified over and over and over again, who always returns with the same hopeful and human message of liberation.

This co-option of the multiracial messiah extends to the *Matrix* franchise itself: right-wing culture has twisted *The Matrix*'s notion of "redpilling"—rejecting the authoritarianism and conformity represented by the false reality of the Matrix—to instead refer to those who exit the liberal/progressive sphere and jump onto the proto-Nazi neofascist bandwagon of institutionalized hatred. C. Richard King and David J. Leonard explore how white supremacists have adopted the language of *The Matrix* to promote white nationalist projects in "Racing the Matrix: Variations on White Supremacy in Responses to the Film Trilogy."[18] Fascinatingly, part of how white supremacists are able to subsume the language of this multicultural allegory is through the whitewashing of Keanu Reeves's actual racial identity.*

The reactionary take on Keanu's multiracial messiah is particularly valuable to analyze because race is most commonly discussed from the perspective of people of color themselves, as we call out a variety of racist or racially insensitive behavior. But it's also important to approach race from a perspective of whiteness, as Brette D. W. Kristoff does in

---

* LeiLani Nishime's *Undercover Asian: Multiracial Asian Americans in Visual Culture* offers further insight into these discussions, unpacking the shifting gaze of whiteness as it may or may not land on Keanu Reeves's racialized body in the *Matrix* franchise.

her 2023 master's thesis for the University of Saskatoon's Department of Religion and Culture in "Contextualizing Trumpism: Understanding Race, Gender, Religiosity, and Resistance in Post-Truth Society." By exploring how white supremacist and white nationalist groups online co-opted *The Matrix*'s concept of the "red pill," Kristoff unpacks the variety of perceived grievances of online groups of white men in particular as they often violently reject a racially diverse society.[19]

Multiracial People as the Other

Even when not in the hands of white nationalists, the mixed-race messiah framework can become a tool of Othering, portraying multiracial people as liminal figures who are allowed to exist only in borderspaces. The term "ethnically ambiguous" alone suggests that a multiracial person doesn't have the same fixed identity as monoracial people—that they are neither here nor there. If they are both simultaneously, it can inspire fear and hatred rather than hero identification. In *47 Ronin* (2013), the vengeful samurai Yasuno (Masayoshi Haneda) spits, "I would rather have been killed by that beast than saved by a half-breed!" rejecting Keanu's Kai even though they still share Japanese heritage. Kai's mixed heritage is in many ways deemed a social crime, which keeps Kai literally living at the edge of the kingdom in a thatched hut, far from all the "pure"-breeds.

In a *New York Times* article titled "Keanu Reeves Is Whatever You Want Him to Be," pop culture philosopher William Irwin is quoted as saying of Reeves, "There is an ambiguity about him. . . . He's not androgynous. He's not an alpha male. He's masculine and feminine in a way."[20] None of this is quite the compliment Irwin intends when we examine it in light of Keanu's multiraciality, as each of these statements positions him as a kind of the ultimate Other: different enough to be attractive, but not so different that he can't be relatable to white people in particular. Because Reeves has effectively been claimed by white audiences and critics, LeiLani Nishime advocates "reading race back into Reeves"[21] as an important tool in any analysis of Keanu as a person or a performer.

Doing so confirms how frequently this multiracial Othering happens in Reeves's movies. For example, in *The Bad Batch*, Keanu's the Dream is a cult leader who heads a hedonistic town called Comfort in the deep desert and controls the community through a specialized hallucinogenic he himself created. The Dream has a harem of young, pregnant women of all races who are creating that blended postracial future of utopian visions. Except the Dream uses coercion and violence to maintain his status and position of power. In light of Reeves's multiracial identity, this scenario taps into a fear of the Other as a colonizing and authoritarian force that should be feared and obeyed without question.

When we bring Reeves's Asian and Indigenous heritage into his role as Shane Falco in *The Replacements* (2000), we get an extension of *Point Break*'s Johnny Utah (see chapter 2), but Shane's Otherness is heightened: he's the de facto leader of the ragtag second-string team of scabs brought in to play for professional football players on strike. Here Reeves's multiraciality adds to the hodgepodge of identities on display, from a Japanese sumo wrestler to a hearing-impaired man to a wiry Welsh football—a.k.a. soccer—player subbing in for kicker.

In *Constantine* (2005), the title character's suicide attempt as a teenager condemned him to hell, and now he hunts demons to redeem his soul. John Constantine is thus a spiritual halfling of sorts, operating on the margins of not just human society but also the literal underworld of hell itself. Keanu's mixed-race identity adds to Constantine's already marginalized position in the story. Similarly, though Jonathan Wick isn't multiracial in the narrative, the fact that John is set apart from all other assassins in the series' criminal underworld also falls in line with an Othering, even among an entire underworld who have been Othered by mainstream society.

The New Face of America?

Back in 1993, *Time* magazine's cover featured a computer-generated portrait that composited the images of people of multiple races to create an imaginary person of the future called Eve, whom they dubbed THE NEW FACE OF AMERICA.[22] Gerald Sim points out in *The Subject of Film and Race* that Keanu Reeves could easily be Eve's brother in his similar racial and ethnic ambiguity.[23] While the early 1990s was supposed to be a moment that heralded the eventual pluralizing of the United States as a multiracial and multicultural society—the melting pot myth made into physical and genetic reality—in fact we've seen quite the opposite happen in the USA, with the rise of open white nationalism, neo-Nazism, and proto-fascism. Mixed-race folks exist at the nexus of these two opposing dynamics: the postracial future many predicted and the violent movements to enshrine white supremacy before that multiracial society can fully blossom.[24] It leads to a paradoxical quantum mechanics in which we're asked to hold two contradictory beliefs to be true simultaneously. First, that each multiracial person is a unique bridge between cultures tasked with forging cross-cultural understanding as a low-key messianic messenger. And that multiracial people are to be seen as complicated Others whose mixed backgrounds embody the anxiety of people who would prefer a return to the days when interracial relationships were illegal in the USA.

The Keanu Reeves movies I've discussed in this chapter highlight the tension between how multiracial people like him are tasked with being the future charge of societies that have moved beyond race and discrimination, while at the same time also set apart from the majority in uncomfortable new hierarchies rather than being subsumed into a collective. The mixed-race messiah trope is problematic from the get-go, mainly because it suggests that one day the racial and ethnic signifiers that have defined human experiences (including inequity, inequality, and injustice) will simply disappear, thereby erasing thousands of years' worth of race-based social structures and the accompanying violence, including genocide.

The bottom line is that multiracial people aren't saviors or Others set apart. We are just humans, each with a unique upbringing and heritage. While Keanu often makes an excellent poster boy for multiracial representation, and his racial heritage is a foundational theme in any Critical Reeves Theory, he brings much more than discussions of race and multiraciality to the table in his catalog of work. I'll begin deep-diving into less-examined themes of his work in the chapters to come.

7

I WILL SEARCH FOR YOU TO A THOUSAND WORLDS AND TEN THOUSAND LIFETIMES

Keanu and Conceptualizing
the Perfect Leading Man

IN A 2021 APPEARANCE on the talk show *The Drew Barrymore Show*, Keanu Reeves tells his host (who was also his costar in one of his earliest projects, the 1986 TV movie *Babes in Toyland*), "If you're a lover, you've got to be a fighter . . . because if you don't fight for your love, what kind of love do you have?"[1] Both he and Drew burst out laughing at the corniness of the comment. But there's a lot of truth to that statement when it comes to Reeves's career as a romantic leading man. While critics and academics focus almost exclusively on debating Keanu's ethnic heritage, racial identity, and proximity to whiteness, a gender analysis of Reeves's catalog of films—not just the romantic comedies—reveals that he's been quietly working as a feminist trailblazer in so many regards.

Atypically among romantic male leads, his characters will admit they are wrong (*Permanent Record*), graciously accept an apology instead of being an ass about it (*Something's Gotta Give*), and acknowledge that they don't know everything (*Speed*, *The Lake House*). A Keanu character will cover a drunk colleague with a blanket rather than hitting on her (*Chain Reaction*), bring his girlfriend breakfast in bed (*Flying*), and let his partners control their own desires by being on top (*River's Edge*, *Feeling Minnesota*, *Siberia*). And, of course, there are the tender lines, like in *47 Ronin* when he says, "I will search for you to a thousand worlds and ten thousand lifetimes." *Sigh*. (OK, yeah, I know he commits seppuku almost immediately afterward. Still, that line is romantic AF.) Keanu Reeves's characters offer a universe of both admirable and swoon-worthy behavior that doesn't rely on tired gender stereotypes—unless the tiredness of those stereotypes is the point of the story.

The world certainly appreciates the effort. Keanu's reputation as everyone's dream boyfriend continues to grow, with references popping up in the most unlikely places. For instance, in Frances Koncan's 2020 stage play *Women of the Fur Trade*, about a group of nineteenth-century Indigenous Canadian women, the characters' discussion of who they have crushes on includes Keanu Reeves, as his image is projected onto a screen behind the actors.[2]

This is a good moment to remind you of what *John Wick* screenwriter Derek Kolstad noted: Keanu has hundreds of scripts on his desk at any given moment, carefully choosing his projects. His on-screen record of boyfriends and exceptional leading men reflects the foundational goodness of Keanu Reeves the human being. As the #MeToo movement has exposed so many serial predators in the film and TV industry, it has uplifted Reeves as one of the only celebrities to emerge from the scrutiny of #MeToo without a single negative mark by his name. The closest he has come to the Playboy Mansion—the anything-goes celebrity hangout where the A&E documentary series *Secrets of Playboy* (2022–2023) exposed numerous and gruesome sex crimes—is wearing Dolly Parton's iconic Playboy Bunny outfit for Halloween when he was a teen. Keanu's mother, Patricia Taylor, designed the costume for Dolly in the first place, which is why it was at his house at all.[3] And he doesn't even touch fans, or sometimes even costars, when he takes pictures with them.[4] This personal sense of respect and decency finds its way into the kinds of stories Keanu leads, and the kinds of people who star alongside him. The consistency of that influence will become clear as we examine Reeves's personal outside-the-norm leading man tropes.

A Leading Man Who Doesn't Always Get the Girl

Breaking with the precedent set by other leading men, Reeves often doesn't end up with the leading lady at the end—certainly much more than other actors in his cohort, such as Tom Cruise, Matthew McConaughey, and Hugh Grant. The trend starts early in Keanu's career: the dark dramedy *The Prince of Pennsylvania* (1988) ends with Keanu's Rupert Marshetta choosing not to ride off into the sunset with his lady love Carla (Amy Madigan). And as a love interest of main character Sissy (Uma Thurman) in *Even Cowgirls Get the Blues* (1993), his Julian Gitche is only a masturbatory blip in what will be mostly same-sex pairings for Sissy going forward. These transitory pairings persist as Reeves's star rises. In the romantic drama *Sweet November* (2001), Nelson (Reeves) and Sara (Charlize Theron) ultimately part ways as Sara decides to end her run with cancer alongside her family rather than with a love interest. And in Nancy Meyers's *Something's Gotta Give* (2003), Reeves's Dr. Julian Mercer realizes his girlfriend Erica Barry (Diane Keaton) is still in love with her ex and chooses to let her go.

Even in action movies, where women are too often treated as prizes to be won by the hero, Keanu doesn't always get the girl. *Constantine* (2005) oozes with sexual tension between Reeves and his costar Rachel Weisz, but they never kiss. The *John Wick* series, of course, begins with the death of John's beloved wife, and despite the parade of apparent former lovers, as discussed in chapter 3, none of them ever take her place in his heart.

What's fascinating about this particular rejection of leading man precedent is how much agency it affords the women characters Reeves plays against. It's a subtle way he shows he's equal to women, and that they have their own minds and plans for where their story will end up. Contrast this to the films of Matthew McConaughey, for example. In rom-coms such as *How to Lose a Guy in 10 Days*, *Failure to Launch*, and *Fool's Gold*, McConaughey's characters go through a much shallower arc, starting with utter contempt and disdain for not just relationships but women in general, and eventually learning that women are humans who are worthy of respect, not just naked desire. By clearing this very low bar, McConaughey's character wins over his love interest for good. In his catalog of seventy-eight films at the time of writing, the closest Reeves comes to this kind of narrative misogyny is as Frank in *Destination Wedding* (2018). But Frank is a man who hates everyone equally and women are no exception—at least at first.

Flipping the Savior Script

In chapter 4 we discussed Keanu's pattern of being saved by other people, particularly women, in his action films. That tendency carries through into Reeves's non-action roles as well. His life is saved by Sandra Bullock's Kate Forster in the time travel romance *The Lake House* (2006). And in the crime thriller *Siberia* (2018), Keanu's Lucas Hill gets the shit beaten out of him by two jealous factory workers who leave him for dead in the middle of a Russian winter. He is saved by the local bartender Katya (Ana Ularu), who brings him out of the cold.

Another technique Keanu uses to demonstrate that he's an equal to women in his action movies—bending over so he can be at their eye level, exchanging intense eye contact at his own expense—also carries over into his work in other genres. In his romantic comedies *Something's Gotta Give* and *The Private Lives of Pippa Lee* (2009), Keanu's character often gets down into eyeline of his love interest to make sure she knows he is not just focusing all his attention on them but really sees them and is listening. In rom-coms as well as in action movies, most leading men go to a lot of trouble to make sure they're taller than the women they play opposite, even going so far as standing on blocks or having holes dug for their leading women to stand in to make them appear shorter on-screen. Keanu does none of that nonsense. The opposite, in fact.

Keanu As the Younger Man

Keanu Charles Reeves was born September 2, 1964. Further breaking with movie tradition, he consistently defies the notion that older male stars should be paired with female love interests who are significantly younger. Think, for example, of Tom Cruise in the *Top Gun* movies: In the original *Top Gun* (1986), Cruise's love interest was Kelly McGillis, who was five years older than him. But when Cruise reprised his role more than thirty years later for *Top Gun: Maverick* (2022), his love interest was played by Jennifer Connelly, a woman eight years his junior. The script even tries to pass her off as the same age as Maverick, since she plays an old flame mentioned in the first film—though Connelly herself would've been sixteen years old at the time. And Connelly is actually more age appropriate than many of Cruise's recent female costars, who echo Matthew McConaughey's famous line from *Dazed and Confused*: Tom Cruise is allowed to age, but his costars remain in their twenties and thirties.[5] The same pattern is true for many actors in Keanu Reeves's cohort who appear opposite twenty- or thirtysomething love interests as they themselves have crossed the sixty-year mark, with the age difference playing no part in the story at all.[6]

Not so with Keanu Reeves. In fact, he has played his fair share of younger romantic interests to middle-aged women, not all of whom were going through any kind of midlife crisis. One of the most famous is his on-screen affair with Diane Keaton in *Something's Gotta Give*, featuring a dramatic eighteen-year age difference between both the actors and their characters. Not only is Dr. Julian Mercer the younger man, he's arguably one of the most perfect men ever put to screen in a rom-com or otherwise. Julian is kind, intelligent, and empathetic, and sees women as whole beings, not a collection of fuckable parts like his rival Harry (Jack Nicholson) does. On his first date with Erica, he only has eyes for her, even as every other woman in the place is strategically trying to place herself in his eyeline. "I knew you'd smell good," he whispers after kissing her neck. He's seen all her plays, some of them more than once, and loves them. He calls to make plans the day after their first dinner because he doesn't play games. Even after Erica stands him up, he comes to her with flowers. "These are for you to give me when you apologize," he says, fully leaning into the relationship with compassion and forgiveness.

Maybe it's a boomer thing for Erica, but to this day I cannot understand how or why anyone would give up the gorgeous, talented, sweet, loving non-game-player Julian for Harry, an inconstant womanizer asshole and emotionally unavailable prick who dated Erica's own daughter. *Something's Gotta Give* ends up reading as a peculiar warning to older women: that you can have your fun with a younger man, but your destiny is tied up with an old codger from your own generation who will most certainly hurt or even abandon you again when you're least expecting it. Worse, the film never properly addresses the profound disgust Harry expresses at the aging woman's body, a sentiment that never even occurs to Julian once. Yet Erica doesn't just end up with Harry, she actively chooses him. Classifying *Something's Gotta Give* as science fiction is the only way to make it make sense.

Thankfully, though, thirteen years earlier Reeves starred as the younger man Martin to Barbara Hershey's Julia in *Tune in Tomorrow* (1990). With a sixteen-year age difference both on-screen and off, this chaotic adaptation of Mario Vargas Llosa's metatextual melodrama gives us the *Something's Gotta Give* ending we deserve: Martin and Julia live happily ever after in Paris, where "all the women are older than the men." It's another case where events and themes in Keanu's early films were ahead of their time.

In fact, the pattern goes back to the very start of Keanu's career, in *Young Again*, a Disney TV movie from 1986 in which he plays Michael Riley, a forty-year-old man who magically becomes seventeen again. Even as a teenager, he's still in love with Laura (Lindsay Wagner), a woman fifteen years Keanu's elder in real life but playing significantly older.* Teen comedy caper *The Night Before* (1988) features a young Winston Connelly (Reeves) making out with a beautiful sex worker named Rhonda (Theresa Saldana) ten years his senior. In *The Prince of Pennsylvania*, Reeves's love interest is intense diner owner Amy Madigan, who's fourteen years older. The pattern continues in 2009's *The Private Lives of Pippa Lee*, but with a caveat: Robin Wright has been aged to somewhere around forty-five and Keanu has been de-aged to thirty-five—in real life the actors are only two years apart.

There's no other actor who has so frequently been the love interest to older women, across the entirety of his career. Although Channing Tatum is certainly taking pages from Keanu's playbook in this regard with a string of older women leading ladies in films like *The Lost City* (2022) and *Magic Mike's Last Dance* (2023).

---

* "Don't you guys have any respect for women?" Michael asks his catcalling new teenage peers, suggesting they should pull over and talk to the women instead of just screaming at them and driving by. "Just a thought," he says as they give him the stink eye.

Keanu's Appropriately Aged Leading Ladies

Keanu minds the age gap. A quantitative analysis of age differences between Keanu and his women costars demonstrates that the majority of them are on average only five years younger. This appropriately aged cohort includes, at the time of this writing:

- Olivia D'Abo, *Flying* (1986): 5 years younger
- Lori Loughlin, *The Brotherhood of Justice* (1986), *The Night Before* (1988): Same age
- Ione Skye, *River's Edge* (1986): 6 years younger
- Danae Torn, *Under the Influence* (1986): 8 years older
- Jill Schoelen, *Babes in Toyland* (1986): 1 year older
- Michelle Meyrink, *Permanent Record* (1988): 2 years older
- Kimberley Kates, *Bill & Ted's Excellent Adventure* (1989): 5 years younger
- Martha Plimpton, *Parenthood* (1989): 6 years younger
- Lori Petty, *Point Break* (1991): 1 year older
- Chiara Caselli, *My Own Private Idaho* (1991): 3 years younger
- Winona Ryder, *Bram Stoker's Dracula* (1992), *Destination Wedding* (2018), *A Scanner Darkly* (2006): 7 years younger
- Uma Thurman, *Even Cowgirls Get the Blues* (1993), *Dangerous Liaisons* (1988): 6 years younger
- Rajeshwari Sachdev, *Little Buddha* (1993): 9 years younger
- Sandra Bullock, *Speed* (1994), *The Lake House* (2006): Same age
- Dina Meyer, *Johnny Mnemonic* (1995): 4 years younger
- Aitana Sánchez-Gijón, *A Walk in the Clouds* (1995): 4 years younger
- Debra Messing, *A Walk in the Clouds* (1995): 4 years younger
- Rachel Weisz, *Chain Reaction* (1996), *Constantine* (2005): 6 years younger
- Cameron Diaz, *Feeling Minnesota* (1996): 8 years younger
- Connie Nielsen, *The Devil's Advocate* (1997): 1 year younger
- Carrie-Anne Moss, *Matrix* quadrilogy (1999–2021): 3 years younger
- Brooke Langton, *The Replacements* (2000): 6 years younger

- Marisa Tomei, *The Watcher*, (2000): Same age
- Lauren Graham, *Sweet November* (2001): 3 years younger
- Diane Lane, *Hardball* (2001): 1 year younger
- Monica Bellucci, *The Matrix Reloaded* (2003): Same age
- Melody Chase, *A Scanner Darkly* (2006): 4 years younger
- Lisa Marie Newmyer, *A Scanner Darkly* (2006): 4 years younger
- Jennifer Connelly, *The Day the Earth Stood Still* (2008): 6 years younger
- Robin Wright, *The Private Lives of Pippa Lee* (2009): 2 years younger
- Vera Farmiga, *Henry's Crime* (2010): 9 years younger
- Sarita Choudhury, *Generation Um . . .* (2012): 3 years younger
- Bridget Moynahan, *John Wick* franchise (2014–2023): 7 years younger
- Mira Sorvino, *Exposed* (2016): 3 years younger
- Renée Zellweger, *The Whole Truth* (2016): 5 years younger
- Jennifer Garner, *A Happening of Monumental Proportions* (2017): 8 years younger
- Molly Ringwald, *Siberia* (2018): 4 years younger

The fact that Reeves has worked with many of these women on multiple occasions also skews the results toward equitable age averages between him and his leading ladies. Even Reeves's one sort-of male love interest, River Phoenix in *My Own Private Idaho*, was only six years younger.

What makes many of these pairings extra great are the stories surrounding them, in which Reeves often sets new paradigms for leading men who are kind, empathetic, and respectful toward the women in his orbit. This is true not just in a genre like romantic comedy that is geared more toward women; even a violent action movie like *John Wick: Chapter 4* (2023) is surprisingly romantic, as John is buried next to his beloved Helen with the simple inscription LOVING HUSBAND. And unlike many other male leads, who cultivate a gratuitous antagonism toward women in their on-screen roles, in the few cases where Keanu's characters don't have such a healthy attitude toward women, there's almost always a narrative reason why.

Younger Women with a Purpose

Keanu Reeves's first love interest who is more than a decade younger than him is Charlize Theron, first in *The Devil's Advocate* and a few years later again in *Sweet November*. But their eleven-year age gap corresponds with the character Theron is playing—in *The Devil's Advocate*, a naive southern girl in the big city, and in *Sweet November*, a "manic pixie dream girl" whose aesthetic stems from her relative youth.

In bank-robbery/play-within-a-movie dramedy *Henry's Crime* (2010), Keanu's Henry begins the story married to Debbie (Judy Greer), a woman eleven years his junior. But he ends up with Julie (Vera Farmiga), who is only nine years younger. This is a reversal of what usually happens when a male character ends a film with a different partner than he started with. Reeves has only one instance of the typical dynamic, in the diamond heist thriller *Siberia* (2018), where he has an affair with Katya (Ana Ularu), a woman twenty-one years younger, when he finds out his age-appropriate wife Gabby (Molly Ringwald, four years younger) has been having an affair herself.

Often when Keanu is romantically entangled with decades-younger women in his films, it highlights the troubling nature and power imbalance of these kinds of relationships. For instance, in *The Gift* (2000) Keanu plays abusive Donnie Barksdale, a character with much younger love interests. Mistress Jessica King (Katie Holmes) is fourteen years younger, and wife Valerie (Hilary Swank), is ten years younger. This pattern makes sense, since abusers often choose young women whom they believe are easier to manipulate.

As he pursues seventeen-year-old Mary (Gretchen Mol) in the Beat-generation period piece *The Last Time I Committed Suicide* (1997), Keanu's thirtysomething character Harry says, "I *am* a creep. [. . .] Creepiness just so happens to be one of my most powerful traits. Creepiness. And neediness." What's interesting about relative ages in this particular film is that while many of the women love interests—including another of Harry's, Sarah (Meadow Sisto)—are playing sixteen and seventeen, in real life the actors were born in 1972 and are only eight years younger than Reeves. The age differences within the story heighten Harry's role as a perverse agent of chaos, but the making of the film itself had ethical age gaps.

In James Ellroy's police corruption drama *Street Kings* (2008), Grace (Martha Higareda) is nineteen years younger, and it's Reeves's first huge age difference between himself and a leading lady. This serves the story, since his Detective Ludlow is an absolute piece of shit and would seek out a very young woman who doesn't know any better. Further, all of his colleagues also date women twenty-plus years their junior, as their stunted adolescence makes it impossible for them to even conceive of a relationship with an actual peer. These massive age differences between the men and the women add unspoken layers to the character development of this roving gang of cops who operate outside the law and social propriety.

When *Knock Knock* (2015) director Eli Roth throws the entire good-guy narrative out the window in this home invasion horror movie with a twist, he starts by making all of Reeves's love interests decades younger. From his wife Karen (Ignacia Allamand, seventeen years younger), to the interlopers Genesis (Lorenza Izzo, twenty-five years younger) and Bel (Ana de Armas, twenty-four years younger), this sets the film up from the beginning with an ick factor, especially where Keanu's character is concerned. But it's an ick factor that well serves the story.

Generation Um . . . (2012) features Keanu Reeves as John, driver of two erratic, cocaine-addled young sex workers: Violet (Bojana Novakovic, seventeen years younger), and Mia (Adelaide Clemens, twenty-five years younger). John isn't their pimp, but the group vibe is overtly sexual, especially once John pilfers a video camera and begins filming them— sometimes in particularly vulnerable moments, like when the women are showering. Violet seems to be no stranger to cam work as she poses and preens for John, directing his gaze via the camera. While it's uncomfortable to watch these dynamics at play between an adult man and women decades his junior, *Generation Um . . .* makes it clear that it knows what it's doing by introducing the hot diner waitress Lily (Sarita Choudhury), who John is crushing on, a woman only two years younger than him. More on this film in chapter 16, but the age differences all serve a purpose and add levels of meaning to the narrative.

Writer-director Ana Lily Amirpour multiplies the gross age disparity by several dozen in *The Bad Batch* (2016), as Keanu's character the Dream is a cult leader with a harem of very young, very pregnant, gun-toting, brainwashed, drug-cooking wives. As one of the Dream's unnamed girls,

Emily O'Brien is the only bride with a birthdate listed online (1985, the year of Keanu Reeves's first film appearances, as an unnamed teen in the TV movie *Letting Go* and the star of the TV short *One Step Away*), showing a twenty-one-year age difference we can safely assume is the in the ballpark for the rest of them as well. And the Dream's would-be bride Arlen (Suki Waterhouse) was born in 1992, giving them a massive twenty-eight-year age difference. Again, the age disparities here only add to the sense of horror of the desert world to which these ragtag characters have been exiled—a world where the abuse of young women, sexual and otherwise, has been essentially codified.

In *Always Be My Maybe* (2019), Keanu plays himself as the new beau of Ali Wong's Sasha Tran, a woman eighteen years his junior. But based on how heightened and self-parodying this version of "Keanu" is, it tracks that he'd mess around with a much younger woman, which as far as we all know isn't something he's ever done in real life.

The terrible pièce de résistance comes in director Nicolas Winding Refn's Los Angeles horror satire *The Neon Demon* (2016), in which Reeves's Hank is obsessed with Jesse (Elle Fanning), a child thirty-four years younger than him. But Hank is a pedophile who preys on runaway girls, so the age difference between Reeves and Fanning only adds to the grotesquery of events in the story. It's wild to think that others in Reeves's cohort regularly have love interests three decades their junior, but the one time Reeves does it's because he's literally playing a pedophile. What a subtle but powerful message this sends to the established Hollywood dynamics of male-female pairings on-screen.

Keanu Reeves only has three films where a large age disparity is not justified in story terms. *Bill & Ted Face the Music* (2020) recasts Princess Elizabeth—who was age appropriate in both previous films—with Erinn Hayes, who is an obvious twelve years younger. In *47 Ronin* (2013), Keanu's character, Kai, meets his love interest, Mika, when they're both apparently teenagers—but as an adult Mika is played by Ko Shibasaki, an actress seventeen years younger than Reeves. We could read this as Keanu's character, Kai, being much older than he seemed when we first met him, but it's a stretch given the dialogue refers to him as a child when he's found abandoned by the Tengu. And in *Replicas* (2018), a Keanu film that regularly ends up on worst-of lists, William's wife Mona (Alice

Eve) is a whopping eighteen years younger for no good reason. Taken together, in seventy-eight films at the time of writing, to have only three movies that feature a huge, unjustified age disparity is a rather epic feat in a misogynistic industry that allows men to age on-screen but not women. Yet again, Reeves consistently sets himself apart from his peers.

The Lack of Romantic Interest

But this brings me to another fascinating point about Keanu Reeves movies when analyzed through a gendered lens: a sizable chunk of Reeves's films don't feature him with a love interest at all. That's the case in one of his earliest roles, in the short TV movie *One Step Away*, and it continues in higher-profile appearances such as *I Love You to Death* (1990), in which he plays a bumbling hit man and it's his peer River Phoenix who has the love interest. *Much Ado About Nothing* (1993) features Reeves as Don John, one of the only characters who isn't entangled in romantic foibles on-screen (although by my interpretation, he's secretly in love with Robert Sean Leonard's Claudio—more on this in chapter 14). *Freaked* (1993), *Little Buddha* (1993), and *The SpongeBob Movie: Sponge on the Run* (2020) find Reeves as a messiah figure who is beyond sex and romantic interest (his arranged marriage in *Little Buddha* was an economic match, not a love one). *Thumbsucker* (2005) has him in a nonromantic mentor role, as does the teen rom-com *SPF-18* (2017), where he cameos as himself. In another cameo appearance as himself in the L.A. dramedy *Ellie Parker* (2005), Keanu is utterly uninterested when Naomi Watts's aspiring actress character tries to flirt with him after a performance by his real-life band, Dogstar. And Reeves's Batman in *DC League of Super-Pets* (2022) is one of the few big-screen versions of the Caped Crusader without a love interest.

Julian Cha's "'There Is No Spoon'" might connect this long list of nonromantic or aromantic characters with the desexualization or asexualization of Asian men.[7] I instead think it shows Keanu Reeves's range, his talent for choosing characters who defy expectations and break molds that other male stars are more than happy to reproduce. And, on the other hand, his Asian and Indigenous Hawaiian heritage makes the movies where he *does* play a mainstream romantic lead groundbreaking as well, since he's one of Hollywood's only romantic leads of color.

Working with Women Directors

A 2016 survey on gender and diversity by Women and Hollywood identified a shocking *twenty* of the hundred highest-grossing male actors who had never worked with even one woman director. "Among the household names that have never worked under a female director are Sean Connery (64 films) Sylvester Stallone (55 films), Ben Stiller (54 films), Matt Damon (51 films), Tom Cruise (38 films) and Tobey Maguire (24 films)."[8] Even at the time of this writing, many of these top actors have continued making movies only with men directors. To date, the only woman director Brad Pitt has worked with is Angelina Jolie, his then wife.

So, in keeping with Keanu Reeves's status as a Hollywood outlier, it's not surprising at all to note that since the beginning of his career, he has consistently worked with more women directors than his peers, starting with Marisa Silver's teen suicide drama *Permanent Record* in 1988. Kathryn Bigelow directed Reeves in 1991's *Point Break*. Melissa Behr and Sherrie Rose directed and wrote the poignant motorcycle road trip drama *Me and Will* (1999), in which Keanu cameos with his band Dogstar. Rebecca Miller directed *The Private Lives of Pippa Lee*, a complicated portrait of a woman on the verge. Courtney Hunt helmed Reeves's legal family horror pic *The Whole Truth* (2016), while Iranian American horror director Ana Lily Amirpour almost tailor-made a creepy role for Reeves in *The Bad Batch*. Marti Noxon directed and wrote *To the Bone* (2017), based on her own experiences with an eating disorder, and Reeves's *Henry's Crime* costar Judy Greer directed the comedy satire *A Happening of Monumental Proportions* that same year. Nahnatchka Khan directed Keanu Reeves's brilliant ad-libbing in *Always Be My Maybe*. Keanu worked with Lana Wachowski on *The Matrix Resurrections* (2021), making him one of few male superstars to have worked not just with women but with an out trans woman to boot. Clearly, he's actively choosing scripts written and directed by women—this is the quiet feminist trailblazing I'm talking about.

But even among all of this paradigm-shifting stuff, Keanu Reeves isn't perfect. My criticism here is the fact that all of Keanu's costars have been thin, fair-skinned women, the vast majority of them white. He has only had seven Latinx/Hispanic costars and three Asian ones, and the only explicit Black love interests in his entire career were the few unnamed pregnant background women in the Dream's harem in *The Bad Batch*. (As I mentioned in chapter 3, the third *John Wick* movie does imply that Halle Berry is John's former love interest, but that's a subtextual suggestion, not a canonical fact.) This trend, unfortunately, does follow racist, anti-Black, misogynistic, and fatphobic Hollywood patterns that Keanu has yet to transcend, especially in not having even one main Black woman lead in seventy-eight movies and counting.

Thankfully, there's still time in Reeves's career to rectify this oversight, and an entire bevy of Black age-appropriate actresses who would be amazing to see across from Keanu. I'm looking at y'all, Angela Bassett, Regina King, Viola Davis, Vanessa Williams, and Regina Hall, just to name a few. And while we're at it, let's go ahead and pair Keanu and Halle Berry once again, but this time in a romantic dramedy. Reparations, but make it casting.

8

I WILL BE YOUR FATHER FIGURE

Keanu Reeves's Most Triumphant (and Most Heinous) Parenting

IN KEY AND PEELE'S ULTIMATE FAN FILM *KEANU* (2016), an entire subplot centers around the attempts by mild-mannered Clarence (Keegan-Michael Key) to rack up his street cred with a gang of assassins after they find out he's a fan of British pop singer and gay icon George Michael. Clarence convinces them that George Michael is "the real OG" by cheekily straight-washing his song "Father Figure" into a literal interpretation, saying, "My man right here, he didn't have his own positive male role model in his life." Fascinatingly, this gag ends up reflecting some of Keanu Reeves's real-life trauma around his own dad.

It's been no secret that Keanu Reeves suffered a difficult relationship with his father, who abandoned Keanu and his family when Keanu was just a young boy. They never reconciled before his father's death in 2018. While Reeves has spoken about having supportive stepfathers, some of whom helped him in his career, there's a particular kind of pain of rupture that comes from being fully estranged from a birth parent who was once in your life, even briefly. Horribly, Keanu has also experienced the loss of fatherhood from the other side: his daughter with partner Jennifer Syme was stillborn in 1999, and then Syme herself died in a car accident two years later.

In such heartbreaking circumstances, closure can manifest through both the creation and the consumption of art that helps shape those spaces for healing. For instance, Netflix's *Finding 'Ohana* (2021) is a quiet tribute to Keanu Reeves from the island of his father, Hawai'i, that also grapples with father-child relationships via an adult daughter who has been estranged from her father and homeland for decades—a story that resonates with me, too, on multiple levels. It's a vision of what a healthy father-child reunion could be like, if circumstances didn't involve irreconcilable differences.

In a similar way, the presentations of fatherhood in Keanu's own films often involve fantastic triumphs and nurturing masculinity. But they also extend across a huge spectrum, into terrible fathers who never should have been, once again demonstrating Reeves's enormous range as a performer and storyteller.

"I Used to Be a Prince": Difficult Father Relationships

For his first commercial gig at age seventeen, Keanu Reeves starred in a Coke ad featuring a young man's bike race as his father cheers him on from the sidelines, soda in hand for when he crosses the finish line. The best part of the commercial is that Keanu's character doesn't even win the race—he comes in third—and yet his father is celebrating anyway. This sweet father-son moment at the beginning of Reeves's career actually becomes ironic when we recognize that a large chunk of Reeves's catalog includes films in which his character has a negatively charged relationship with his father, one that has ended up shaping the son's life and other relationships.

An early example set a young Keanu opposite a surprising familiar face as his abusive dad. In the 1986 CBS TV movie *Under the Influence*, Andy Griffith stars as Noah Talbot, a violent alcoholic who specifically targets his son Eddie (Reeves) when he's drunk. Eddie also struggles with his own drinking, while his sister Ann (Season Hubley) and mother Helen (Joyce Van Patten) abuse pills. While a bit dated in some aspects, the film's presentation of addiction stands true today. And featuring all-American good guy Andy Griffith as a violent, alcoholic abuser is a powerful moment in American pop culture history that humanizes addiction as an illness, not a personal shortcoming.

A pair of movies from around the same time stand out for another reason: they're two of the only Keanu films about a strained father-son connection in which the relationship metamorphoses into something positive by the end of the story. "My dad left this morning," Chris Townsend (Keanu Reeves) tells his best friend David Sinclair (Alan Boyce) in *Permanent Record* (1988). "You have a dad?" David responds. Marisa Silver's still-poignant teen suicide drama not only gives Reeves's character an absentee dad who travels for work and a missing mom whose absence is never explained but also introduces a surrogate father figure. After David's sudden suicide, David's dad Jim (Barry Corbin) becomes a shoulder for Chris to cry on, giving him a safe space to weep and scream and process so much grief and stress—a role Jim was unable to play with his own son.

Similarly, in *Parenthood* (1989), Keanu plays Tod, whose father is violent and abusive—a fact that inspires Tod to be the exact opposite when presented with fatherhood himself. Tod reveals, "I had a man around. He used to wake me up in the morning by flicking lit cigarettes at my head. 'Hey, asshole, get up and make me breakfast.' You know, Ms. Buckman, you need a license to buy a dog, or drive a car. Hell, you need a license to catch a fish! But they'll let any butt-reaming asshole be a father." In *Permanent Record*, Jim gets a second chance with his son's best friend Chris, and in *Parenthood*, Tod gets to be the father figure he never had— not just for his child on the way but for others in his orbit who need it, including adults.

But this isn't the case in *The Prince of Pennsylvania* (1988), in which Reeves's Rupert Marshetta kidnaps his father Gary (Fred Ward) for ransom after he beats up Rupert's mom Pam (Bonnie Bedelia) for cheating on him. Rupert and Gary have an intense showdown in a remote cabin, where instead of sadness, Rupert's unadulterated rage at his father explodes and their battle of opposing wills comes to a head. Gary wants Rupert to be more like him, down to working in the local mine, while Rupert is a creative soul who wants to make art and live free. Reeves's performance here is moving and vulnerable, as Rupert realizes that not only will he be unable to get the kind of love or even closure that he wants from the strained relationship, he will also never get his father to understand him. And all that's left is to let go. Rupert leaves town without saying goodbye.

My Own Private Idaho (1991), on the other hand, begins with the father-son estrangement. Reeves plays Scott Favor, who has run away from his millionaire family. He'd rather live on the streets as a sex worker than go into the family business of money—at least at first. In *The Gus Van Sant Touch: A Thematic Study—"Drugstore Cowboy," "Milk" and Beyond* Justin Vicari writes, "The need for a father runs throughout the film like the interstate highway where people find themselves stuck, stranded, again and again, searching for a benevolent guiding force which simply isn't there."[1] There's a moment when Scott visits his father Jack (Tom Troupe) in one of his more outlandish hustler outfits and gives him a hug. His father literally gags, so disgusted is he by his son. Contrast this relationship to that with Scott's surrogate "psychedelic papa" Bob (William Richert), who embraces Scott as a whole human and sees only the best in him. But because this is a story about toxic and destructive father-son relationships, Scott ultimately betrays Bob and returns to his life of luxury, leading to Bob's death of a broken heart. And where Scott has two fathers to choose from, his best friend Mike (River Phoenix) has a single figure in dual roles—his older brother Dick, who raised him after their mother abandoned them. It's ultimately revealed that Dick is actually Mike's biological father: he was sexually abused by their mother, and Mike is the product of this incest. It's arguably the most fraught father-son relationship in Keanu Reeves's entire canon, though Keanu's character Scott is only a witness to it.

Scott Favor's own father issues are echoed in *Little Buddha* (1993), as Prince Siddhartha's father the king also wants to control his son and keep him from experiencing the nitty-gritty of life, protecting him behind castle walls until Siddhartha ventures out to see the world for himself. "Your love has become a prison," Siddhartha says to his father, before abandoning his own wife and son to embark on a journey of enlightenment through meditation. While this narrative focuses on the becoming of the Buddha, it's hard to forget that he had an entire family who he up and left without spending any time thinking how his absence would affect them. Siddhartha might have changed the world through his meditation practices, but he was a terrible husband and father.

Two of Reeves's films show the impact of an absentee father on an adult son by maintaining that absence throughout the movie itself. We never meet the father of Jjaks Clayton (Reeves) in *Feeling Minnesota* (1996), but his abandonment has shaped Jjaks's toxic relationship with his older brother (Vincent D'Onofrio). In *Private Lives of Pippa Lee* (2009), Reeves's Chris Nadeau is adopted, and while we don't meet his father either, we learn that their difficult relationship was part of why he left Chris and his mom Dot (Shirley Knight)—the nightmare of divorced kids' self-blaming coming true.

The Devil's Advocate (1997) becomes a competition of bad and absent dads. Kevin Lomax (Reeves) never knew his father, while his wife Mary Ann (Charlize Theron) wishes she didn't know hers. "I tell Kevin, the only thing worse about not having a father was having mine," she says. Kevin finds himself at odds with his boss John Milton (Al Pacino)—who turns out to be both his father and the actual devil, manipulating Kevin to do his bidding in a global takeover. Having the devil as a dad is an apt metaphor for many of the fathers in this section, who put their own needs before those of their family, often wreaking violence on the ones they're supposed to protect.

Yet a portrait of troubled fatherhood doesn't need to be about literal violence or an over-the-top struggle between good and evil. One of Keanu's most poignant moments on-screen is simply about the tragic lack of reconciliation between father and son. In the time travel romance *The Lake House* (2006), his character Alex Wyler comes from a family of architects, headed by his award-winning father Simon (Christopher Plummer). Alex has been estranged from Simon for years because he abandoned architecture for community development, an unforgivable crime to his demanding father. But after his father's death, there's a stunning scene where Alex breaks down while reading a retrospective book about his father's work. It is a moment of raw emotion and sadness as Alex weeps, with director Alejandro Agresti giving Reeves space and time on camera to sit with Alex's immense grief. Here the anguish is in the fact that not only was there no reconciliation, but there wasn't even the start of a discussion about why their relationship was always so strained. And Alex is left to put together these pieces afterward.

Themes of damaged fatherhood extend even beyond Keanu's dramatic films. Though the *Bill & Ted* trilogy is a comedy, it incorporates an incredibly dark story thread in which Ted "Theodore" Logan's cop father plans to send his sweet, unassuming, gentle son to military school just because he's not performing to his father's standards in school. An online meme speculates that "JOHN WICK is the dark timeline where Ted went to military school."[2] While that's not literally true—John Wick wasn't in the military—we can still see in Wick how Ted's personality might have ended up if he had been forced into a life of violence. And his father would've been responsible for that terrible shift.

Most Triumphant Parenting

Just as notable is the way in which the *Bill & Ted* series ultimately reveals the other side of the coin: one of the most striking things about *Bill & Ted Face the Music* (2020) is how much both Bill and Ted seem to like and respect their children. I actually cried during this film because I was so moved by their loving, accepting, and mutually respectful relationship with their daughters. As someone estranged from my own father for many, many years, I found these to be really beautiful moments to witness: Bill and Ted break the generational curse of their demanding and abrasive fathers to become gentle parents whose children will always find a home in their arms. Even more, though the series was always centered around the idea that Bill and Ted would create a utopian future through their music, when they realize it's actually their *daughters'* song that will save the universe, they don't hesitate in helping the girls fulfill their purpose, something their own fathers never quite learned how to do.

It's the roles like this, where Keanu Reeves plays an ideal father himself, that become shining lights in Reeves's catalog. His turn as Tod in *Parenthood* remains ahead of its time for how willingly the character takes on fatherhood, even as a teen. In a story filled with dysfunctional adults, Tod becomes the beacon of rationality and calm amid many storms, a beautiful role that remains as poignant now as it was in 1989.

More recently, even though *Replicas* (2018) often ends up on Reeves's worst-of lists, what I particularly appreciate about director Jeffrey Nachmanoff's movie is how Keanu's William Foster loves his family so much that after a car accident kills them all, he uses every technological advance at his disposal to bring them back. It's fantastic how *Replicas* breaks the mold of sci-fi thrillers in this way, with its male lead motivated not by revenge or anger, just love for his wife and children.

More commonly than literal fatherhood, though, Keanu has been drawn to positive portrayals of *surrogate* fathers—often those who embrace the role by choice.

His first surrogate father role is an unlikely one: as twitchy Nelson Moss in the romantic drama *Sweet November* (2001), he becomes surrogate father to Abner (Liam Aiken), a precocious young boy who is struggling to deal with his father's absence. "You're a father figure now," his free-spirited love interest Sara (Charlize Theron) tells him. "The kid just met me," Nelson scoffs. Sara replies, "Well, when you don't know your dad, you're not that picky." Abner even goes so far as to ask Nelson to adopt him. They strike a compromise by Nelson agreeing to attend father-son day at school as his friend. That same year in *Hardball*, Reeves becomes a surrogate father figure for the young boys on his baseball team, and the theme of absent dads is brought home even further when the boys are shown reading *A Wrinkle in Time* in school. This is a story about a young girl's search for her missing father through the universe—which ends up resonating not just with the kids on the baseball team but with Reeves's character as well, as he takes on fatherly responsibilities.

In the same vein, in *Thumbsucker* (2005) Reeves's Dr. Lyman might only be a dentist dealing with Justin (Lou Taylor Pucci), a teenage boy who still sucks his thumb. But he also tries to undo the damage caused by Justin's father Mike (Vincent D'Onofrio) and his obsession with winning and fear of aging. Justin's thumb-sucking reflects his father's own inability to grow up and leave the past in the past. But unfortunately neither Justin nor his father are ready to move forward as Dr. Lyman pushes too far, too hard, and too fast, effectively breaking the family. What's extraordinary about Reeves's character in this film is that he's an adult who learns. He realizes he went too far with a kid who wasn't psychologically ready to heal, and he accepts the consequences of that overstepping. Dr. Lyman goes back to his own personal drawing board and starts from scratch to figure out who he is and how he wants to help people, and how he simply wants to be in the world. Adults often act like they are fixed in place and that's just how they are now. But Keanu's surrogate dad in *Thumbsucker* shows that adults have as much capacity for change, development, and growth as kids. It just takes adults more work.

In *To The Bone* (2017), Keanu again plays a medical professional who becomes a surrogate dad, this time to his patient Ellen (Lily Collins). Dr. Beckham steps up because Ellen's dad refuses to engage with her anorexia treatment. Her father also seems to be the one who might have inspired her eating disorder, and Dr. Beck gives her the space she needs to begin healing. Oftentimes in therapy the therapist must take on the role of the parent, or parents, who have caused the psychological damage the patient is trying to heal from.

But my ultimate favorite moment of Keanu Reeves as surrogate dad comes in *The Matrix Resurrections* (2021) as Neo, restored to life and once again trapped in a virtual world by machines bent on enslaving humanity. In the decades since *The Matrix* (1999) first hit cinemas, its writer-directors, the Wachowskis, have confirmed that the movies are an allegory for the transgender experience, with the Matrix representing a binary world where people are forced into boxes based on arbitrary physical and social signifiers. Lana and Lilly Wachowski have also both come out as trans themselves. Beautifully, Lana Wachowski's *The Matrix Resurrections* is openly queer in ways the earlier three movies were not, and in that queer community we see Neo and Trinity (Carrie-Anne Moss) as the spiritual mother and father of a new generation of revolutionaries fighting for human liberation. They might not have had babies with their genitals, but their past struggle and their mere existence were the catalyst for the younger folks breaking out of the Matrix and building a new world that is based on equity, equality, and acceptance. This is fatherhood in a queer, chosen-family sense, and it's arguably one of the most beautiful examples in Reeves's career.

Heinous Anti-fatherhood

But Keanu hasn't just played struggling sons and fabulous father figures; he's also devoted a fair share of his film catalog to playing toxic, abusive, and otherwise gnarly father figures himself. And what this indicates about Reeves as a performer is his unwillingness to be typecast, even though people continually try to stereotype his roles. It also demonstrates his huge range as an actor, something else he is often accused of *not* having.

Again starting early in his career, the teen vigilante drama *The Brotherhood of Justice* (1986) sees Reeves's Derek as a leader and hero figure, but there's another, darker side to this role. Derek's parents are absent for the entire film, leaving him and his younger brother Willie (Danny Nucci) with only the supervision of their maid. When Derek finds out that his brother has been using drugs, instead of calmly talking to him about it or even getting in touch with their folks, Derek beats him up and threatens him with worse if Willie doesn't stop. It's a really horrifying moment to watch this domestic abuse at the hands of such a young Keanu Reeves. But when it comes to absentee parents, this is often a violent dynamic that happens when you have a child parenting another child.

This same dynamic follows in *River's Edge* (1986), which has a secondary dark plot concurrent to the main storyline about a dead girl dumped by the side of the river by her boyfriend. Reeves's Matt has a fraught home life with a stepfather who is trying to convince his mother to ship her three kids off so they can start their own family. Like Derek, Matt has been parentified, thrown into a combative surrogate father role with his troubled and antisocial little brother Tim (Joshua John Miller). Matt even beats the shit out of Tim after Tim bullies their little sister, and Tim's resulting rage results in him stealing a gun and almost shooting Matt. This subplot shows the spread of generational violence from (step)father to children, and how easily those patterns can be reproduced.

In *A Scanner Darkly* (2006), director Richard Linklater's critique of the surveillance state, we see how deep such patterns can run. Keanu's Bob Arctor had the perfect family and a beautiful home in Orange County, California, a life that he wanted and worked hard for, the kind of life he didn't have growing up. But as in many of these films, the legacy of abandonment is hard to escape, and he abandons his wife and two young daughters for his job as an undercover policeman, a decision that leads to drug addiction and ultimately ending up alone.

When a superstar like Keanu chooses to play such unflattering roles, it adds dimension to the films' portrayal of toxic fatherhood. Take director Eli Roth's home invasion horror film *Knock Knock* (2015), which takes place on Father's Day. And what does Reeves's Evan Webber do while his wife and children are away? Has a threesome with two much-younger strangers who randomly show up at his door. The women turn out to be psychopaths, and as their violence escalates, Evan tries to remind them, "I'm a good father!" But one of his captors, Bel (Ana de Armas), smirkingly corrects him: "Until yesterday." By the end of *Knock Knock*, video footage of Evan and the girls—among so much more—will have ruined his life for good. One of the most effective parts of this film is its casting of Keanu Reeves; this beloved pop culture figure goes from hero to fallen angel well beyond redemption, and it all happens in gruesome and grisly detail. Had somebody else played the role, we very likely could have sided with the two girls and their vengeance fetish rather than continuing to feel empathy for Keanu as he in fact helps destroy his perfect life before our eyes.

Similarly, in the last section I mentioned Keanu's William Foster in *Replicas* as an example of a role that showcases the best of fatherhood—but it also shows fatherhood at its worst. After his family is killed in that brutal car accident, William has access to technology that can pull human consciousness into a synthetic body, but it has not been perfected. Yes, he brings his family back after their tragic deaths, but he essentially uses them as human lab rats to test out his tech. Worse, he can't bring them all back and must choose one of his children to let go, by erasing all traces of her from their family home and his family's actual memories. We feel for William as his immense grief crushes him while he erases all of his daughter's drawings from walls and tables around the house and removes all photographic evidence of her. At the same time, this is a deeply disturbing choice that William has made, especially knowing that the technology he's relying on is not fully functional. He's a good dad and a bad dad at the same time.

And even when Keanu is playing a father figure who's all bad, it's a testament to his range and talent as an actor. In the apocalyptic wasteland of *The Bad Batch* (2016), Keanu's cult leader the Dream is not just a husband to his harem of hugely pregnant, extremely young women who he collects and brainwashes—he's also a father figure to his child brides. We can predict nothing but the worst for all those babies, including potentially being a fresh food source. *Shudder*.

The enormous gulf between Tod from *Parenthood* in 1989 to the Dream in *The Bad Batch* almost thirty years later confirms that Keanu Reeves is not content to play to only one part of the spectrum of human experience. His character choices bring balance to the creative universe he's part of, reflecting both the best and worst of people simultaneously. He is the tarot in living archetypal motion, and the roles discussed in this chapter alone are more than enough to demonstrate Keanu's massive range as an actor, not just in the variety of genres that they represent but also in the nuanced portrayals of fatherhood that they embody.

PART II

THE DEVIL

IN A TAROT CARD READING, whenever the Devil appears, it changes everything. Unlike Death and the Tower, two cards that look and sound scary but actually signify change and awakening, the Devil always arrives with a warning that someone or something might be actively working against you. This can be an external force or another person, or even your own shadow self sabotaging you from within. The Devil card signals an obsession with power, money, sex. But not loving, healthy sex; this is a sadistic, abusive, perverse sexuality that often intersects with addictions of all kinds. This card asks, *What have you been doing to chip away at your own purest self of light?* And it demands you take stock of your bondage to things, uncontrolled passions, toxic relationships, and even money. It indicates that somewhere close is a lack of essential connection to humanity that results in self-centeredness, selfishness, and spite—and that ends in annihilation. The films of Keanu Reeves often serve this same purpose, confronting the viewer with their shadow self and exposing the dark places and urges that lurk within. Speak of the devil, and Keanu Reeves often appears.

9

I'LL SEE YOU IN HELL, JOHNNY

Keanu Reeves and the Underworld

WHEN ASKED BY STEPHEN COLBERT what he thinks happens after we die, Keanu Reeves had a thoughtful response: "I know that the ones who love us will miss us."[1] It's a sentiment that is perfectly in keeping with Keanu's kind and down-to-earth persona—and in direct opposition to the numerous visions of an archetypal hellish afterlife that Reeves himself has helped to bring to the screen.

There's a fantastically apt bit of imagery in *Much Ado About Nothing* (1993) when Keanu's Don John wears a red devil mask at a masquerade ball, both echoing and foreshadowing Reeves's various and deep descents into hellscapes both literal and metaphorical. In some of Keanu's films, hell is an actual place, like in *Constantine*, *The Devil's Advocate*, the *Bill & Ted* franchise, *47 Ronin*, the *Matrix* films, and even the Christmas comedy musical *Babes in Toyland*. But often the hellscapes are earthly tests of survival under some pretty grim circumstances, as in *John Wick*, *A Scanner Darkly*, *The Bad Batch*, *My Own Private Idaho*, and many more.

Considering Reeves's impeccable reputation in real life, there's a dark poetry when it comes to the portrayal of the devil and the underworld in his movies. Especially when we take into account all the religiously inspired fan iconography that has essentially made a saint of Reeves, reverently placing his image on candles, pillows, shirts, posters, and more. Our heavenly prince does love to dance with the devil in the pale moonlight, and the results often produce a singular kind of dissonance that comes from someone fully playing against type and expectation.

Unlike many of his peers, Keanu Reeves has never treated his onscreen personas as precious. Dwayne Johnson tanked his DC Comics film *Black Adam* (2022) by reworking his antihero character into a straightforward heroic one, because he can't stand to be seen as a bad guy even when he's acting. Tom Cruise is guilty of this as well; just compare his self-tormented portrayal of the vampire Lestat in *Interview with the Vampire* (1994) with Sam Reid's deliciously villainous Lestat in the 2022 television remake. When Keanu goes in for a character, he goes all in—all the way to demonic depths if necessary. And so do we along with him.

Hell Is Real

"Are you still trying to buy your way into heaven?" Tilda Swinton's androgynous angel Gabriel asks the title character of *Constantine* (2005), set in a world defined by Catholic dogma and its rigid binaries. By attempting suicide as a teenager, John Constantine consigned himself to hell, and he has made it his personal mission to kill as many demons as possible in hopes of eventually redeeming his soul. The phrase "committed suicide" sprinkled throughout *Constantine* is no longer in favor by mental health professionals due to the simple fact that killing oneself isn't a crime, it's a tragedy. But in the specific Catholic context embraced by the film, suicide *is* a crime, one punishable by eternal suffering in a fiery pit of brimstone.

This same vision of hell—souls writhing in flame—appears briefly at the end of *The Devil's Advocate* (1997), as Reeves's Kevin Lomax makes his fateful choice to reject the temptation of his devil father. Though he does so by shooting himself in the head, his righteous choice allows him to escape perpetual damnation—at least for a moment. And while the portrayals of hell and the devil in *Constantine* and *Devil's Advocate* are indeed similar, there are some troubling details in *Advocate* that render its version problematic. For example, before revealing himself to be the devil and Kevin's father, John Milton (Al Pacino) takes Kevin to a flamenco club, where he shows off his ability to perfectly perform this hard-to-learn traditional Romani Spanish dance. Unfortunately, throughout history the Roma have been stereotyped as agents of the devil, both in popular stories like Bram Stoker's original novel of *Dracula* and in real life. Romani folks across Europe faced pogroms and genocide centuries before other groups like Jewish people were targeted. So it's troubling that this scene suggests a special familiarity between Satan and the Roma. Similarly, *Devil's Advocate* presents several unhoused men as agents of the devil; Milton calls on them to beat one of the few good guys in the story to death. Again, the narrative connects a hugely marginalized group with demonic forces—a tendency that has allowed and continues to allow groups like the Roma and unhoused people to be criminalized not just legally but socially and culturally as well.

Though many such Judeo-Christian visions of hell are sprinkled throughout Keanu's catalog, a few of his films bring in a hellscape based in Eastern cultures. In the criminally underrated samurai action adventure *47 Ronin* (2013), Keanu's Kai was adopted by the Tengu, forest demons with magical powers who are widely feared and respected throughout Japan and beyond. The Tengu live in what seems to be a parallel dimension accessed via a forest that everyone knows not to go through. Why was Kai chosen by the Tengu? And why was he ultimately rejected by them? We don't rightly know. But their reputation as creatures of hell, based on their grizzled appearance, supernatural strength, and battle prowess, follows Kai through the entire story, since he was raised by them.

Visions of hell from the Indian subcontinent are seen in *Little Buddha*, presented in two ways. First, hell is figurative, represented in the poor and sick people who live outside Prince Siddhartha's opulent palace. Later, it is literal: as Siddhartha walks his path to enlightenment with a marathon meditation session, Mara (Anupam Shyam) the Lord of Darkness sends an entire army of demons, not unlike the Tengu from *47 Ronin*. Mara himself emerges from a hell portal through water, and the Buddha ultimately defeats him.

The Matrix (1999) and its sequels present their own unique vision of hell, in which humans serve as living battery power for the artificial intelligences that now rule the planet. Like the visions in *Constantine* and *Devil's Advocate*, this hell is deep underground. But it's not fiery; instead it is cold, sleek, and sterile. It's still a particularly chilling vision of an

actual hellscape on Earth, where humans are tortured, milked, and ultimately discarded and recycled—a grotesque techno-cannibalism no one
can escape. True to the setting's hellish implications, *The Matrix Reloaded*
(2003) also features a character named Persephone (Monica Bellucci), a
nod to the character of the same name in Greek myth: the daughter of
the goddess Demeter, who was kidnapped by Hades and forced to spend
half of every year in hell.

It is wild that even Keanu Reeves's comedies feature visions of Hell.
In the made-for-kids Christmas comedy caper *Babes in Toyland* (1986),
there's an entire hellscape underneath Toyland called the Forest of the
Night that's filled with monstrous creatures and a diabolical ruler, Barnaby
Barnicle (Richard Mulligan), who eventually gets his hands on a bottle
of distilled evil that threatens not just Christmas but the very fabric of
reality as the characters know it. Keanu and company, including a ten-
year-old Drew Barrymore, must sing their way out of this hell and restore
the balance of goodness.

But on-screen visions of hell in Keanu movies go even more bananas
with the time-traveling adventures of the *Bill & Ted* series, in many ways
unsettling our expectations of who ends up in hell and why. As far as we
know, the only people Bill and Ted negatively affect at first are themselves,
as their hapless natures and low ambitions find them at the bottom of their
class—and Keanu's Ted potentially on his way to military school. And yet,
when Bill and Ted are killed by robot doppelgängers in *Bill & Ted's Bogus
Journey* (1991), they go directly to hell. But why, though? They've done
their share of silly, but nothing bad enough to send them to the genuinely
disturbing pits of hell they end up in, tormented by the horrifying figure
of Beelzebub, a deranged Easter Bunny, a crazed military school instructor,
and of course their showdown with Death himself (William Sadler) in order
to restore their bodies. There's a lot I love about this franchise, but one of
my favorite things is how hell is a completely arbitrary place to end up, just
as heaven is elsewhere in the same story. Unlike narratives like *Constantine*, which insist that our actions in life determine where we go after we
die, *Bill & Ted* is like, "You just end up *somewhere*, dude. [*shrug emoji*]"
It's a wonderfully freeing notion, somewhat echoed in the popular sitcom
The Good Place (2016–2020), in which a terrible woman accidentally ends
up in heaven, unsettling the notions of goodness and badness altogether.

What's extra fascinating about Keanu's cinematic experiences with hell and its denizens is that many of these films—particularly *Constantine*, *The Devil's Advocate*, and *The Matrix*—receive ongoing academic attention from scholars in religious, race, gender, and cyber studies, just to name a few of the interested disciplines. For example, because of *The Devil's Advocate*'s overt links to John Milton's epic poem *Paradise Lost*, from its exploration of Satan and the fall of humanity to naming the devil character after the writer, academics often compare the two; Ryan Netzley's essay ""Better to Reign in Hell than Serve in Heaven," Is That It?': Ethics, Apocalypticism, and Allusion in *The Devil's Advocate*" uses the film as a jumping-off point to discuss a variety of interpretations of the original *Paradise Lost* and what has been both added and lost in *The Devil's Advocate*, such as the twisting of the concept of free will.[2] In Regina M. Hansen's "Lucifer, Gabriel, and the Angelic Will in *The Prophecy* and *Constantine*," Hansen likewise explores the notion of free will as it relates to angelic beings' own self-determination in a deep religious reading of *Constantine*.[3] And David Hauka's "Advocating for Satan: The Parousia-Inspired Horror Genre" discusses the particularly American version of Satanism presented in *The Devil's Advocate* and *Constantine*, in a cross-cultural examination of US history, Puritanism, and end-of-days narratives.[4]

Jeffery A. Smith uses both *The Devil's Advocate* and *The Matrix* in his essay "Hollywood Theology: The Commodification of Religion in Twentieth-Century Films" to explore the Hollywoodification of religious themes such as good and evil, and how these themes are often oversimplified on-screen to a point that they're no longer useful as parable. Smith also implicates these films in the kind of cultural commodification that both of them seem to criticize within their own narratives.[5]

On the other hand, Andy Porter and Jessica A. Albrecht find deeper meaning in the *Matrix* series' visions of hell. In their fabulous article "Nonviolent Utopias: Heroes Transgressing the Gender Binary in *The Matrix Resurrections*," they explore how the binary hellscape of the first three *Matrix* films, with its religious underpinnings of Neo as a savior figure, transforms into a feminist utopia by *Resurrections* as the story reveals that Neo's power is dependent on Trinity's. Their analysis makes for great reading, recontextualizing the entire franchise in important gender-critical and gender-forward ways.[6]

And in a piece of fascinating quantitative research, Williams Sims Bainbridge's "Expanding the Use of the Internet in Religious Research" compares *Constantine* to Mel Gibson's *The Passion of the Christ*, noting that the Gibson film "has some aesthetic similarities while being theologically more orthodox." That's because in *Constantine*, he argues,

> the major theological premise of the film is dualist, comparable to the theology of The Process Church of the Final Judgement. . . . The Process promoted the unity of Christ and Satan, beyond good and evil. The protagonist of the movie, John Constantine, battles against demons invading the Earth from Hell, but he considers God to be no better than Satan.

This religious distinction is meaningful enough, Bainbridge argues, that he can compare audiences of these two films based on Amazon.com recommendations and determine potential links to viewers' spiritual predispositions in the algorithm.[7] Whoa, right?

Metaphorical Hellscapes

"Welcome to hell," Ortiz the Dawg Boy (Reeves) drawls in Alex Winter's directorial debut *Freaked* (1993), and when it comes to less literal hellscapes in Keanu Reeves's extensive catalog, we have a plethora of examples on the table. In *Freaked*, a political satire about unchecked capitalism and environmental devastation, Ortiz leads a group of hybrid humans who have been experimented on by Elijah C. Skuggs (Randy Quaid), the owner of a remote carnival in the jungles of South America where he displays his collection of mutated prisoners. Hell might look like paradise in this case, with the tropical setting and lush backdrop of the fictional country of Santa Flan. But the process of becoming one of Skuggs's creatures, via exposure to the toxin Zygrot 24, looks as hellish as it must feel as we watch Alex Winter's Ricky turn into a drooling half-demon-looking monster. That the human hybrids are all kept in cages adds to the horror of their situation. And vain and egotistical Ricky lives his own personal hell as he becomes physically ugly for the first time in his life, forcing him into a personal reckoning that ends up being almost as painful as his monstrous transformation. As it takes its cast into the depths of science-experiment hell, *Freaked* aligns in many ways with of one of Keanu's own favorite films: the horror comedy *Young Frankenstein* (1974),[8] albeit in a bright color palette as opposed to black and white.

In contrast to the verdant backdrop of Santa Flan, hell appears in rocky mountainous form for Keanu Reeves's Jonathan Harker in *Bram Stoker's Dracula* (1992) as he journeys into the wilds of Transylvania. What begins as a business trip descends into a literal pit in Dracula's castle where Harker is held prisoner, tortured and fed upon by Dracula's demon brides. But Harker's hell doesn't end there, as Dracula's thrall enmeshes his fiancée Mina (Winona Ryder), forcing him to confront evils that literally turn his hair white.

Hell in *The Bad Batch* (2016) is the barren desertscape where unwanted citizens are released to fend for themselves amid scarcity and grotesque cannibalism in this society of the abandoned. *The Bad Batch* takes place in a version of the United States where citizens are summarily ejected from the country for a variety of transgressions, the real world's punitive "three strikes law" taken to an exponentially violent extreme. In this sepia-toned dystopia not unlike that of *Mad Max: Fury Road* (2015), hell is starvation, thirst, and a constant battle not just for bodily autonomy, as bands of cannibals rule the roost, but also for the imaginations of cult leader the Dream, played by Keanu Reeves, whose endless supply of hallucinogens distracts the bad batch from their horrific reality.

Then there's the frozen icescape of *Siberia* (2018), where the cold is as much a villain as the cast of characters trapped in freezing purgatories of their own making. "In heaven we'll all speak Russian," mob boss Boris (Pasha D. Lychnikoff) says in Russian to Reeves's Lucas Hill as they come to terms in the midst of a diamond heist. Lucas fittingly responds, "In hell, too." Hell, in this case, is not the usual fiery pits of perdition but rather the bleak and desolate landscapes and frigid arctic temperatures Keanu's character must constantly pass through, wearing just a thin wool coat for most of the film. It's a place that feels like a netherworld far away from the rules and conventions of the West. As Lucas falls deeper and deeper into the enormous snowdrifts of Siberian corruption and international gem smuggling, he's totally unprepared for not just the weather but also the brutality of the people he meets there—a place where Americans are certainly not welcome.

Other Keanu movies focus on a figurative hellscape much closer to home. In *Act of Vengeance* (1986), based on a true story, we receive an education in the hell of coal mining, as the film opens with a horrific disaster underground that takes the lives of many workers due to cost-cutting measures by the corporation that owns the rights to the mine. Jock Yablonski (Charles Bronson) is a former miners union leader who decides to run for office again, in order to hold the corporation account-able for the recent slew of deaths and install new protections for all of the mine workers. In retaliation, the corporate powers that be call out a hit not just on Jock but on his entire family in an effort to put their profits ahead of the people who work for them. In one of his first roles, Reeves plays the chillingly jovial hit man sent to murder Jock. Just two years later, another movie in Keanu's filmography echoed these same themes: *The Prince of Pennsylvania*, which this time actually goes down into the mines with Keanu's Rupert Marshetta and his abrasive father (Fred Ward), in similarly dangerous conditions for the men who are being ignored for profits. In these two films, living under capitalism is as much a hell as the dangerous mines themselves.

Early in *Permanent Record* (1988), popular teen David (Alan Boyce) goes to everyone's favorite cliffside hangout overlooking the ocean and jumps to his death, turning a suburban California community upside down. While David's life may have seemed charmed on the surface, under-neath he was grappling with a great deal of social and other pressures that eventually got the better of him. Suicide was his way out of the hell of his own life, the hopelessness about what kind of future he might have, especially living under the kind of expectations he was putting on himself without asking for help. This was the late '80s, long before it was accept-able to even talk about the idea of anxiety and depression, let alone admit that you're feeling them. But it's not just the hell of suicide that *Permanent Record* unpacks, it's also the hell of having witnessed it, like David's best friend Chris, played by Reeves, and the intense pain of survivor's guilt as he and his peers find themselves in the hellscape of extreme and acute grief. The survivors' agony is only deepened by the fact that nobody will talk about what was really going on with David. The teens all ponder the ways they could have saved him, and a flock of adults just wants the problem to go away, even discouraging the young people from talking through their suffering. Through her compassionate direction, Marisa Silver explores the hell of grief in a way that feels timeless, in spite of clothes and tech firmly situating this film in the '80s.

Where death in *Permanent Record* is self-inflicted and we witness the community ripple effect of grief, 1986's *River's Edge* takes us into the hell of apathy after weirdo senior Samson (Daniel Roebuck) strangles his girlfriend Jamie (Danyi Deats), leaving her naked corpse on the riverbank. It's an unforgettably unsettling scene as Samson brings their friends to see her dead body, none of them reacting in horror or shock except for Keanu's Matt. All of them just go about their days afterward as if everything is just fine, not telling their parents or anyone at school—leaving Jamie's corpse to rot as if she were garbage dumped by the riverside. Matt is the only one visibly affected by not just the horrific sight of a dead body but also the fact that someone he considers a friend would do something so atrocious while being so nonchalant about it. And no, it isn't just shock on everyone else's part; Jamie's friends just don't care enough about her to feel anything. As Samson ropes in Layne (Crispin Glover) to help him cover up his crime, Matt goes to the police, who disbelieve him and accuse him of orchestrating the whole thing. There's more murder and attempted killing before this dark tale of teenage desensitization ends. And all of it raises the question of whether the kids were capable of feeling anything at all, in a quiet indictment of American suburban culture

Another Keanu film from 1986, *The Brotherhood of Justice*, spotlights a different kind of teenage psychological descent, as a group of popular seniors at a California high school go vigilante in response to a crime wave. Their vigilantism begins with good intentions as they target known criminals in their community. But as they get drunk on power, the brotherhood quickly devolves into petty grievances, violence against romantic rivals, and targeting folks they simply don't like, culminating in an almost fatal stabbing and attempted murder by car bomb. *The Brotherhood of Justice* also introduces a concept that may have seemed novel in the mid-'80s but that we are now well familiar with today: the militarization of school campuses. For Principal Grootemat (Joe Spano), a police presence on campus is tantamount to the school becoming an educational hell, and he does everything in his power to prevent this situation. But by the end of the film there is a police car parked on campus, with an ominous feeling that something fundamental in the American youth experience is about to drastically shift. In real life we have seen this shift play out to often violent ends, as law enforcement on campus often clashes with students even as young as six or seven, arresting and handcuffing them for perceived unruly behavior, all across the US.

This early Keanu movie about protecting young citizens from police also foreshadows Reeves's later films that dive all the way into the particular hell of law enforcement violence, especially how it's often committed against the very people the police are supposed to protect. Cowritten by the godfather of modern noir, James Ellroy, *Street Kings* (2008) is a harrowing plunge into the underworld of corruption that shapes the Los Angeles Police Department. Keanu's Detective Tom Ludlow is accused of killing a fellow officer, turning himself into the new public enemy number one until he shoots his way to clearing his name. *Street Kings* in many ways reflects the reality of LAPD corruption up and down the ranks: a *Rolling Stone* exposé chillingly mirrors the events of the film as it examines the variety of actual gangs that make up the LAPD.[9]

Similarly, in *Exposed* (2016), Reeves's Detective Galban is part of an enormous web of violence and corruption, this time on the East Coast with the NYPD. After Galban's rapist of a partner, Cullen (Danny Hoch), is found brutally murdered, the hunt for the killer reveals the history of extreme sadism and almost total impunity that shaped his career. Cullen's most infamous crime was sodomizing a young Dominican man with a broomstick, an act that becomes the emblem of his deep depravity, well known to both the communities he polices and his colleagues. The film further highlights his devilishness by having one of his victims, a young woman named Isabel (Ana de Armas), see visions of angels as she disassociates from the horrific crimes she's survived at his hands. While narratively confusing, *Exposed* still touches on what is often a hellish immigrant experience in the United States—especially when you're not white—and the terrible intersection of police violence with these particularly vulnerable communities. Reeves's Galban himself is no saint, using police brutality at every turn and often threatening Black and Brown men with his service weapon, crimes that he too gets away with.

Exposed and another 2016 Keanu film, *The Neon Demon*, touch on the hell of gender-based violence such as rape, sexual assault, and domestic violence, but this theme is featured so extensively in Reeves's catalog that it gets its own chapter, coming up next.

Speed (1994) is about the extended hell that is a hostage situation, from the nightmare of being trapped in an elevator that's about to fall or a bus that's about to explode if the driver goes below fifty miles an hour. But it also touches on the dark underbelly of US law enforcement: as discussed in chapter 4, the motivations of bomber Howard Payne (Dennis Hopper) are intertwined with his neglectful treatment as a former police officer who was disabled in the line of duty.

And then there's the uniquely American hell of gun violence, which is actually so normalized in Keanu Reeves movies that the line "Guns. Lots of guns" from *The Matrix* has become an in-joke for fans, and Keanu's own movies call back to it in a variety of ways. (As mentioned in chapter 4, *John Wick: Chapter 3* even quotes it directly.) Even his comedies and dramedies like *Parenthood* (1989) and *Henry's Crime* (2010) are not immune to featuring firearms in the most unlikely of contexts, like the shoot-'em-up cowboy birthday party with replica guns that Gil (Steve Martin) throws for his son in *Parenthood*, while Gil himself has dark fantasies that his child will become a mass shooter. And as Keanu's most recent action franchise, *John Wick* features such shooting-heavy fight scenes that it inspired the phrase "gun fu" to describe them. Fittingly, the franchise's gunplay occurs alongside numerous references to hell, and Dante's *Inferno* in particular, as its title character traverses the criminal underworld of the High Table.*

My Own Private Idaho (1991) is inspired by another pillar of the Western canon, Shakespeare, and his plays *Henry IV, Part 1*; *Henry IV, Part 2*; and *Henry V*, which are about the horror of battle and war. *Idaho* itself unpacks several circles of hell: of being unhoused, of extreme poverty, of

---

* *John Wick: Chapter 3* references Dante's journey in the *Inferno*—"The path to paradise begins in hell"—while *Chapter 4* opens by quoting the sign over the gates of hell that Dante describes: "Abandon all hope you who are about to enter here." The name of the late Lance Reddick's character, Continental concierge Charon, references the ferryman of the dead in Greek and Roman mythology. And John's own nickname Baba Yaga refers to a witch, but she's also often presented as a demonic force who calls on the various entities of the underworlds to empower her magic. By the end of *Chapter 4*, the Bowery King (Laurence Fishburne) even outright asks at John Wick's grave, "Where do you think he is? Heaven or hell?" The answer, from John's sometime ally Winston (Ian McShane) is "Who knows."

homophobia. In particular, young gay sex worker Mike Waters, beautifully played by River Phoenix, has struggled through a hellscape of violence, abandonment, and illness ever since birth. And when we bring Keanu Reeves's Indigenous background into a reading of the film, we also see a quiet commentary on the horror of Indigenous genocide in the Pacific Northwest. When we first see Portland in the film, the camera lingers on a statue of an Indigenous man riding an elk, with the inscription THE COMING OF THE WHITE MAN. There is a double entendre here, as the film opens with a blow job and a climax of a white man. If, as discussed in chapter 6, Keanu's character is read as half Indigenous on his mother's side, the reference can be extended to the barbaric sexual violence that was inflicted mainly on Indigenous women, not just during the early colonial years of war and mass killing as whites seized tribal and ancestral land but also in the decades since, as things like forced sterilization and the kidnapping of indigenous children by state actors also proceeded from the coming of a white man. Keanu Reeves's own Indigenous ancestors in Hawai'i had very similar things happen to them, and his presence in this film is a good moment to take a beat and honor all those lives lost because of the hell of settler colonization—a hell that continues today, as many Indigenous communities across America continue to live in abject poverty; their struggle to survive continues.*

It is a corresponding hell of poverty, this time in Hong Kong, that leaves Tiger Chen (Hu Chen) open to the financial manipulations of Reeves's snuff filmmaker Donaka Mark in Reeves's directorial debut, the action film *Man of Tai Chi* (2013). This martial arts version of *The Devil's Advocate*, with hints of *Hostel* (2005), *Fight Club* (1999), and *Unleashed* (2005), features Keanu playing his most devilish character yet, with a dead-eyed shark stare as he metaphorically vampirizes all those around him, exploiting fighters for a twisted video project that results in their murder. Tiger Chen, whose parents live in one of the lowest-income neighborhoods in Hong Kong, begins the story as one of the last two

---

* It's also interesting to note that when we see the COMING OF THE WHITE MAN statue in *Idaho*, it serves as the backdrop for a shot in which Keanu's character is cradling Phoenix's. This could be read a nod to the good faith in which Indigenous ancestors first treated the colonizers—helping and protecting them—before the settler-colonizers' genocide projects began in earnest.

people to practice tai chi as a nonviolent martial art. Tiger is idealistic, romantic, and kind. He quickly becomes the perfect target for Mr. D, who systematically strips him of all his previous morals and ethics, almost until the point of no return. All because the monstrous Donaka Mark gets off on watching his victims' loss of innocence in real time, as do the uber-wealthy audiences to whom he sells these prolonged snuff tapes. *Man of Tai Chi* provides an action-horror look at how capitalism creates hellscapes wherever it goes.

So do the Reeves films that explore the connection between capitalism and high rates of addiction, such as *Under the Influence* (1986), *Johnny Mnemonic* (1995), and *A Scanner Darkly* (2006), in which alcohol and drugs pull large groups of humans into depravity, despair, and ultimately death. Interestingly, it is the earliest of these three films, *Under the Influence*, that does the most to destigmatize addiction, framing it not as a moral failing or a failure of self-control but as an illness. *Johnny Mnemonic* and *A Scanner Darkly* make less of an effort, so that the characters' addictions can be seen as a reflection of their moral turpitude, rather than situational behavior provoked by a series of complicated internal and external influences.

Even Reeves's comedies and romance films end up descending into metaphorical hellscapes. *The Night Before* (1988) is a teen comedy adventure in the big city like *Adventures in Babysitting* (1987)—but much grittier, as hapless nerd Winston (Reeves) ends up in the wrong part of town, having accidentally sold his senior prom date to a pimp after being roofied. The sheltered Winston is forced to confront aspects of Los Angeles society he would never otherwise have any contact with, including sex workers, drug dealers, and mob bosses.

Weirdly in the same vein as *The Night Before*, *The SpongeBob Movie: Sponge on the Run* (2020) also finds its hapless main character in a downward spiral as he tries to find his pet snail Gary and instead gets sucked into the crass commercialism and consumerism of the Lost City of Atlantic City. It's a surprisingly deep topic for a children's cartoon, and Reeves's Sage is the God figure who counterpoints the enormous variety of devils on-screen.

In the romantic drama *Sweet November* (2001), we experience the hell of cancer alongside Reeves's Nelson and his paramour-for-a-month Sara

(Charlize Theron). Sara has terminal cancer, and while her struggles with her mortality are agonizing, she's able to sidestep another common health care nightmare: Sara comes from a wealthy family and has the financial means to treat her cancer and extend her life as much as is medically possible. This is a privilege that a majority of Americans in real life cannot afford, as a cancer diagnosis can also bring about absolute financial ruin for the average American citizen. As they say, you're one cancer diagnosis away from bankruptcy, and we've already discussed the hell that is poverty and the kinds of horrible desperation that come with it.

Another of Keanu's romances confronts an all-too-common horror head-on. The period drama *A Walk in the Clouds* (1995) examines the hell soldiers face not only in war but also in the form of the PTSD upon returning home. Reeves is Paul Sutton, a soldier turned chocolate salesman who poses as the husband of a young Mexican American woman, Victoria (Aitana Sánchez-Gijón), who finds herself pregnant and alone, with a conservative father who will not accept her single parenthood. During the course of their romance, Paul often has flashbacks to his experiences in World War II, which collage with his turbulent childhood raised in an orphanage and often have him waking up in terror and cold sweat. What's particularly special about this moment of honesty about PTSD on-screen is that the film was made in the mid-'90s, when open discussions about such mental health issues were rare. Choosing to tackle this subject in a sensitive way is absolutely unusual for romantic dramas of this era.

When one steps back to consider this collection of figurative descents into hell throughout Reeves's catalog of films, what's striking is the sheer number of them that have been panned by critics and audiences alike, including *The Bad Batch*, *Street Kings*, *Exposed*, and *The Man of Tai Chi*. It's often the films in which Keanu himself plays a metaphorical devil. Could it be that these films didn't fare well because Keanu is so convincing at portraying the dark side of humanity on-screen that it makes viewers uncomfortable in ways they might not even consciously acknowledge?

Many of the panned projects are fairly recent Reeves films, so it's again important to keep in mind that since becoming a superstar, Reeves has not been limited by the particular scripts offered to him; each of these films was a conscious choice that he made amid many other potential options. And what's also interesting is how particularly these darker tales in his catalog correspond to his list of movie recommendations that he thinks everyone should see, published by *Esquire*. This list includes his own frequently panned movie *The Bad Batch*; 2016's *The Neon Demon*, in which he plays a pedophile; and the following films by other artists:

- *Amadeus* (1984)
- *The Big Lebowski* (1998)
- *Blazing Saddles* (1974)
- *A Clockwork Orange* (1971)
- *Dr. Strangelove* (1964)
- *The Evil Dead* (1981)
- *La Femme Nikita* (the original French version, 1990)
- *Mad Max 2: The Road Warrior* (1981)
- *Monty Python and the Holy Grail* (1975)
- *The Outlaw Josey Wales* (1976)
- *The Professional* (1994)
- *Raising Arizona* (1987)
- *Rollerball* (1975)
- *Rosencrantz & Guildenstern Are Dead* (1990)
- *Seven Samurai* (1954)
- *Young Frankenstein* (1974)[10]

When I consider this list of Keanu's must-watch films and compare it to the films under discussion in this chapter and the rest of part 2, it becomes easy to see why he's chosen the darker roles and projects in his filmography, even if critics and audiences don't always appreciate them. I am also hoping that my analysis here and following might help audiences who didn't appreciate these films on first viewing to see them in a new light and recognize the deeper meaning they bring to Keanu's stupendous collection.

White Devilry

But there's still another vital level to unpack when it comes to devils and hellscapes on-screen in Keanu Reeves movies: white devilry. This concept is brilliantly explored in a 2018 episode of performance artist, poet, and activist Terence Nance's HBO series *Random Acts of Flyness.*[11] The episode connects white devilry to the archetype of the antihero—that is, a character who is driven to do bad things in pursuit of good ends, and often gets a free pass because of it. Nance narrates:

> The white devil, also known as the antihero, is an archetypal character trope. White devils are white men and women thrust into situations in which they are surrounded by other white characters who do not possess their preternatural level of genius or skill. The wrinkle is that the white devil is his or her own antagonist. Often some embodiment of their Jungian shadow consistently pervades their life and relationships. The power this shadow generates is the key source of the white devil's exceptional technical genius. The white devil's narrative function is to win in the battle against his or her shadow self and make sure the dark energy that their shadow self generates is used for good. [. . .] Have you thought about what makes these characters compelling? Why them? Why their stories? [. . .] Is it because white people are the best at everything? Not only the best cops but also the best drug dealers?

This narration is accompanied by images of antiheroes and the extreme violence they perpetrate in TV series such as *Dexter* and *The Sopranos* and films such as *The Wolf of Wall Street* and *American History X*—and, crucially, highlights the fact that all these characters are white.[12] There are hundreds and hundreds of examples of white antiheroes in television and film, but only a small handful of antiheroes of color.*

Why is this? White antiheroes abound, Nance says,

> because the white devil archetype in contemporary film and television functions as yet another display of white male dominance and social power, by framing the Jungian shadow as a source

---

* Films and TV series that do feature Black antiheroes include *Beverly Hills Cop*, *Black Monday*, *Black Panther*, *The Chi*, *Claws*, *The Fast and the Furious*, *The Girlfriend Experience*, *Godfather of Harlem*, *Hustlers*, *I May Destroy You*, *John Wick*, *Ma*, *Obi-Wan*, *Pitch Black*, and *The Wire*.

of white male cultural and social centrality. Its function is to peacock. To put on display a shadow-fueled virility and acumen. The desired effect is for the melanated masses to hesitate before challenging white supremacy. Their hope is that in any moment of resistance, no matter how big or small, they, us, *we* will remember that the white person or institution they are resisting has a devil inside them. An amoral devil that will not concede defeat under any circumstances.

As John Milton puts it in *The Devil's Advocate*, "Freedom, baby, is never having to say you're sorry." This could be the motto for most white antiheroes, as they rarely see real consequences for their illegal and immoral actions, often including murder.

Communities of color, meanwhile, are pathologized in ways that white folks are not—and not just on-screen. White criminals are presumed innocent, given the benefit of the doubt, and treated with kid gloves. Folks of color, especially Black people, are immediately treated with a presumption of guilt. A white mass shooter gets taken for Burger King after murdering people; an unarmed and innocent Black man gets shot in the back for existing in public.[13] You can't be an antihero if your very existence is considered a criminal act by the white supremacist powers that be. You don't have the privilege of doing bad things for good ends and expecting to get away with it—unless you're white.*

All of this makes Keanu Reeves a fascinating figure—one of the few actors of color who gets to be an antihero on-screen. In films like *John Wick*, *A Scanner Darkly*, *Henry's Crime*, *Siberia*, *My Own Private Idaho*, *Hardball*, *Constantine*, and even the comedies *Destination Wedding* and *Always Be My Maybe*, Keanu has delighted in playing dark and morally complicated characters. For example, Eli Roth's home invasion horror film *Knock Knock* (2015) begins with Keanu's Evan Webber, a perfect husband and father turned adulterous antihero, initiating a threesome with two young strangers, who then relentlessly punish him for the transgression. Yet we root for him in this role when we might not have with another

---

* It's important to note that the white devil trope has a flip side: the white savior. White savior behavior in places like Africa and Asia is also experienced as an extension of white supremacy and white paternalism.

actor. The same goes for *Street Kings*, where as much of a dirtbag as his Detective Ludlow might be, we still want to see him come out on top. And for many audiences it's much more than just personal goodwill at work here. Is Keanu in this particularly privileged position because the industry has often whitewashed Reeves's ethnicity? Very possibly.

In some cases, whitewashing Reeves's Asian and Indigenous racial identity has led to him playing actual white devils—unambiguously white characters in movies such as *The Night Before*, *The Brotherhood of Justice*, *The Prince of Pennsylvania*, and *The Devil's Advocate*. For those of us who have never seen Keanu Reeves as white-passing, it's almost a kind of shared delusion among industry people, critics, and audiences alike that they've quietly agreed to experience Keanu as a white person even if he's not. Which again brings us back to the white supremacy that Nance calls out in *Random Acts of Flyness*, by which white people can confer passing status on certain folks of color they have claimed, and those people get afforded privileges other, even similar-looking people of color don't get.[14] At the same time, just because he's playing white doesn't mean he *is* white. To have an actor of color playing an antihero at all breaks the molds of the film industry and society at large that pathologize the behavior of nonwhite people who do bad things for good reasons, while giving white people the benefit of the doubt when they do the same.

None of this changes the dark legacy of white supremacy, which has been another kind of hell for marginalized groups around the world— whose lands, cultures, and even bodies were brutalized by the violent crimes of white devils and their colonization projects. Speaking of Keanu's Indigenous heritage, Hawai'i was invaded by an OG white devil, Captain James Cook, a violent sadist whose policies were so grotesque he was eventually murdered by a group of Indigenous Hawaiians. The postcolonial experience is also a purgatory of liminality, especially in places like Hawai'i where tourism and a military presence not only deplete and pollute resources for Indigenous Hawaiians but also put their lives in direct danger, as I'll discuss further in the next chapter.

While it may not always be pleasant to explore the darker themes of Keanu Reeves's work, they reflect a spectrum of realities that too many people must struggle with in their daily lives. And sitting with our discomfort reveals how brilliantly Reeves has challenged and continues to challenge his audiences' expectations. It's not every day that a performer beloved for his kind and down-to-earth real-life persona would opt to spend so much time in hell and among devils in his creative work. That Reeves often chooses to play the devil himself is just another testament to his fearless creative range as an actor.

10

MEN WERE DECEIVERS EVER

Gender-Based and Sexual Violence as a Recurring Theme

IN REAL LIFE, Keanu Reeves would never hurt a woman. (It's not actually his fault if you were upset when he and visual artist Alexandra Grant, with whom he's collaborated on several art books, went public with their romance in 2019.) But in a number of Reeves's movies, he plays characters who delight in their violence against women. If chapter 7, which looked at Keanu's exceptional qualities as a leading man, represented the Lovers tarot card, this chapter represents the Lovers reversed and crossed with the Devil card, which indicates sex offenders, domestic abusers, and intra-relationship violence of many kinds.

There is something uniquely shocking about many of these films and roles, mainly because they contrast so starkly with the real-life persona of Keanu that everyone has come to respect and love. This chapter will be disturbing to read, so survivors of domestic and other sexual violence might want to do a quick body check to make sure you're in a good place to absorb these themes. And even though the majority of gender-based violence like rape outlined here is against women, it's certainly not exclusive to them.

What I present to you here is a chronological overview of all Reeves's films to focus on themes of gendered and sexual violence. Why chronological? To emphasize that these themes have been part and parcel of Keanu's artistic output from the very beginning of his career to the present day. I'll get to why this is important at the end of the chapter.

Gendered Violence Through Reeves's Movies

In one of Keanu's first roles, in the 1986 TV movie *Act of Vengeance*, he plays distressingly jovial hit man Buddy Martin, who nonchalantly asks his bosses, "Did either of you ever put your hand, I mean, your whole fuckin' hand, inside a lady?" accompanied by a mimed demonstration. Buddy tells them that after they've completed their hit job, he'll take them to a place where they can try it. Buddy's colleagues are revolted— which is really saying something, since one of them admits he shot his own wife *and* brags that he got her not to press charges. It's a repulsive moment, especially for a made-for-television movie in the 1980s; Keanu really came through the gate already defying expectations. Incredibly, that same year Reeves's Christmas adventure *Babes in Toyland* features a plotline in which a teenage girl is being forced into marriage with an old, cruel, and violent man, which is as bizarrely uncomfortable in this holiday film as it sounds.

Also jarring is the statutory rape in Keanu's hockey drama *Youngblood* (1986), at the hands of nymphomaniacal boardinghouse matron Miss McGill (Fionnula Flanagan), who "welcomes" newcomers in their beds whether they like it or not. When teammates witness seventeen-year-old Dean Youngblood (Rob Lowe) getting his "greeting," Reeves's French Canadian Heaver looks troubled as he confesses, "She do it to me last year." It doesn't sound like he consented. That's not cool, Miss McGill. That's rape.

In 1988's *The Night Before*, the disturbing content is the themes of sex trafficking and sex work, when Reeves's Winston accidentally sells his prom date Tara (Lori Loughlin) to a pimp, and she ends up in the hands of a human trafficker who makes a huge show of testing "the merchandise" before he transports it. The threat of "white slavery" in a comedy romp is very 1980s and shocking by today's standards, especially since Loughlin's character, a junior in high school, spends the latter half of the movie in only her underwear.

Also in 1988, *The Prince of Pennsylvania* features graphic domestic violence: Pam Marshetta (Bonnie Bedelia), the mother of Reeves's main character Rupert, gets beaten up by her husband Gary (Fred Ward) once he finds out she's been having an affair with one of his fellow miners. And to round off the year's violence-against-women theme we have director Stephen Frears's *Dangerous Liaisons*, in which French nobleman Valmont (John Malkovich) plays complicated, manipulative, and often nonconsensual sex games with young women—one of whom is the would-be fiancée of Keanu's Chevalier Raphael Danceny—in the court for fun, leading to ostracism and even death.

The toxic masculinity is subtler in the 1989 made-for-TV short *Life Under Water*, which aired on PBS's *American Playhouse*. In it, Keanu plays Kip, a restless young man in the Hamptons who sexually and otherwise manipulates two best friends, played by Haviland Morris and Sarah Jessica Parker.

I Love You To Death (1990), likewise, starts out focusing on toxicity rather than overt violence, with Kevin Kline playing Joey Boca, a serial cheater with absolutely no shame. But when his wife Rosalie (Tracey Ullman) finds out about it, she plots to kill him with the help of a string of ineffective accomplices, including Reeves's dim-witted hit man Marlon. While the physical violence in this film originates with Rosalie, the emotional violence began with Joey, in the quietly destructive way that adulterous liars make fools out of everyone who loves them. Joey's toxic masculinity is so poisonous it almost leads his own family to murder. By the end of the film, we meet Joey's overbearing mother (Miriam Margolyes), who proceeds to beat him around the head—where he's just been shot—after finding out about all his infidelity, highlighting how cycles of domestic violence are often passed down generationally, by men *and* by women.

The next year in *Point Break*, the violence against women is subtler still. It begins with FBI agent Johnny Utah (Reeves) casually manipulating Tyler (Lori Petty) to get her to help him with his investigation of the surfing bank robbers known as the Ex-Presidents. Relationships built on lies and false pretenses are not fully consensual, so any sexual encounters that result end up in a gray area of consent too, painting a different portrait of our hero Johnny. And by the end of *Point Break*, Tyler is also being used as a pawn by Ex-Presidents leader Bodhi (Patrick Swayze), who leaves her hostage with sexual sadist Rosie (Lee Tergesen). While we are not told or shown on-screen if Rosie sexually assaulted Tyler, based on her subsequent body language and the way that she behaves completely unlike the Tyler we've known the entire rest of the movie—suddenly desperately clingy, fearful, and emotionally broken—we can very well read it as a yes. With that implied act of violence, Bodhi punishes Tyler by surrogate for bringing the law right to his doorstep. After all, she's the one who agreed to teach Johnny Utah how to surf, giving him the key to their world. This adds a grim shadow over the film that you can't unsee once you've recognized it.

My Own Private Idaho (1991) gives us an important reminder that sexual violence is not only a women problem. In the film, we hear a number of disturbing stories of rape from the various male sex worker friends who hang around with Mike (River Phoenix) and Scott (Reeves). They discuss how they were raped their first time selling sex, and while the stories are painful on their own, the casual way in which these young men laughingly share these tales adds a fresh level of horror to their experiences. It wasn't necessarily common knowledge back in 1991, but today we very well know that gay men are disproportionately at risk of being sexually assaulted compared to heterosexual men, and a huge part of this is due to their marginalized status in society—especially when you add sex work into the mix. But sexual violence against boys and men in *Idaho* does not end with the dangers of sex work: Mike himself is a product of his mother sexually abusing his brother when he was a teenager. While familial sexual violence perpetrated by men is much more common, mothers are just as capable of it.

Even the comedy romp *Bill & Ted's Bogus Journey* (1991) features evil robot versions of Alex Winter's Bill and Keanu's Ted who are verbally abusive to the real Bill and Ted's girlfriends, the princesses. At one point the robots try to coerce the women into unwanted sexual contact. It's actually Ted's stepmom Missy (Amy Stoch) who helps the princesses stand up to Evil Bill and Ted, literally placing her body between the robots and the girls. Missy, I mean Mom, is a feminist hero who never gets the credit for it.

In *Bram Stoker's Dracula* (1992), Count Dracula (Gary Oldman) has a murderous obsession with Mina (Winona Ryder) that leads to him

sexually abusing her best friend Lucy (Sadie Frost), then ultimately killing Lucy and turning her into a vampire. He hypnotizes Mina herself
into nonconsensual sexual contact that leads to her temporarily taking
on vampiric qualities as well. And let's not forget Mina's fiancé, Jonathan
Harker (Reeves), who is held captive and sexually assaulted by Dracula's
brides. The movie is so beautiful and captivating that it's really easy to
forget about all of this nonconsensual sex that takes place throughout.

Much Ado About Nothing (1993) features Keanu not as a victim but as
the self-professed villain, Don John, who sets in motion a plot to implicate
Hero (Kate Beckinsale) in a premarital affair and thus ruin her betrothal
to Claudio (Robert Sean Leonard). But in this adaptation of one of Shakespeare's comedies, it's actually Claudio who is the real bad guy. How quick
Claudio is to reject Hero on the basis of a rumor, even going so far as to
call for her death because he suspects she's not a virgin. That's fucked.
And then they still end up together? That's abuse. The fact that any of
this would be considered the stuff of comedy, not only in Shakespeare's
time but in the 1990s—and even more recently, when there have been
several additional film adaptations that retain this aspect of the plot—
speaks to how normalized violence against women is, and how casually
our humiliation becomes entertainment.

Following Much Ado, Keanu took a three-year break from these sorts
of narratives, but he returned with a bang, literally, with 1996's Feeling
Minnesota. Echoing Babes in Toyland's forced marriage, the film opens
with Freddie (Cameron Diaz) being chased down the train tracks in a
wedding dress as she's being forced to marry Sam (Vincent D'Onofrio)
by a mobster, Red (Delroy Lindo), to whom she owes $10,000. Red has
gone so far as to brand Freddie with the word SLUT, and Freddie is even
raped by Sam—thankfully off-screen, but we still hear it happen. And the
violence against her doesn't end there. Freddie ends up shot by Sam and
buried by his brother Jjaks (Reeves), who loves her but thinks she's dead
and is trying to dispose of her body. Yet somehow she manages to survive
all this male violence. Good for her and only her. As with Much Ado About
Nothing, it's distressing that these grim events would be considered funny
or romantic, yet the film is classified as a romance and dark comedy to
this day. The handful of sweet moments between Jjaks and Freddie in no
way makes up for the violence that is done against her.

The Last Time I Committed Suicide (1997) is based on the real life of Neal Cassady, a friend of Beat poets and writers Jack Kerouac, Ken Kesey, and Lawrence Ferlinghetti—and an all-around hot mess of a human being. Thomas Jane plays him as a twenty-year-old, in a "relationship" with a sixteen-year-old girl named Mary (Gretchen Mol), a girl he later tries to pass off to thirtysomething pervert Harry (Reeves) before eventually getting arrested for statutory rape himself. But it's not just Mary who Neal's selfishness and hedonism affects profoundly. The film opens with his girlfriend Joan (Claire Forlani) just after she's attempted suicide, partly because of Neal's treatment. And while this film is a love letter to the exploits of the Beat generation, the misogyny inherent in their vibe is also crystal clear here. How many other women did Neal and his cohort use and discard, effectively ruining them in the eyes of 1950s society? How much more rape was there, statutory and otherwise? How many did they leave pregnant? How many more tried to kill themselves? From a woman's perspective, this film has many shades of gender-based horror. And from that same perspective it's gut wrenching how all of this violence against women is filtered through the rose-colored glasses of men's sexual desires, even as those desires are absolutely perverse, extending the romanticization of the Beat poets that continues to this day.

Also in 1997, Reeves released another film that's essentially wall-to-wall violence against women: *The Devil's Advocate*. The film opens with a young girl testifying against her abuser, who's defended by Reeves's lawyer Kevin Lomax. Kevin wins the case by smearing the young victim's reputation. A later client, Alexander Cullen (Craig T. Nelson), murdered his wife, maid, and son, and is sexually abusing his teenage stepdaughter; Kevin presents his alibi in court knowing it's a lie, and gets him acquitted too. Cullen's gold-plated New York penthouse actually belonged to an unscrupulous businessman turned US president with whom the character shares disturbing similarities. That president has since been found liable for the sexual abuse of E. Jean Carroll, and there's even footage of him confessing his desire to date one of his daughters if she weren't blood related.[1] Outside the courtroom, Kevin helps gaslight his wife Mary Ann (Charlize Theron) to the point where she is institutionalized and kills herself—this is after we find out she grew up with an abusive father and Al Pacino's devilish John Milton violently rapes her. Milton himself is abusing his own daughter, and we eventually learn that Milton raped Kevin's mother too. By the end, we also discover that the original case Kevin won on a technicality led to that same child molester murdering a ten-year-old girl. This one is a lot. But once you learn that *The Devil's Advocate* was adapted from the novel by Andrew Neiderman, prolific ghostwriter for *Flowers in the Attic* author V. C. Andrews, all the *Flowers*-esque incest and violence against women starts to make a fetishistic narrative sense.

"What good is a phone call if you're unable to speak?" Agent Smith (Hugo Weaving) asks as Reeves's Neo finds his mouth disappearing in *The Matrix* (1999). Smith and his fellow agents then hold Neo down and impregnate him with a slithering mechanical creature that burrows into his navel. Neo thinks the whole thing was a dream until Trinity (Carrie-Anne Moss) and Switch (Belinda McClory) pull the "tracking bug" from his belly. This sequence of events is disturbingly reminiscent of a rape scene: many survivors of sexual violence mention how they were too scared to even scream, making Agent Smith's erasing of Neo's mouth a terrible metaphor for the side effects of rape.

Keanu opened up the 2000s with *The Watcher*, playing a serial killer who exclusively targets women. We can be grateful that there is no rape involved, at least. This is also the one film that Keanu Reeves wishes was not in his catalog, as he himself was coerced into making it through a forged signature. In order to avoid a prolonged legal battle, Reeves decided to go ahead and just do the movie. So we have the additional nasty factor that Keanu is not in this movie entirely consensually himself.

Also in 2000, *The Gift* has Keanu convincingly playing wife beater, adulterer, and murder suspect Donnie Barksdale. The scenes of domestic violence at the hands of our beloved Keanu Reeves are really hard to take. In fact, instead of using stunt performers, Keanu actually performed the punching scenes himself opposite Cate Blanchett and Hilary Swank—with their consent, of course—and the results are like the difference between practical effects and CGI. The scenes are ageless and chilling, just as gender-based violence continues to be. *The Gift* also features sexual violence against men, as Buddy (Giovanni Ribisi) finally comes to terms with the abuse he's survived at the hands of his father since he was a child—by dousing his father with gasoline and setting him on fire. Yes, it's a crime to attempt to murder the person who abused you. But as we saw in *The*

Devil's Advocate (and, well, real life), the legal system is not always on the side of victims of sexual violence. In the case of Buddy, this was the only justice that he would ever see for the grotesque crimes committed against him by his own father.

Reeves's next film with a theme of violence against women comes in 2005 with *Constantine*, which centers on a demonic plan to use a woman's body as a vessel to bring Satan's son Mammon to Earth, and hell along with him. Rachel Weisz plays twins, one of whom killed herself to avoid becoming Mammon's vessel. Interestingly, in David Hauka's essay "Advocating for Satan," he discusses how women are used as passive vessels for the Antichrist in both *Devil's Advocate* and *Constantine*, a critique that accurately notes how these films entirely deprive women of their agency.[2] In another example of this lack of agency, a series of horrific crimes against women are reduced to whispered news stories echoing in the head of psychic priest Father Hennessy (Pruitt Taylor Vince), as he runs his hands over a pile of newspapers in search of information to help Reeves's demon hunter John Constantine (Reeves). It's monstrous.

The Private Lives of Pippa Lee (2009) is a much more direct look at the unraveling of a woman's life, as she looks back on her experiences from middle age. The title character (played at different ages by Blake Lively and Robin Wright) is sexually abused when just a teenager by her aunt's girlfriend (Julianne Moore), who also takes pictures of the assault. This betrayal becomes a turning point in Pippa's life, leading her to drug abuse and more sexually abusive encounters. This film is a great example of how just one instance of sexual abuse as a child can have lifelong implications for all kinds of interpersonal and social difficulties. Also, we see the quiet violence that adultery can wreak on a family, as Pippa's relationship with Herb (Alan Arkin) leads his wife Gigi (Monica Bellucci) to kill herself in front of him and his very young girlfriend. Abuse is never a single act; it always has an enormous ripple effect outward from the person who has been hurt—this is one of many tragedies of this specific kind of violence.

Keanu returns to this theme three years later in *Generation Um . . .* An example of what's now called the "mumblecore" school of film, the movie follows Reeves's John, a driver who works with Mia (Adelaide Clemens) and Violet (Bojana Novakovic), two very young sex workers. While this is a darkly sex-positive film, the girls do have some gnarly tales to tell about their histories of abuse. Like Mia talking about how her father's beatings killed her sibling in utero, and how her mother would burn her with an iron when she wasn't being abused herself. "When I was growing up, I even felt that . . . I did not feel that I was human." Mia confesses. Similarly, Violet has cigarette burns on her butt, the positioning suggesting this isn't the result of self-harm and might possibly be a service that she offers to her more sadistic clients. And when we finally see Violet and Mia at work toward the end of the film, it's clear that the boundaries of consent are tissue-paper thin, putting everything we have seen up to that point into question. We see Mia disassociating as her body is used as a collection of holes, no humanity. Sexual violence can be contagious for survivors, as we witness a non-consensual moment between Violet and John as she coerces him into a blow job he clearly doesn't want. The interplay of consent versus assault in this film is intense and layered in ways that interrogate a variety of power dynamics, as well as the insidiousness of sexual violence in certain industries such as sex work.

In *47 Ronin* (2013) an illusion produced by a witch disguised as a nobleman's concubine (Rinko Kikuchi) makes it look like the heroine Mika (Ko Shibasaki) is being sexually assaulted. Its purpose is to trigger Mika's father, Lord Asano (Min Tanaka), into breaking feudal law—which leads to his death by seppuku and the expulsion of Mika's love interest, Kai (Reeves), and the rest of the forty-seven ronin. With Asano's death by dishonor, all of his lands can be temporarily seized by the witch's lover Lord Kira (Tadanobu Asano), until such time as he can marry Mika himself. That part of the plan is why it's so important for the assault to be a mere hallucination; if Mika had been actually raped, she would have no future in the hugely patriarchal world of feudal Japan. This scene creates a scenario where there is no actual victim of assault, thus allowing the narrative to focus on toxic patriarchy without a woman being physically hurt in the process. While it's still a gruesome situation all around, this assault, like many of the examples in this chapter, serves as an important plot point and not just as gratuitous sexual violence.

In a disturbing role reversal, Keanu Reeves is the one who receives the sexual violence in *Knock Knock* (2015), as his character, loving husband and father Evan Webber, is seduced then graphically assaulted on-screen by two young female visitors (Lorenza Izzo and Ana de Armas). Director Eli Roth's casting here was quite a genius move, because Reeves's goodwill as an actor and public figure helps ensure that we empathize with him as he's going through all of this horrific torture. Had Evan been played by someone not so beloved both on- and off-screen, we might actually have found ourselves siding with the girls—who from a feminist perspective are retributive figures punishing men for their infidelities and other crimes—rather than experiencing this prolonged degradation from his point of view.

Clearly inspired by Gaspar Noé's *Irréversible*, the police drama *Exposed* (2016) utilizes its own narrative trick that essentially makes the story unfold backward: we find out that Isabel (Ana de Armas), who is convinced she's been impregnated by an angel, was actually raped by a cop; she subsequently killed him and blacked out the memory. The story also has a twist ending that highlights how Isabel's psychotic break was provoked not only by the cop's sexual assault but also by repressed sexual trauma from her childhood—trauma she's now able to act on as an adult woman, leading to another death of a man who abused her. Unfortunately, though, the film's production was marred by studio meddling and incoherent rewrites (more about that in chapter 16), which prevented it from successfully exploring the nuances of police violence through rape and its intersection with childhood abuse.

Far more successful as nightmare fodder is Nicolas Winding Refn's *The Neon Demon* (2016), which features Reeves as Hank, a pedophile motel owner who preys on the young runaways who seek shelter in his establishment. In one of the most harrowing moments in Reeves's career, he inserts a huge, serrated hunting knife into the mouth of sixteen-year-old Jesse (Elle Fanning) as if it's a penis, telling her to open wider as she chokes on steel. This scene ends up being a dream, but the imagery is no less haunting. Hank goes on to attack the thirteen-year-old girl in the room next to Jesse's, and while the violence is off-screen, as in *Feeling Minnesota* we can still hear what's happening and it's truly revolting—especially when we consider it's Keanu Reeves playing and voicing this role. *The Neon Demon* also opens with a murder tableau of a thin, blonde white woman that feels very much like a nod to Reeves's *River's Edge*, which features similar imagery, albeit nude, of the murdered Jamie.

In Ana Lily Amirpour's *The Bad Batch* (2016), Keanu plays another abuser of women: the Jonestownesque cult leader the Dream, who has a harem of extremely young followers, and most of them are pregnant with his babies. These young girls are also being used to manufacture drugs (which they also seem to be taking while pregnant, yuck) and serve as the Dream's security detail, presumably because aggressors might hesitate to attack pregnant girls. It totally makes sense that Keanu would play a cult leader given his global status. Once again, this is a brilliant bit of casting that subverts all of the goodwill Keanu has accumulated as a public figure, perverting it into this disgusting creature who is human in theory only.

In addition, *The Neon Demon* and *The Bad Batch* both feature the on-screen cannibalism of a young woman—commentary on the commercialization of young flesh that treats young women as disposable collections of body parts, not full, autonomous human beings. This dehumanizing view lies at the very heart of violence against women.

Another 2016 film, Reeves's legal drama *The Whole Truth*, has at its core an abusive marriage between Loretta (Renée Zellweger) and Boone (Jim Belushi)—featuring some graphic rape scenes, to boot—that ends in Boone's murder. The couple's son Mike (Gabriel Basso) is charged with the crime, and it's up to Keanu, yet again playing a morally flexible defense attorney, to keep him out of prison. Over the course of the trial, it emerges that Boone may have also sexually abused his own son, potentially leading Mike to kill him. But as Loretta's motives become cloudy toward the end of the film, it's unclear whether we can trust the events that we've seen via flashback, or whether she is manipulating the situation knowing how people react to such scenes of domestic violence against mothers and sons. Yes, this twist seems to echo the highly troubling phenomenon by which real-life women who come forward with accusations of sexual abuse are accused of lying. But this highly underrated film is actually more nuanced than that. It's implied that Loretta is indeed being abused, though maybe not in the exact way she's been claiming; her allegations are similar to the witch's rape illusion in *47 Ronin*, in that she games a patriarchal system to her advantage. And even so, the way events spiral out of her control calls into question the wisdom of Loretta's actions. All this complexity is in contrast to most rape-revenge narratives, which tend to be exceedingly straightforward.

As of this writing, Reeves's final film to feature violence against women is 2018's *Siberia*. The crime thriller features a particularly loathsome scene in which Boris (Pasha D. Lychnikoff), the mobster contact of diamond smuggler Lucas Hill (Reeves), seals their alliance by forcing Lucas's girlfriend Katya (Ana Ularu) to give him a blow job while one of Boris's women does the same for Lucas. The twist: Boris requires Lucas to look him in the eye as he orgasms. Using women as sexual pawns in this way only adds to the many layers of discomfort in this scene, and thankfully the film cuts to the aftermath just as the act begins.

In fact, it's notable how many of the sexual assaults and rapes that I've described here do not actually happen on-screen, shielding audiences from experiencing that violence in great visual detail. The same cannot be said for the similar-themed films starring many of Reeves's peers and colleagues.

MMIW and Violence Against Women and Girls

Aside from admiration for Keanu Reeves, there is very little in the world that is actually universal. But one of the other universal facts of life that transcends economic status, race, culture, and all other social signifiers is sexual and other violence against women. What's particularly important about the Keanu films discussed in this chapter—yes, *important*—is how each of them reflects actual realities for women and girls around the world when it comes to familial abuse, rape, domestic violence, and other sexual assaults.

In 2023 the Centers for Disease Control issued a shocking press release, "U.S. Teen Girls Experiencing Increased Sadness and Violence," which noted that according to a recent survey, sexual violence against teenage girls was up 20 percent from 2017 and the numbers of those who had been raped was up 27 percent.[3] This same year, Showtime released the three-part documentary series *Murder in Big Horn*, which focused on the epidemic of Missing and Murdered Indigenous Women (MMIW) on Indigenous reservations across the US, but in particular Big Horn County, Montana.

While I'd been aware of the MMIW problem for some time, it actually took another entertainer of Indigenous Hawaiian heritage like Keanu, *RuPaul's Drag Race* season 15 winner Sasha Colby, to draw my attention to the astronomical rates of violence experienced by Indigenous Hawaiian

women. Colby has spoken publicly about the postcolonial violence perpetrated against queer Indigenous Hawaiians, known as māhū. Moved by
her stories, I did my own research and learned that Indigenous women in
Hawai'i face the same threats, often by the same perpetrators: members
of the military and law enforcement, in connection with human traffick-
ers. The Hawaiian MMIW epidemic is even more severe than in areas
like Big Horn on the US mainland. While Indigenous women on the
mainland make up 2 percent of the population but have a murder rate
ten times the average,[4] Indigenous Hawaiian women represent two out of
every three human trafficking victims in Hawai'i despite making up only
10 percent of the state's population.[5] A 2018 report from the Office of
Hawaiian Affairs noted that almost 21 percent of Indigenous women on
the islands between the ages of eighteen and twenty-nine had experienced
interpersonal violence, a figure that's almost twice the statistic for non-
Indigenous women.[6] Horrifyingly, 75 percent of the girl children who went
missing in Hawai'i during 2020–2022 were Indigenous Hawaiian. And
worse, it seems that US military forces are among the largest perpetrators
of rape of teenage Indigenous Hawaiian girls as young as thirteen, often
grooming the girls online first.[7]

I would not have learned about any of this if not for Sasha Colby's
activism. Celebrities like her aren't just entertainers, especially when
they represent a marginalized identity. They also become educators and
social justice advocates, sometimes just by their mere presence on-screen.
As we've seen throughout this book, that's certainly the case for Keanu
Reeves, even when it's not necessarily intentional.

#MeToo

In some cases, though, Keanu's advocacy seems quite deliberate. Things
are not getting better for women and girls out there—the opposite, in
fact—but awareness of this ongoing scourge of violence stretches as a
narrative thread across Keanu Reeves's entire career, from some of his
earliest films in 1986 to his current superstar era, when he chooses to
play against type in projects like *The Neon Demon* and *The Bad Batch*
that he counts among his most recommended films.[8] This through line
feels like quiet feminist activism.

Put another way, it's actually a vital public service for well-liked actors to play abusers of all stripes, because it demonstrates just how insidious these crimes are to those experiencing them. Abusers are often incredibly charming to everyone but the person they are hurting, making it all the harder for women and children especially to extricate themselves from these awful situations. Like, remember how upset folks were when beloved Chucks-wearing *Doctor Who* star David Tennant played a rapist with mind control powers on *Jessica Jones* (2015–2019)? That's the same kind of social justice work Reeves does in his collection of roles, reminding us that abusers and monsters often hide behind handsome faces and charismatic personalities.

Where it gets next-level creepy—as if this chapter isn't unsettling enough already; my apologies—is when we look at the negative counterexample: the handful of Reeves's costars and past directors who have abused women:

- In her memoir *I'll Scream Later*, actress Marlee Matlin outlines years of vicious abuse from Reeves's *I Love You to Death* costar William Hurt.[9]
- Among Keanu's costars in *Point Break*, Gary Busey was accused of sexually assaulting and sexually harassing women at a fan convention, and Anthony Kiedis has a terrifyingly long history of sexual abuse and assault allegations, including against minors.[10]
- Gary Oldman, star of *Bram Stoker's Dracula*, was accused of domestic violence by his ex-wife Donya Fiorentino.[11]
- Reeves's *Little Buddha* director Bernardo Bertolucci orchestrated the sexual assault of actress Maria Schneider by Marlon Brando on the set of *Last Tango in Paris* during a rape scene that quickly became horrifyingly unscripted for the actress.[12]
- The omniscient narrator voice of everyone's dreams and *Chain Reaction* costar Morgan Freeman has been accused of sexual harassment by eight women.[13]
- *Constantine* costar Shia LaBeouf has been in and out the news for a variety of erratic behaviors, including allegations of abuse,

sexual and otherwise, against former partner FKA twigs and even current partner Mia Goth.[14]

- Two of Keanu's *Bad Batch* costars have faced varying levels of accusations: Jason Momoa was caught on camera making disgusting rape jokes about his stint as Khal Drogo on *Game of Thrones*, and Jim Carrey has been accused of some heinous domestic violence that allegedly led to the suicide of his ex-girlfriend Cat White.[15]

- *Always Be My Maybe* star Ali Wong hired self-described rapist David Choe on her 2023 Netflix show *Beef*, and when she finally addressed the controversy, gave a disappointing nonapology for the decision.[16]

Moreover, a number of Keanu Reeves's women costars have "come out" as survivors of rape, sexual assault, sexual harassment, and domestic violence, including Brooke Shields (*Freaked*), Uma Thurman (*Even Cowgirls Get the Blues*), Debra Messing (*A Walk in the Clouds*), Robin Wright (*Private Lives of Pippa Lee*), Mira Sorvino (*Exposed*), and Molly Ringwald (*SPF-18, Siberia*).[17] A number of his costars came forward about having been sexually harassed by infamous Hollywood predator Harvey Weinstein,* including Heather Graham (*I Love You to Death* and *Even Cowgirls Get the Blues*), Kate Beckinsale (*Much Ado About Nothing*), Claire Forlani (*The Last Time I Committed Suicide*), Connie Nielsen (*The Devil's Advocate*), and Rosanna Arquette (*SPF-18*).[18] And several of Reeves's male costars have also come forward as victims of sexual violence. *Street Kings*, *A Happening of Monumental Proportions*, and *John Wick: Chapter 2* costar Common revealed that he was molested as a child, sharing the story when he starred in the child abuse drama *The Tale* (2018).[19] And another *Street Kings* costar, Terry Crews, also disclosed that he had been sexually assaulted by a film executive, who then threatened to tank his career.[20]

---

* Thankfully, Keanu himself has had minimal contact with Weinstein in his career: *Little Buddha* (1993) was produced by Weinstein's original production company, Miramax, and two decades later the Weinstein Company's subsidiary Radius-TWC distributed *Man of Tai Chi* (2013), though it was not involved in the film's production. Keanu was also slated to star in the Weinstein Company's *Passengers*, a glorified rape fantasy that was eventually shifted over to Sony and was released in 2016 with Chris Pratt in the starring role instead.

Unlike other industry peers and colleagues who might play villains and also *be* villains in real life, thankfully Keanu Reeves has never actually done any of these things. I wouldn't be writing this book if there'd been even a hint of suspicion Reeves has harmed women. As Claire Dederer, author of the moving essay "What Do We Do with the Art of Monstrous Men?," put it, *the antidote to fallen idols is to not create idols in the first place.*[21] And this is a huge reason why throughout this book, if you haven't noticed already, I do call out a number of different problematic elements of Keanu Reeves's body of work. But thankfully, when it comes to gender-based and sexual violence, the man himself is a thoughtful advocate for victims and not a perpetrator. Whew, amirite?

11

IF WE'RE GONNA WASTE THE DUDE, WE OUGHTA GET PAID FOR IT

The American Dream Gone Wrong

"THE AMERICAN DREAM" is a term first coined in 1931 by historian James Truslow Adams to describe the distinctly USian notion that anyone who works hard enough can rise from humble beginnings into fame, fortune, success, and more.[1] For decades, this term was used uncritically, by white Americans in particular, to suggest that if you're not making it in America, you just aren't working hard enough. But in recent years, as racial literacy has added an intersectional perspective to the discussion, we have come to understand that the American Dream is a myth, especially when it comes to Black, Indigenous, and many other marginalized communities of color for whom upward economic and social mobility are simply not possible due to structural barriers.[2] In fact, a poll in 2020 found that only 54 percent of Americans find the American Dream even "somewhat attainable" for them personally; among millennials, it's not even a majority, at 46 percent.[3] Worse, in their own scramble toward the American Dream, a small number of wealthy people have not just consolidated huge wealth but have embraced unethical and inhumane corporate and labor practices and set in motion irrevocable planetary damage in the form of climate change.[4]

Keanu Reeves's movies engage with all of this, frequently confronting us with visions of an American Dream that has gone off the rails in a spectrum of terrible ways. What I present to you here is an overview of those visions—again in chronological order, to spotlight the bleak persistence of the rot within certain segments of American life, and Reeves's commitment to exploring that decay in ever-deepening ways.

1980s

Keanu's journey through the dark side of the American Dream begins with a horrifying true story. In the 1986 TV movie *Act of Vengeance*, Charles Bronson plays real-life labor activist Jock Yablonski and Reeves is Buddy Martin, one of the killers who was sent to murder the working-class opposition leader before he won an election to lead the United Mine Workers of America. In his post-coal-miner career, Bronson's Yablonski is living a charmed life in rural Pennsylvania with his family, until a horrific mining accident takes the lives of eighty miners in one fell blow and the United Mine Workers' new president, Tony Boyle (Wilford Brimley), sides with the company over the workers. In a rage, Jock decides to run for union president once again, setting off a horrible chain of events as the corporate hacks put out a hit on Jock and his family. As the quiet hero of *Act of Vengeance*, Charles Bronson plays fully against his revenge-thriller type as a devoted family man who fights only with words, and for the people. Also playing out of type is the grandfatherly Wilford Brimley, as the cartoonishly evil villain who murders his rivals with no remorse. In one of his first movie roles, Reeves is absolutely chilling as a cheerful psychopath, pervert, and cold-blooded killer. While all guilty parties do see consequences, Jock and his family's American Dream is shattered regardless. This film is a great reminder that unions have been the things that help Americans protect their dreams of safe employment, homeownership, work-life balance, and so much more.

Similarly playing against type in 1986's *Under the Influence*, the all-American figurehead of kindness and decency Andy Griffith stars as abusive alcoholic Noah Talbot. Noah leads a charmed life as the owner of the local hardware store, beloved by everyone in town. But his family, including son Eddie (Keanu Reeves), see behind the curtain into his cruelty and physical violence every time he drinks. Eddie himself struggles with alcohol and resulting rage, following in his father's terrible footsteps. The film illustrates how even those who seem to have achieved the American Dream—a supposedly perfect suburban life and family—can be destroyed by the dark forces that ideal is designed to keep hidden. That's as apt a message today as it was in 1986, showing the insidiousness of addiction as it ripples outward to everyone in the family and beyond. And as mentioned in chapter 8, what's especially great about this film is how it humanizes addiction, presenting it as an illness not a moral failure and asserting that through treatment you can still go on to live a healthy and happy life even if you are an addict. That's a healthier future to aspire to than an idealized American Dream that allows no room for imperfection.

Considering these are two of Keanu's earliest films, it's fascinating that they featured three older, established actors—Griffith, Bronson, and Brimley—all playing against type. It's a tendency Reeves himself would be quick to embrace.

Another 1986 film, *The Brotherhood of Justice*, stars Keanu as Derek, the de facto leader of a group of popular and wealthy high-school seniors. After vandals trash their school, Derek and his friends form a vigilante gang that at first targets people in the community who are legitimate criminals, like the local drug dealers. But their sights quickly devolve into petty grudges that lead to the stabbing of a football teammate who might have been dealing drugs, and the wiring of a romantic rival's car to explode upon ignition. While these young men seem to have it all, especially money, nice cars, and mansion homes, by the end of *The Brotherhood of Justice* they've risked everything for the rush of power that the brotherhood gives them. But considering their economic status, all of these young men will likely have their records expunged with their parents' help. This blip in their past might determine future behavior, but they will likely not have to face any real consequences for it. While terrorizing a party, one of them even wears a Nixon mask and flashes Nixon's trademark V-for-victory sign—a fitting reference to the "law and order" president who was himself a crook (and a moment that's directly echoed five years later in one of the Ex-Presidents' bank robberies in *Point Break*). So although *The Brotherhood of Justice* certainly shows the dark side of the American Dream, it's the rare case on this list where the dream would still be attainable to the characters who succumb to that other side, whereas if these young criminals were of a different race, it would likely have resulted in a prison sentence.

River's Edge might have been made in 1986, but it has retained its power as a parable of the American Dream gone all the way wrong. One day, totally randomly, Samson (Daniel Roebuck) nonchalantly tells his friends he's murdered his girlfriend Jamie (Danyi Deats) and left her naked body on the riverbank. What's most disturbing about this film is the lack of response Jamie's friend group has to her murder, with the exception of Keanu Reeves's Matt, who eventually is the first and only one who goes to adults for help. While the group embodies apathy to Jamie's murder, there would eventually be psychological and social repercussions once a bigger circle of people found out what happened and how they did nothing about it until it was almost too late. For this group, in some ways Jamie's death marks the end of dreams altogether, not just the American Dream.

David Sinclair (Alan Boyce) appears to have it all in *Permanent Record* (1988). He's talented, handsome, well liked by all, and has a loving, caring family in suburban Portland. All of which adds to the absolute shock when one day, seemingly out of nowhere, he jumps off a cliff, killing himself. While his best friend Chris (Reeves) grapples with what went wrong and how he could have fixed it, entire community is thrown upside down as the young people act out in grief and hopelessness. Marisa Silver's thoughtful portrait of teen suicide, as relevant now as it was in the late '80s, speaks to the value of dismantling notions like the American Dream for all the pressure they put on people—young people in particular—to live up to impossible social and cultural expectations.

The Prince of Pennsylvania (1988) begins as a potentially dark comedy, but devolves quickly into domestic violence, kidnapping, and attempted murder. Rupert Marshetta (Reeves) is a quirky, creative young man whose father Gary (Fred Ward) is one of the head miners at the local coal mine—and one of the wealthiest men in town. After Gary finds out his wife Pam (Bonnie Bedelia) has been cheating on him and goes nuclear,

Rupert devises a plot to kidnap Gary and hold him for ransom—money that would help him and his mother escape Gary's American Dream and their nightmare. "I used to be a prince," Rupert says at the close of the film, rejecting the status his father as self-named king bestowed on him, and riding off to find a different kind of American dream entirely, one that better suits his creative nature. Because another problem with the American Dream is that it leaves no room for people who don't exactly fit a certain mold, and that includes bohemians like Rupert.

Aspects of the American Dream include upward mobility, the ability to save, a good education, and of course those 2.5 children that make up the demographics of the perfect American family. *Parenthood* (1989) takes all these notions and flushes them down the toilet, as we see dysfunction upon dysfunction play out among the Buckman siblings and their messy families. Incredibly, Keanu's character, Tod—a teenage drag-race driver facing his girlfriend's unplanned pregnancy—ends up being the most mature of anyone, as this kid with a heart of gold embraces parenthood as a chance to be the kind of father he never had.

1990s

"If we're gonna waste the dude, we oughta get paid for it, man. That's the American way, right?" Reeves says as bumbling hit man Marlon in *I Love You to Death* (1990), and his call-out of the capitalist impetus lurking within the American Dream is way telling. Marlon and his cousin Harlan (William Hurt) have been hired to murder philandering pizza shop owner Joey Boca (Kevin Kline), on the orders of his wife and business partner Rosalie (Tracey Ullman). What's ironic about this movie's view of the American Dream is that Joey Boca is literally living it, as a recent Italian immigrant who owns his own business and fucks any young woman who catches his eye. But Joey's American Dream isn't Rosalie's, and when she discovers his rampant infidelity, she taps into capitalist desperation, finding people to pay to murder her husband instead of simply divorcing him. "In America people kill each other left and right, it's like national pastime. Nobody gets caught," Rosalie's Yugoslavian mother Nadja (Joan Plowright) says, a statement that often remains true today. However, unlike most of the other films in this list, *I Love You to Death* actually does end with a twisted happily ever after, because Joey and Rosalie decide to stay together: he decides she must really love him if she cared enough to kill him, and promises to be faithful from now on. Even stranger, the same is true of Tony and Frances Toto, the real-life couple the movie was based on. They were still together as of 2023, forty years after their marriage nearly ended in murder.[5] It seems that for some, the compulsion to live out the American Dream of marriage, children, homeownership, and entrepreneurism supersedes logic and even basic safety considerations. That's how deeply rooted the dream can be.

In *Point Break* (1991), the financial promise of the dream provokes a backlash, as Bodhi (Patrick Swayze) and his gang turn to a life of crime to fund their thrill-seeking lifestyle. For them, robbing banks is as much about the adrenaline rush as the money, and it's also their form of social commentary: by wearing masks of former presidents like Ronald Reagan and Richard Nixon during their crimes, they highlight the government policies that have made crime the only option for some. "We've been screwing you for years, so a few more seconds shouldn't matter," Bodhi as Reagan says during a robbery. "The money's insured, so it's not worth dying for." Bodhi, however, fails to take into account the trauma of surviving gun violence of this kind, which can have horrific repercussions on the lives of innocent bystanders, who in that moment have no idea if they will live or die.

My Own Private Idaho (1991) sees another shortsighted rebellion against the American Dream as Reeves plays Scott Favor, a wealthy young man who temporarily rejects his family's wealth and goes on an urban walkabout as a sex worker. For Scott, it's all just poverty tourism; he returns to the manor born on his twenty-first birthday, and even after spending so much time with genuinely suffering people like Mike (River Phoenix), who he claims to love, he doesn't take any of them with him on his journey back to the upper classes. There's a heart-crushing moment when Scott, riding in his mayor father's limousine through downtown Portland, passes Mike lying unconscious on the sidewalk. He gives no indication he ever even knew him. Scott has the ability to yank every single one of his unhoused former friends out of poverty without it affecting his bottom line and he chooses not to, because the American Dream isn't about sharing, it's about hoarding what you believe is yours and yours alone. At the end of the film, the abandoned Mike passes out on an unnamed highway. As passersby rob the helpless young man, "America the Beautiful" begins playing. Another car stops and this time a man carries Mike out of the road and into the vehicle—to safety we can only hope, but with Mike's past experiences we can't entirely be sure. The film closes with a colorful HAVE A NICE DAY cue card, that uber-American catchphrase becoming ominous in this particular context. Because by watching this film from the comfort of our wherever, we are in effect aligned more with Scott than with Mike. And some of us will also go about our day as if we never met him, as we selfishly pursue our own American Dream.

A woman with enormous thumbs named Sissy traverses the United States as a master hitchhiker in *Even Cowgirls Get the Blues* (1993), meeting a host of strange and wonderful characters along the way, including Keanu as short-term love interest Julian Gitche. But it's not until she arrives at Rubber Rose Ranch and meets all the fabulous cowgirls, including Bonanza Jellybean (Rain Phoenix, in a film dedicated to her late brother River), that she finally begins to understand that the ranch could be all their American Dream, if only the men of local law enforcement would let them be. Which they don't, resulting in murder and the dissolution of this female-centered utopia—because, like I mentioned, the American Dream has certain parameters, and a lesbian dude ranch doesn't fit. Still, the movie ends on a note of hope that the dream may be reborn in a more sustainable form.

Johnny Mnemonic (1995) takes place in an imaginary 2021, when one of the only ways to attain even a basic semblance of the American Dream has become people renting out their own brains to carry digital data, even though the procedure is often deadly dangerous. At the same time, the overabundance of technological signals "poisoning the airwaves" has created a seizure-like syndrome in the public at large that ends in death and that has no cure. Capitalism kills, and the free city of Newark is as far from a dream as a place can get, with its crumbling infrastructure and pervasive violence. It's a world where real-life American nightmares are exponentially heightened—especially when we find out that the corporations do have a cure for the deadly disease, they would just rather people continue to suffer, because "treating the disease is far more profitable than curing it." Those at the top are certainly living all the glories of the

American Dream, as they actively prevent the majority of society from living that way too. Sounds a lot like the actual 2021.

From a strangely familiar future to an all-too-real past: While away on the front lines of World War II, Paul Sutton (Reeves) wrote to his wife every day about his dreams for their future, and the picket-fence life they would build together in *A Walk in the Clouds* (1995). Instead, they divorce, which eventually allows Paul to build a new dream with Mexican American vineyard owners. Interestingly, Paul's American Dream also becomes an extension of an immigrant's dream of landownership and upward mobility in the country.

Feeling Minnesota (1996) explores a present-day setting where, once again, that hope has withered: a nowhere town where crime is the only thing that pays. To get his American Dream, Sam Clayton (Vincent D'Onofrio) kidnaps Freddie (Cameron Diaz) and forces her to marry him, while planning to buy her a plush home in a planned community development near Las Vegas. Sam is sexually and physically violent with Freddie, and seems to think all of that bad behavior will somehow be wiped clean if he just buys her a perfect house in a perfect town. Once again, one person's American Dream is another's nightmare. And while Sam's brother Jjaks (Reeves) in theory has love and empathy to offer Freddie, Jjaks squanders this potential by leaving her for dead and helping Sam cover up her attempted murder. Ultimately, Freddie's American Dream is fulfilled when she becomes a self-sufficient Vegas showgirl, but on her flesh she carries many scars of the male violence it took to get there.

The Neal Cassady biopic *The Last Time I Committed Suicide* (1997) is an often-uncomfortable romp through the freewheeling world of the beatnik subculture that began in the 1940s. While Neal (Thomas Jane) has dreams about a perfect American life, complete with picket fences and a happy wife and family, he continually manages to shit on every opportunity to actually live that dream. He is helped in blowing up aspects of his life by Harry (Reeves), a decade-older pervert who functions as the voice of Neal's id, rejecting the banality of a "fenced-in happily ever after," as Harry calls it. In this film, we see the tension between an "innate" wanderlust that characterizes the Beat generation and that sociocultural pull of the settled-down American Dream. At the same time, we see Neal's collection of discarded women, beginning with Joan (Claire Forlani), who opens the story with a suicide attempt, followed by the several teenage girls whose futures were effectively shattered by their entanglements with Neal and his friends. In fact, every iteration of Neal's life results in nightmares for the women around him: they receive the brunt of consequences for his noncommittal ways, poor choices in friends, and more. More often than not, men's dreams become women's nightmares.

Closing out the '90s is *The Devil's Advocate* (1997), in which Keanu's Kevin Lomax realizes that the price to pay for the standard version of the American Dream—great job, huge pay, penthouse apartment, gorgeous wife—is his actual soul. He agrees to the price before ultimately realizing the fallacy inherent in the entire process and opting out of the bargain, only for the dance with the devil to begin again.

2000s

Keanu's first look at the American Dream in the new millennium, *The Replacements* (2000), tackles the dream's attainment and maintenance from two different perspectives. First, the striking NFL players are positioned as greedy multimillionaire thugs who don't care about football outside a paycheck. And the team of ragtag players who replace them want nothing more than just to play football, even though they are being underpaid and exploited as they cross a picket line. In actuality, labor activists and union leaders would definitely label Shane Falco (Reeves) and his replacements as the villains of the movie for not respecting the players' strike. But instead they are framed as underdog heroes, in a distinctly anti-union messaging that encourages scab labor. What's interesting about how this film portrays the American Dream is that there is plenty of money for everyone to succeed in this scenario, the existing NFL players as well as the replacements. But predatory team owners hoard all the profits for themselves, denying opportunity and pitting worker against worker.

As with many narratives in Reeves's catalog, *Sweet November* (2001) begins with its main character, Reeves's Nelson Moss, living a charmed life: he's a high-powered executive who has achieved the American Dream and then some. But after he's unexpectedly fired and his girlfriend breaks up with him, Nelson finds himself at a loss. Until he meets manic pixie dream girl Sara (Charlize Theron), who shakes up his notions of what a dream life might be. Also like many stories in this list, *Sweet November* does not have the happily-ever-after ending we hoped for; we find out Sara has terminal cancer, and she leaves Nelson to spend her last days with her family. However, Sara's family is wealthy and she has the means to die with dignity, which is an American Dream that average Americans do not have access to given the poor state of US health care.

Reeves's character in *Hardball* (2001), on the other hand, does not start the film on top. Conor O'Neill suffers from a gambling addiction that regularly puts his life in danger. But it's not until he's tasked with coaching an inner-city baseball team of determined but underprivileged Black children that he has his first wake-up call to the realities of the American nightmare for people much worse off and much younger than him whose futures hang in the balance. All of which comes to a terrible head when one of his youngest charges, sweet G-Baby (DeWayne Warren), is killed in a random act of gun violence. When we talk about people being left out of the American Dream, it's often not by accident, evidenced in the housing projects where G-Baby and the rest of the teammates live— segregation by race might be officially over, but the structural violence it has left behind means it continues in practice if not in theory, leaving many Black neighborhoods in poverty and particularly vulnerable to a variety of negative influences like gangs and drug dealing. The American Dream doesn't exist for people like G-Baby, his family, and his friends, simply because they're Black.

Thumbsucker (2005) looks at some of the subtler dangers of the American Dream, even for a white, middle-class family. Justin Cobb (Lou Taylor Pucci) has a bizarre thumb-sucking habit that has followed him into his teenage years. His father, Mike (Vincent D'Onofrio), is a former football star whose light shone briefly (echoing Johnny Utah's backstory in *Point Break*), and who is mentally stuck in those long-gone glory days to the detriment of his family. Justin's orthodontist Dr. Lyman (Reeves) tries an experimental hypnotherapy procedure to cure him of his thumb-sucking, but it ends up having some wild consequences, upending Lyman's own middle-class existence and kicking off his quiet quest for more than just materialism. Through Justin's reckoning with himself and his family, everyone in his orbit is forced to reassess the kind of life that they want versus the kind of life that they are living. And by the end of the film, all of their notions of what a dream life or dream future might be have in many ways dissipated. Without the blueprint provided by the American Dream, they have a lot of blank space to dream all kinds of new dreams—or to go into a new crisis because their future is no longer mapped out. The problem is that the American Dream can make you lazy and complacent. It sets false limits on where your life can go, when often the most interesting things that can happen are beyond those boundaries.

In *A Scanner Darkly* (2006), Reeves's Bob Arctor is a man who tried to look past those limits. Having grown bored with his perfect suburban American life and beautiful family, he abandoned them to become an undercover cop and drug addict living in filth and squalor. Bob is sure that there must be something more—something more exciting or more fulfilling or simply more interesting than an existence mapped out by a picket fence and a beautiful yard. The shame here is the way that he abandoned his family in order to seek that out.

On the complete flip side, in *Street Kings* (2008) Reeves's Detective Ludlow embraces the worst of the American Dream, as a police officer who's all too familiar with casual and extreme police brutality. One important aspect of the dream is its emphasis on safety and security, and in theory police and other law enforcement are supposed to be helping maintain these functions for the good of society. But as we see in *Street Kings*—and in real life—these institutions (the LAPD in particular) work as a roving gang whose members only look out for themselves first and their colleagues second, unless a fellow boy in blue isn't toeing the line of corruption everyone else is. *Street Kings* is a narrative that details, often painfully, the myth of law and order being championed by the police, and just how broken the system is all the way to the top, and beyond.

2010s

The 2010s is the decade when Keanu Reeves really went all in on demolishing the myth of upward mobility, with a grand total of nine disturbing movies that particularly highlight the impossibility of attaining this thing called the American Dream.

Henry's Crime (2010) opens with Reeves's Henry Torne living a mediocre existence as a tollbooth attendant, but still with a nice house in the suburbs and a loving wife who wants to grow their family. When he's tricked into serving as a getaway driver for a bank heist and is the only one arrested, the police give him the opportunity to rat out the actual robbers and return to his life. ("You got a wife, you got a job. Don't you care?") He chooses to remain silent and do the time instead. While the film is not as violent as other prison narratives, what it reveals is how prison makes better criminals, not rehabilitated citizens, as when Henry gets out he decides to commit the crime he was imprisoned for. He ends up with an unlikely ally in Frank (Bill Duke), the security guard who got him arrested. Frank's dream was to retire to the Loire Valley in France with his wife. But she got cancer, medical bills wiped out all their savings, and she died—all while Frank's employer did nothing to help soften the financial blows for their employee of thirty years. One of the key messages here is, once again, how American families are one illness away from financial desperation—and how quickly any dreams at all slip out of grasp for working-class folks once a health crisis enters the picture.

Generation Um . . . (2012) is a portrait of disaffected America, following young and drug-dependent sex workers Violet (Bojana Novakovic) and Mia (Adelaide Clemens) and their driver John (Reeves) over the course of a "normal" twenty-four hours. While both girls are sex workers by choice, there's an underlying tension as they grapple with what's being done to their bodies and the often-dehumanizing situations their clients put them in, even though they might be financially well compensated. As auditory wallpaper to this scenario, we hear radio pundits arguing about unemployment rates and a decided lack of "proper" and "suitable" jobs for people to be able to attain the American Dream. This disturbingly suggests why the girls would continue with this line of work when they seem ambivalent about it at best: the money is too good not to. How do they go from making several hundred dollars an hour only working a few hours a week, to a forty-hour-plus workweek that pays tens of dollars an hour? They won't until age or disability forces them to retire from their current line of work. More American Dreams ending in nightmares.

In Eli Roth's *Knock Knock* (2015), Evan Webber is an architect whose quiet existence is upended when two young women appear at his door on a night his family is away. In the course of twenty-four hours, Evan throws away his beautiful life as he's seduced by the sexual attention of women who are decades younger than him. By the end, Bel (Ana de Armas) and Genesis (Lorenza Izzo)—who wears a shirt that says It Was All a Dream—become retributive figures who test supposedly good men, draw them out from behind the facades they've cultivated, and expose them to anyone who trusted them, ruining their futures irrevocably. The American Dream is great when you have it, but as we see in so many of these stories, the lure of what's beyond the picket fence is too strong to ignore—which makes Genesis's tagging of Evan's house with the phrase It Was Not a Dream resonate on multiple levels.

As in 2008's *Street Kings*, in *Exposed* (2016) police brutality happens with scary frequency at the hands of Keanu's character, Detective Galban. And like in *Street Kings*, we see law enforcement function as a barrier preventing hardworking immigrant families from living their own American Dreams of upward mobility, financial security, and acceptance in their new home. Corrupt cops meddle in their lives, bringing gruesome levels of violence and shattering families. Law enforcement exists to uphold the American Dream, but only for certain segments of American society—namely, those who can pay for it. And yet film and television sell the myth of the American Dream around the world, encouraging immigrants to come here. In *Exposed* we ourselves are exposed to the nightmare that they often find.

The Neon Demon (2016) looks at another group led astray by the myth of American opportunity: young starlets fresh to Hollywood. From start to finish, it explores the price these young women pay, often literally with their flesh, in pursuit of fame. Motel owner Hank (Reeves) lives his twisted pedophile dream as he uses his rooms to prey on the young women runaways all in town in search of a better life; their own dreams are quickly torn apart by Hank's sexual violence. All the while Hollywood churns out movies and shows that paint the town as glamorous as can be, weaving a deceptive web that continues to draw young women into its carnivorous fold. *The Neon Demon* is a scathing commentary on the Hollywood industrial complex.

The Bad Batch (2016) is about people who have been expelled from the USA's borders altogether. They're literally locked out of any potential life there, let alone a dream one. Playing with the irony, Reeves's cult leader is ironically named the Dream, and he offers drugs, music, and twisted community as he exploits all the young women in his orbit. One of them, Arlen (Suki Waterhouse) even has a tattoo reading SUICIDE, which recalls the particular death of the American Dream seen in *Permanent Record*.

Legal family drama *The Whole Truth* (2016) and anorexia memoir *To the Bone* (2017) bring us back to earlier Reeves narratives in which, from the outside, everything looks hunky-dory and amazing in the lives of the main characters. But peel back the curtain and it's an entire mess of abuse, violence, eating disorders, and more that threatens entire family systems with emotional and psychological annihilation. In both films, achieving the American Dream doesn't repair dysfunction but merely hides it, even once you have bought the house and have the perfect family and kids.

And in *Replicas* (2018), the Foster family's idealized existence is shattered when a car accident takes the lives of the mother and their three children. In a haze of grief, father William (Reeves) uses experimental cybernetic technology to bring his family back, but without enough body pods he has a *Sophie's Choice* moment and must erase one of his daughters. And yet again a man's dream becomes a woman's nightmare, as his wife Mona (Alice Eve) realizes she isn't real and had no say in returning to her life as a cyborg. She has an important moment of anger as she grapples with her consciousness nonconsensually being placed into a synthetic body. I can't help but wonder: What kind of dreams will she have now? This is a question that Phillip K. Dick asked in *Do Androids Dream of Electric Sheep?*, the novel on which *Blade Runner* (1982) is based, and the answer remains murky. But William Foster did not consider any of this when he resurrected his family without their consent.

2020s

With all this context, it's really no surprise that Keanu Reeves would sign up to play the sage named Sage in *The SpongeBob Movie: Sponge on the Run* (2020), a children's cartoon with unexpected sociopolitical subtext. SpongeBob is forced to venture out from his enchanted corner of the ocean to find his pet snail Gary, who's been kidnapped to the Lost City of Atlantic City. Even though Sage warns SpongeBob and his friend Patrick to not be dazzled by the city's hedonistic offerings, they can't help but lose themselves in the harried displays of capitalism, overindulgence, and greed, to the point that they even forget why they are there at all. In some ways this version of the Lost City of Atlantic City has become a new form of the American Dream, one where excess and vanity are prized over substance and stability.

And the final installation of the *Bill & Ted* trilogy, *Bill & Ted Face the Music* (2020), finds the hapless duo once again at a loss to complete their song to heal the universe and on the verge of giving up. While they continue to live a suburban lifestyle that's lovely on the surface, Ted (Reeves) complains about being tired of their grind, and Bill (Alex Winter) agrees. As the duo is sucked back into the universe-saving business, we see iterations of their life that all end tragically, while not just their American Dream but also their musical dreams die. As in *Sponge on the Run*, the anti-capitalist subtext in *Face the Music* runs deep, and ultimately evolves into a tale about community engagement in collective and shared futures. Where *Sponge on the Run* gives us a toxic vision of a new American Dream of excess and consumerism, *Face the Music* instead offers an American Dream of collective solidarity and support, not just in the United States but globally, that could serve as a future model for a more ethical and even sustainable vision for an American future.

Revisiting Anti-copaganda

In this chapter, I've talked about how one of the pillars of the American Dream is safety, which in theory is upheld by the work of various law enforcement agencies. This chapter has also discussed several films in Keanu's catalog that call into question this law enforcement role, instead making it clear how the police destroy the promise of the American Dream. And in chapter 4, I looked at how his action films defy the genre's usual tendency toward copaganda. But there are several more bad cops in Keanu's filmography to add to this discussion.

Tune in Tomorrow (1990) features an abusive cop father (Paul Austin) who puts his own son Martin (Reeves) in a choke hold and threatens to arrest his lover for a crime she didn't commit. Later, contemplating his own crime of passion, Martin steals his father's service weapon because he doesn't have it locked up. Similarly, in *The Night Before*

(1988), Reeves's love interest has a cop father (Michael Greene) who threatens to shoot him if anything bad happens to his daughter. And *The Prince of Pennsylvania* (1988) features a corrupt cop (Jay O. Sanders) who not only stole the baby of his mistress, he gave the baby to his wife, who then proceeded to adopt the child, not allowing the birth mother access to a child she never willingly gave up. All of these cops are operating outside the legal system they are supposed to be upholding, and by taking the law into their own hands they undermine the very system that they claim to protect.

In *Bill & Ted's Excellent Adventure* (1989) and *Bogus Journey* (1991), Reeves's character again has a father who's a police officer; Captain Logan is cruel, quietly abusive, and sexually inappropriate with a former classmate of his son's, Missy (Amy Stoch), who in *Bogus Journey* has become his wife. By *Face the Music*, Ted has rejected the disciplinarian style of his father's parenting for a gentler approach with his own daughter.

And the scab football players in *The Replacements* include Jon Favreau as Bateman, a batshit insane cop. His violence on the field is so single-minded he ends up smacking down his own quarterback more than any opposing team's.

And finally, while Keanu's PI detective series *Swedish Dicks* (2016–2018) is a comedy, almost every episode calls out corrupt cops, police brutality, unethical politicians, incompetent prison wardens, and more. You don't need private investigators if law enforcement is doing its job, right? Thus, the very existence of PIs is anticop. Further, at one point when the titular Swedish PIs Ingmar (Peter Stormare) and Axel (Johan Glans) need help, a policeman refuses because nobody is dead yet. "You mean you would get quicker service if you actually killed someone?" Axel asks the desk cop incredulously. The cop confirms, ending the all-too-American encounter by quipping, "Keep that in mind for next time!"

In none of these examples are cops, or law enforcement in general, presented as the good guys in the end. This is yet another thing that sets Keanu Reeves's work apart from not just his contemporaries but also generations of actors since.

American Nightmares

In this wide selection of films from throughout Keanu's career, striving for the American Dream results in violence, robbery, suicide, murder, rape, and more. It raises the ultimate question: What is this dream good for when so many of those primed to attain it cannot, and those who do must often pay such a terrible price? Keanu's films also illustrate how organizations created to protect Americans and their dreams for a better future, like law enforcement, in fact often help dismantle that dream instead. And the fact that so many of these dark narratives are set amid a career better known for action and comedy (more on the latter in chapter 17) sets Keanu Reeves apart as a performer who's committed to challenging audience expectations.

Further, many of these stories land all the harder when we think of them in the context of Keanu's Indigenous Hawaiian heritage. Indigenous Americans were the first stewards of many US territories, yet they've been denied the basic foundations of the American Dream, like cultural and social autonomy. Let's never forget that during the American colonial takeover of the Hawaiian Islands it became illegal to speak native languages, among many more examples of colonizer violence.

And in the context of Keanu's Asian ancestry, we also see how the myth of Asian Americans as a "model minority" is regularly thwarted, often by state-sponsored forces that gatekeep who gets to thrive in the USA and who doesn't. We also see the internalized racism by which many real-life Asians try to code themselves as white or align with whiteness in ways that throw other people of color under the bus. Amid all of this, let's also not forget that while he plays Americans more often than not, at the end of the day Keanu Reeves is actually a *Canadian* citizen, whose projects regularly call out the dark sides of the American Dream and the reality of the United States' so-called exceptionalism. That's a quiet political statement in and of itself.

12

THE DESERT OF THE REAL

The Perils of Technology
in Keanu Reeves's Cyber Cinema

For better or worse, we are all in a parasocial relationship with Keanu Reeves. A parasocial relationship is the skewed dynamic between audiences and famous on-screen figures that often convinces regular folks they have more of an actual connection with a celebrity than they really do.[1] At best, it's what happens when we fans bond over a shared love and respect for a public figure like Mr. Reeves; we might talk about him like we know him or one day will, but we are acutely aware that in reality he's a stranger. At worst, parasocial relationships can lead to toxic behaviors like stalking a celebrity, breaking and entering their home, or even sexual assault and murder. Parasocial relationships between celebs and norms have always been a thing. But many people, like me, grew up in eras when a celebrity encounter was a rare coincidence or required careful calculation on the fan's part, like finding out that they were staying at a certain hotel and staking out the lobby. With the advent of the internet and the proliferation of social media, the parasocial celebrity relationship has become more intense, because now everyday people can peek into the lives of celebrities and maybe, if they're lucky, even have a conversation with them online. This access has made some fans thankful and appreciative. It has also created a surge of entitlement, as segments of fan bases straight-up demand attention from the objects of their affection in ways that often run celebrities off social media altogether.

But the internet hasn't only turbocharged the parasocial relationship between average people and celebs. It has also contributed to various forms of social decline, the bottoms of which we have not yet reached:

- The proliferation of fake news and misinformation online has had very real political ramifications around the world. For instance, as discussed in chapter 6, the way that white supremacists turned the obvious left-wing, anti-capitalist, and anti-binary allegory of *The Matrix* (1999) into propaganda for their own hateful ideology.
- Recent years have seen the rise of artificial intelligence programs capable of creating "original" art and writing by digesting and recombining the work of human creators, often without the creators' permission and with no credit or compensation. Hollywood studios have even begun toying with the idea of using AI to make movies and television, eliminating the roles of actors and writers altogether.
- Police forces regularly use robot dogs and other mechanized, sometimes humanoid machinery in the surveillance of communities across the United States.
- Researchers in Switzerland are working on the Blue Brain Project, attempting to reconstruct the brain of a mouse digitally to see if it can be translated into a cybernetic organism.[2]
- Technology monitors our every move and word these days as a norm—as evidenced by the fact that if you talk about a particular product near your smartphone, you'll likely see an ad for it the next time you open up a website.

"This is a world getting progressively worse," James Barris (Robert Downey Jr.) says in Keanu's film *A Scanner Darkly* (2006). And it's true. For instance, when Elon Musk bought Twitter/X, he converted it from a global town hall that everyday folks used to connect with one another, especially during crises like political uprisings and war and natural disasters, into a propaganda tool for the billionaire class. In an increasingly hostile social climate where it's the uber-rich against the proletariat masses, Twitter/X is a great example of how technology is weaponized against the people who have found it the most useful.

Given the troubling trends of our digital age, it's interesting that many of Reeves's films spotlight analog technology:

- Time travel via the red phone booth in the *Bill & Ted* series
- The compass on the car dashboard in *The Night Before* (1988) that gets borked by a magnet
- The Victorian-era suction-and-rubber-tube blood transfusions in *Bram Stoker's Dracula* (1992)
- All the handwritten letters sent to loved ones in *A Walk In the Clouds* (1995), *Feeling Minnesota* (1996), and *The Lake House* (2006)
- In-person bar gambling on paper chits in *Hardball* (2001)
- The paper-trail-based accountants of the Administration who manage the High Table's affairs in the *John Wick* series, introduced in *Chapter 2* (2017)
- And of course Keanu's 2012 documentary *Side by Side*, which is a love letter to movies made on film as opposed to their digital counterparts

In contrast, Reeves's cyber cinema has often predicted some of the dark turns our real-life society has been going through, as technology advances faster than we can control or regulate it.

AI

The *Matrix* franchise pulls us into a world where humans are used by artificially intelligent machines as a sustainable energy resource after human society loses its battle to maintain stewardship of the Earth. While in real life we aren't exactly at the level of *The Matrix* yet, we are a number of troubling steps closer. In the past, we conceived of AI and robotics as tech-based labor sources that could free humans from certain dangerous jobs, like defusing bombs, exploring mines, or investigating the deep sea. But the tech hasn't stopped there. Instead, AI applications have been expanded to perform the most human of activities, replacing flesh-and-blood artists and musicians with machines that essentially copy humans' existing creations. This is the opposite of how it should be; robots and AI should be taking on the banal tasks, leaving humans with more time to be creative and enjoy their lives. Instead, before long regular people may have to work three jobs to barely scrape by while AI is out there making art and writing songs. It's a danger Reeves himself has warned of, speaking to the *Hollywood Reporter* in 2023: "The people who are paying you for your art would rather not pay you. They're actively seeking a way around you, because artists are tricky. Humans are messy."[3]

We are also seeing a growing disparity in who has access to these technologies and who is being left behind, as the wealthy find new ways to leverage AI for their own benefit, often to the detriment of others. Keanu's film *Replicas* (2018), while critically panned, offers an advance look at the kind of AI wealth gap we may have to worry about in the nearish future. Reeves's character, William Foster, has created a program that in theory could transfer the actual consciousness of a human being into a synthetic body, potentially allowing that person to live forever as an AI. What's particularly chilling about *Replicas* is its ending, when it's revealed that this chance at eternal life is intended for only the wealthiest of the wealthy. Imagine if the millionaire and billionaire families we have today were the exact same ones we'd have in fifty years, or a hundred years, or longer, because of a medical monopoly like this one. The implications of this are as staggering as they are disturbing, especially when you take into account the fact that life expectancies for average people—communities of color in particular—are steadily decreasing each year, and only partly due to the ongoing COVID-19 pandemic.

In the 2020 video game *Cyberpunk 2077*, Reeves's character Johnny Silverhand illustrates another dark possibility for this sort of technology: the military applications. Johnny is a mercenary for hire whose cybernetic "upgrades" make him a more efficient killer. He sports a robotic left arm after losing the original on the battlefield as a US soldier. And even after his death, his consciousness is transferred into another body, where it may or may not be peacefully coexisting with its human host.

All the while in the time travel comedies *Bill & Ted's Bogus Journey* (1991) and *Bill & Ted Face the Music* (2020) we see people in positions of great power using robotic technology for nefarious purposes, including assassinations of world leaders. While events haven't necessarily played out similarly in real life, we have indeed seen unmanned drones targeting and sometimes killing high-level political targets around the world.

Johnny Mnemonic and the Gig Economy

Today we're in the midst of an increasingly precarious "gig economy," which has turned so many Americans into self-employed service workers hustling from one job to the next on behalf of tech companies like Uber and Instacart. But years before the advent of this system, Keanu Reeves was warning us about its dangers to mental and physical health in the 1995 film *Johnny Mnemonic*. Based on a short story by father of cyberpunk William Gibson and set in 2021, it stars Reeves as a wet-wired data courier who had to sacrifice a huge chunk of his own memories—namely, the entirety of his childhood—to make room for the data port in his brain. He's now trying to complete one last delivery job so that he can get out of the business and get his memories back, even if the job requires him to overload his data port and dooms him to death if he doesn't get the data out of his head in time. Unfortunately, in order to unlock the data he needs to access three of what we would now call non-fungible tokens (NFTs), and their transmission is interrupted, further risking Johnny's life.

Decades later, we have seen similar dangers play out within the gig economy. More and more workers are forced to capitalize on their own resources—like their personal car or their own body—in order to find flexible contractor work to make ends meet in a United States where the cost of living rises monthly but wages in many fields have remained stagnant. (The federal minimum wage, in particular, is only a few dollars higher than it was when *Johnny Mnemonic* first came out.) These gig workers also receive no employment protections, no health insurance, no other benefits, and sometimes not even wage guarantees as they often put themselves in harm's way to deliver groceries and perform other services in an increasingly gun-crazed America. For instance, in 2023 an Instacart delivery driver was shot at when he went to the wrong address.[4] And the following year, an Uber driver was shot and killed by an elderly man who thought she was trying to scam him, after the real scammers sent her to pick up the money they were trying to extort.[5]

But the dangers inherent in the gig economy also apply to consumers. An epidemic of rapes and sexual assaults committed by Uber and Lyft drivers has led to multiple lawsuits.[6] There have even been cases where male rideshare drivers have stalked their rides[7] and attempted to kidnap them.[8] The growing fear of being kidnapped by a rideshare driver even led a Texas woman to shoot an Uber driver dead.[9] The gig economy of today predicted by *Johnny Mnemonic* is as safe as having a wet-wired data port in your brain.

Addiction and Tech

As we discuss the perils of technological advancement, we also have to discuss how it promotes addiction and addictive behaviors. *A Scanner Darkly* examines "a culture of addiction" that has arisen because of the proliferation of Substance D, a hallucinogenic and highly addictive drug that has wreaked havoc even on elite communities such as Orange County, known for being a Republican pocket of extreme wealth within the Democratic state of California. In the movie, the government and all levels of law enforcement are complicit in this drug epidemic: they promote Substance D on the streets, produce it in dedicated facilities, and then force people into state-sponsored rehab centers after they've fried their brains. It's an indictment of the way America's real-life War on Drugs enables a culture of addiction by responding to drug addicts with authoritarianism instead of compassion. *Scanner* ends with a quote by the author of the original novel the movie is based on—Philip K. Dick, another father of the cyberpunk movement: "This has been a story about people who were punished entirely too much for what they did. I loved them all. Here is a list, to whom I dedicate my love."

Johnny Mnemonic takes the technology and addiction metaphor to the next level with its Nerve Attenuation Syndrome (NAS), a seizure disorder that affects the entirety of the human population due to society's overuse of technology. These seizures are violent, debilitating, and ultimately deadly, and there is no known cure. That is, until Johnny finds out the data overloading his own brain is, in fact, the cure to NAS that Big Pharma doesn't want publicly accessible, as they profit off the illness running unchecked.

And in a decidedly different take on the intersection between addiction and technology, Cypher (Joe Pantoliano) in *The Matrix* finds himself addicted to the lie that is the virtual world in which machines have enslaved humanity. He sells out his fellow humans to return to it, preferring to exist as a battery for his AI overlords than deal honestly with life on a ruined Earth. For a film made before smartphones and easy internet access, Cypher's arc scarily echoes the addiction to social media and other online distractions that now plagues huge segments of society, not just in the USA but across the globe, as people desperately look for ways to avoid the discomfort of the real world.

The Surveillance State

While all of these technological dangers are uniquely terrifying for a variety of reasons, there is something particularly insidious about the surveillance state in Keanu Reeves's movies—both in his cyber tales and beyond.[10] The surveillance state constantly reminds us that we are being watched, recorded, and judged at all times, often through the use of specialized technologies such as biometrics—something that was only a theoretical notion back when films like *Johnny Mnemonic*, *The Matrix*, and *A Scanner Darkly* came out but has become increasingly real and prevalent in recent years.[11]

In *Johnny Mnemonic*, the surveillance state functions largely on biometric data. At one point Reeves's Johnny is scanned while traveling, and the computer announces, "Dyslexia prosthesis implant. Government approved." Did Johnny once have a dyslexia implant, and that's what he used to wet-wire his brain with the data smuggling port? Or has the wetware been jimmied so it registers as a dyslexia prosthesis to scans? We never find out. But what's fascinating here is the reference to it being "government approved," which suggests that law enforcement is tracking everyone's implants and an unapproved one would subject the bearer to arrest and imprisonment.

In the world of *A Scanner Darkly*, the surveillance state is such a constant threat that undercover agents have to wear a "scramble suit," a device that makes the wearer appear to others as the "vague blur" of an "Everyman," to protect their identities even from other law enforcement. The scramble suit is only available to a privileged few. In real life, to avoid surveillance you can also employ a variety of tech-based tools like burner phones, VPNs to hide your internet history, and more. But these anti-surveillance technologies always end up getting subsumed into the state surveillance machine, or being outlawed.

In the world of *The Matrix*, the surveillance state is everywhere—because the whole world is shaped by the machines who have enslaved humanity. It's sadly not so different in the real world. Government agents aren't the only ones keeping tabs on regular folks anymore. Corporations now monitor consumers. Criminals are constantly looking for their next mark online through identity theft, credit card scams, and so much more. And the rest of us are forced to monitor each other, vetting our digital communications for AI attacks, threats to our physical safety, and even just people being pervs like Cypher.

Ana Lily Amirpour's *The Bad Batch* (2016) takes place in a future USA where such surveillance has gotten completely out of control. Citizens are carefully monitored for certain types of behavior, and repeated breaches get you labeled as "Bad Batch" and summarily exiled from the country into a desert wasteland with no recourse for return. Already in our world people's social media profiles and online behaviors put them at risk of losing their current jobs or missing out on new prospects. So-called revenge porn and AI-created sex videos ruin women and girl's lives daily. Further, I'm writing this book from Florida, where if I were a teacher it would actually be against the law for me to talk with my students about many of the themes I've discussed thus far—even basic ones like race, gender identity, queer theory, and even some of the historical anecdotes about people of color. Nobody sets out to write a banned book, and yet that's what I ended up doing as I researched and pulled together these chapters inside Florida's neofascist borders.[12]

Considering all these real-world examples, it's not surprising that the surveillance state features significantly in some of Keanu Reeves's more grounded dramas as well:

- In *Point Break* (1991), Johnny Utah (Reeves) goes undercover to identify a team of bank robbers, but it is bank surveillance footage of one of their tanned asses that first tips off Johnny's partner (Gary Busey) that the robbers are surfers.
- *Even Cowgirls Get the Blues* (1993) has law enforcement spying on Rubber Rose Ranch, and it results in a dramatic standoff between the boys in blue and a cadre of badass cowgirl bitches.
- *Speed* (1994) shows serial bomber Howard Payne (Dennis Hopper) using the police force's own surveillance technology against them, bugging his rigged bus with a camera and monitoring other key locations in order to get the jump on the cops.
- In *Chain Reaction* (1996), we watch the coordination of state actors including law enforcement and politicians, the media, and even private citizens to spy and report on machinist Eddie (Reeves) and scientist Lily Sinclair (Rachel Weisz) as they attempt to democratize energy production.
- Other Keanu cop dramas *Street Kings* (2008) and *Exposed* (2016) also feature many different aspects of the surveillance state, using both high and low-fi technology.
- Keanu's villainous American businessman Donaka Mark in *Man of Tai Chi* (2013) uses copious surveillance footage to entrap not just the men for his murder fight club but also the enablers in the police force who help him get away with murder.

Law enforcement surveillance even makes an appearance in *John Wick* (2014), despite the fact that it spends most of its time in a criminal underworld seemingly outside the bounds of any law. In the aftermath of a deadly confrontation at the titular assassin's home, friendly cop Jimmy (Thomas Sadoski) shows up at John's door asking whether he's working again.

In many of these examples, the surveillance technology has been put in place with an implicit message that it's here to keep us safe—that we're being watched for our own good. But as we see, it often does quite the opposite. While there's definitely something comforting about knowing you're never alone, when it's the government or a corporation (or a would-be criminal) spying on you, it almost makes you wish for the pre-internet days when it wasn't so easy to access almost every human on the planet.

Environmental Destruction

When it comes to the environment, modern technology has been one of the main drivers of both localized environmental destruction and the bigger picture of climate change. Keanu himself narrated the documentary *The Great Warming* (2006), a terrifying look at the catastrophic changes in climate that are happening primarily due to human activities like drilling for oil, deforestation, and carbon emissions.

The Great Warming isn't the only Reeves film with an environmental message. In Alex Winter's 1993 social satire *Freaked*, the environment is being ravaged by the EES (Everything Except Shoes) corporation and their chemical Zygrot 24, which is being developed with the secret purpose of genetically engineering more effective workers. "Effective" like a factory worker without a mouth or digestive system so it can't talk and doesn't need bathroom breaks. Or a secretary with six arms, four mouths, and a hot figure who doubles as a sexbot. Much like in the real world, the corporation is indifferent to all the disastrous side effects the substance will have when it makes its way into the world's water systems, affecting ecosystems all the way up and down the food chain.

Chain Reaction features a team of scientists who have found a sustainable energy source (based on burning hydrogen extracted from water) that would entirely replace the human need for oil and gas. Of course, both government and corporate forces violently attempt to prevent this information from getting out into the world, since a solution to the climate crisis isn't profitable to those at the top.

In a plot twist from the original nuclear war parable, director Scott Derrickson's 2008 remake of *The Day the Earth Stood Still* shows the consequences of unchecked environmental destruction on Earth, featuring an alien being who has come to wipe humans off the planet in order to allow it to heal. The alien, Klaatu (Reeves), ultimately decides to give humans a second chance, and I'm patiently waiting for the sequel where he returns super pissed that we kept on squandering all our natural resources and finishes the job he started.

Fascinatingly, while Keanu Reeves hasn't really been all that public about the causes he supports—other than a cure for leukemia, which his sister Kim survived—he's been dubbed a "reluctant eco-celebrity" because of these roles and his occasional comments on environmentalism.[13] Unlike many other celebrities, he does make a quiet environmental statement by eschewing private jets; he's known to fly commercial airlines more often than not. And while he might not be as vocal an environmentalist as other celebrities, environmentalists and scientists have claimed Keanu anyway: in 2023 researchers named a group of powerful fungus-killing chemicals *keanumycins* after Reeves himself, in honor of his work as a killing machine in *John Wick*.[14]

Deepfakes and Fake Keanu Quotes

A final technological danger relates not to Keanu's on-screen roles but to his real-life public persona. The viral video mentioned in chapter 1, which claimed to show a heroic Keanu Reeves stopping a robbery in progress but was in fact a hugely convincing deepfake, is one of hundreds of fake Keanu Reeves moments concocted from thin air and posted online. Deepfakes are also responsible for spreading more significant misinformation on issues from health to politics around the globe—but what's particularly ironic about deepfaking Keanu Reeves's face is that the camera technology used to create it is the same one that was used to create the animation in *A Scanner Darkly*. And Keanu Reeves himself is so fed up by deepfakes that he even includes a clause in all his contracts that prohibits filmmakers from digitally altering his performance.[15] And who can blame him?

Especially since there is an entire anonymous online industry that has tasked itself with producing and proliferating another brand of Keanu-related fakery: fabricated quotes. For example, what's wrong with this paragraph posted on Facebook?

> Once Keanu Reeves left a post on his Facebook page addressing all his followers and fans. The message spread online at great speed, already counting hundreds of thousands of likes and shares. "Can you see the people behind me? Everybody running

to work, not paying attention to anything. Sometimes we get so absorbed in our daily routine that we forget to pause for a moment to enjoy the beauty of life. We are turning into real life zombies. Lift your eyes, look directly in front of you and remove your earphones. Say hello to someone passing by or hug someone who feels unwell. Lend a helping hand to someone. Live everyday as if it were your last. Not many people know that I suffered from severe depression several years ago. I have never told anyone this. I had to find a way to get past her. And I realized the bitter truth: The person who did not let me be happy was myself! Every day we live is priceless. So let's live by it. Tomorrow is not guaranteed, so start living today!"[16]

First, Keanu Reeves doesn't use social media for work or in his personal life, so we know that this post is fabricated from the jump. Second, Googling portions of the text only leads to quote aggregator websites, not to Keanu's supposed original post or even a reliable news outlet reporting on it. Checking the database at the Keanu Reeves fan site Whoa Is (Not) Me (http://www.whoaisnotme.net/), which has the largest collection of digitized articles about Reeves going all the way back to the 1980s, provides no evidence that Keanu ever said anything remotely like this.

And this is just one of dozens of fake inspirational posts circulating over social media attributed to Keanu Reeves and taken as actual gospel in certain circles. Here are some others you may have seen:

- "Every struggle in your life has shaped you into the person you are today. Be thankful for the hard times, they can only make you stronger."
- "Even in the face of tragedy a stellar person can thrive. No matter what's going on in your life you can overcome it. Life is worth living."
- "None of us are getting out of here alive, so please stop treating yourself like an after-thought. Eat the delicious food. Walk in the sunshine. Jump in the ocean. Say the truth that you're carrying in your heart like hidden treasure. Be silly. Be kind. Be weird. There's no time for anything else."

- "When you truly understand karma, you realize you are responsible for everything in your life."
- "Common sense is not a gift, it is a punishment. Because you have to deal with everyone who doesn't have it."
- My personal favorite: "I'm at that stage in life where I stay out of discussions. Even if you say 1 + 1 = 5, you're right, have fun."
- Finally, "Try to be wrong once in awhile, it'll do your ego good."

Sorry, folks. There is no evidence he actually said any of these statements. And there are so many more; some of them have even been published in books like *Be More Keanu* and *What Would Keanu Do?*—essentially legitimizing them.

With all this misinformation out there, what's a fan to do when encountering a supposed Keanu nugget of wisdom? Googling for a reliable source is always a good idea. But some quotes are so off-base that it's possible to immediately recognize the fakery. Take this example:

> Someone told me the other day that he felt bad for single people because they are lonely all the time. I told him that's not true, I'm single and I don't feel lonely. I take myself out to eat, I buy myself clothes. I have great times by myself. Once you know how to take care of yourself, company becomes an option and not a necessity.

The clothes-buying comment is a dead giveaway that Keanu never said this, since we know from photographic evidence over the years—and the occasional media call-out of his low-key fashion sense—that the actor's daily wardrobe consists of worn jeans, T-shirts, boots or sneakers, and nondescript coats for inclement weather.[17] Whenever Keanu is fancily dressed, it seems to be because he's walking a red carpet.

Here's another easily disprovable faux Keanu quote: "I dream of a day where I walk down the street and hear people talk about morality, sustainability, and philosophy, instead of the Kardashians." First, Keanu isn't known to talk shit about other people. Instantly suspicious. Second, he's not a misogynist. Why would he be dunking on the Kardashians? The closest I found to this supposed Keanu quote was something his partner

Alexandra Grant said to *Vogue* in March 2020: "'I'm a 6' 1" woman with white hair,' says Grant brightly. 'You know, the idea of fitting in . . . If I wanted to look like Kim Kardashian, I would have to have surgery removing about a foot off my legs.'"[18] Somehow Grant's quote has morphed into a Keanu criticism of the Kardashians, one that is constantly making its way around the internet.

The last example I'll share here is arguably the most ironic. Often presented as an infographic with Keanu's face, it claims that he said, "The truth is, *The Matrix* was a documentary." The nearest quote I could find was in comments Keanu made in 2008 at a Night at the Movies event by the American Film Institute, in which he discussed what drew him into the world of *The Matrix* when he first read the script. What Keanu actually said was:

> I went to the Warner Bros. lot in Burbank to meet [the Wachowskis], the writers and directors of a film entitled *The Matrix*. I was excited to speak with them. They had written something that I had never seen. But in a way something that I had always hoped for. As an actor. As a fan of science fiction. The script that they wrote synthesized to me, you know . . . it had Gibson—I'm gonna be a little "inside baseball" here, as they say. But, I mean, it had Gibson, it had Verne, it had K. Dick, Frank Miller, anime, Kurosawa, Peckinpah. It was, um, Nietzsche, it was Buddha, it was Christ, it was themes and levels, it was dualities, modalities, realities, dreams, will. Um, destiny, freedom, slavery of the mind, of the body. The construct, who lives, who dies? Identity, sexuality, viruses, and love. It was mythology, philosophy, technology, and truth. What truth.[19]

I guess Keanu's poetic actual words were too difficult to fit neatly into a meme. So an anonymous person out in the cybersphere distilled all of this nuance to "The truth is, *The Matrix* was a documentary."

Sigh.

But here is something else very real that Reeves told the *Hollywood Reporter* in 2023, about deepfake technology as it's used both in online fakes and in film and TV productions: "What's frustrating about that is you lose your agency. When you give a performance in a film, you know you're going to be edited, but you're participating in that. If you go into deepfake land, it has none of your points of view."[20] Which is why recognizing all the fake quotes and fake news people spread about Reeves is about more than just not being personally gullible. Putting words in the man's mouth and spreading them as truth is breaching Keanu's own agency and ultimately is a quiet act of violence. A cute Keanu meme with puppies or a film character is one thing, but fans need to stop sharing false posts and amplifying their reach. And actors who impersonate Keanu Reeves online need to stop putting "real" in their social media handles.

But there is a simple, immediate solution to end all of these online fakes, and it rests in Keanu Reeves's own hands: He needs to have his PR and management teams set up official Keanu Reeves accounts across social media platforms and go through the appropriate verification processes. We as users cannot report instances of impersonation without a link to the verified person being impersonated. Creating official Keanu Reeves accounts would cut down fake accounts and fake news about him exponentially, within days. The unfortunate truth is that Mr. Reeves not having any social media only contributes to misinformation, scams, fraud, and fake news around his image and person. For everyone's online safety, it really needs to stop. And with just one hand gesture, Keanu Reeves could do it.

"We live in a world where there is more and more information, and less and less meaning," Jean Baudrillard writes in the seminal philosophical work (and *Matrix* influence) *Simulacra and Simulation*—and all these deepfakes and false quotes are only adding to the noise.[21] But ultimately, as Konstantin A. Pantserev notes in his chapter in *Cyber Defence in the Age of AI, Smart Societies and Augmented Humanity*, the increasingly malicious use of deepfake technology is a critical threat to both political and psychological safety, and should be treated as such.[22] And not just when it comes to Keanu Reeves.

13

A ROLE MODEL WITH A NASTY HABIT

Keanu Reeves's On- and Off-Screen Smoking

WHAT'S ONE QUICK AND EASY WAY to introduce a villain in a movie? Feature them with a cigarette in their hand and a cloud of smoke billowing around them. So it seems a fitting subject to end our discussion of the Devil—the tarot card that, in addition to the other dark forces discussed in part 2, signifies addiction of all kinds.

Yes, some of Keanu's more villainous characters smoke, like diabolical Harry in *The Last Time I Committed Suicide* (1997), diamond smuggler Lucas Hill in *Siberia* (2018), crooked cop Galban in *Exposed* (2016), and opportunistic Scott Favor in *My Own Private Idaho* (1991). But his heroes and antiheroes also light up and puff away with their left hand, like gambler turned baseball coach Conor O'Neill in *Hardball* (2001), the sex-workers' driver John in *Generation Um . . .* (2012), the titular demon hunter in *Constantine* (2005), drug-addled Bob Arctor in *A Scanner Darkly* (2006), and even his New Age dentist character in *Thumbsucker* (2005), who by the end of the film is smoking right in his dental office.

Reeves started smoking on-screen in some of his earliest roles, like 1986's *Under the Influence*, where he plays a young alcoholic, and *River's Edge*, the dark tale of murder and apathy in which the only thing Reeves's Matt has in common with his peer group is their collective cigarette habit. Ten years later, when he played Jjaks Clayton in *Feeling Minnesota*, Reeves's character had a smoking gimmick where he throws a cigarette up in the air and catches it in his mouth—and it's in this film that Reeves himself got addicted to smoking. He hasn't been able to shake the habit in all these decades since. Keanu even told the *Irish Examiner*, "I didn't start smoking until I was 30. Now I'm just in prison," which really speaks to the terrible power of addiction as an illness.[1] Even Reeves himself struggles to overcome this one.

This addiction is truly one of the most unfortunate aspects of Reeves's persona both off- and on-screen. In the real world, Keanu is considered so wholesome and kind, and a role model to so many all over the planet. Yet he continues with a habit that is incredibly damaging to the human body. From a certain perspective, though, his on-screen smoking may be doing even greater harm.

Back in 2001, a team of social scientists conducted a large survey on how on-screen smoking habits of movie stars affected adolescents' own smoking habits, and found a terrible correlation: youngsters whose favorite stars smoked on-screen were significantly more likely to be smokers themselves.[2] A decade later, even as smoking in movies had become much less commonplace (except in period pieces), another study confirmed that movie smoking was still influencing kids to take up the habit.[3] This is not the way to be excellent to yourself or each other, dudes.

But this also raises a fresh question: How is Keanu Reeves the only lifelong smoker who hasn't aged terribly? Could this be more evidence for the ongoing online theories that he's actually an angelic being or an immortal? We could go with yes, but only if we ignore the image of a clean-shaven Reeves in *Bill & Ted Face the Music* (2020), which reveals in unflinching detail the effects that smoking—and his many motorcycle accidents—have had on his face. He's still beautiful, of course, but he's no longer immaculate perfection. Which is another reason why if Keanu's going to smoke, he should be smoking alone.

PART III

THE WORLD

IN THE TAROT, the World card is one of openness and expansion, and the arrival of a logical conclusion. When the World appears in a reading, it's the signal of the closing of a chapter in a positive way that also sets the stage for growth. It can also represent travel and a global perspective, which is my particular entry point into this card as a multiracial woman who has lived all over the world and has a tendency to find the patterns that connect art and culture and social justice. And that is the context in which *Much Ado About Keanu* reaches its own endpoint: this final part delves deeper into the global impact of Reeves's work and how it connects with universal themes within culture and society, whether via queer representation, his unique take on comedy, or his films' inclusive portrayals of world history, or even via the supposed missteps in Keanu's career and the variety of criticisms that have been lobbed his way, both with and without merit.

14

PAINTING THE SKY WITH RAINBOWS

Keanu Reeves and Queer Representation

ANTI-QUEER SENTIMENTS HAVE BEEN ON THE RISE around the globe thanks to the neofascist movements gaining steam everywhere. You might think this ever-looming homophobia would rattle a popular leading man like Keanu Reeves, who has publicly dated only women but faced rumors of being gay or bisexual throughout his entire career. But unlike other stars whose latent homophobia emerged after they were rumored to be queer, Reeves has handled these moments with his characteristic kindness and charm. For example, when people in Hollywood and beyond were convinced that Keanu was in a secret marriage with producer David Geffen, Reeves told *Vanity Fair* he'd never even met Geffen but refused to unequivocally deny being gay: "Well, I mean, there's nothing wrong with being gay, so to deny it is to make a judgment. And why make a big deal of it? If someone doesn't want to hire me because they think I'm gay, well, then I have to deal with it, I guess. Or if people were picketing a theater. But otherwise, it's just gossip, isn't it?"[1] Responses like this are one of many reasons he's become a queer icon, beloved by the LGBTQ+ community, even though he's never actually played a gay man on-screen.

This "crossover stardom," as Michael DeAngelis calls it in his book *Gay Fandom and Crossover Stardom: James Dean, Mel Gibson, and Keanu Reeves*, has been embraced by Reeves in the "construction of his own ambiguity,"[2] which is a fancy way to say Keanu Reeves has been able to maintain a queer-friendly persona without having to necessarily be gay himself. But in Leilani Nishime's book *Undercover Asian*, the chapter "Queer Keanu" points out a sinister side to this phenomenon. Nishime notes that of the few times when Reeves's Asianness has been commented on in mainstream media, several have been in response to instances when he challenged the accepted norms of gender and sexuality. Like the time Keanu was photographed in drag makeup for *Vanity Fair* in 1991 and the caption read "Kabuki Keanu," even though his makeup had nothing to do with Kabuki—nor is Reeves Japanese. It's at moments of queer gender expression when Keanu Reeves gets both racialized and feminized by a mainstream media that otherwise pretends he is white.[3]

But Keanu's actual cultural heritage provides a more nuanced and positive perspective on queer sexuality. In traditional Indigenous Hawaiian culture, queer folks, or māhū, have historically held an elevated cultural position.[4] Before accepting her winning crown for *RuPaul's Drag Race*'s fifteenth season, Sasha Colby noted of the heritage she shares with Keanu, "Māhū, in Hawaiian, it's the third gender in Hawaiian culture. People in the community trusted queer people, and māhūs, to handle their kids, because what is more divine than knowing both feminine and masculine energy?" As in most places around the world before colonization, in Hawai'i there existed a variety of accepted genders, a recognition of gender fluidity, and an understanding that same-sex relationships were part of everyday culture. That is, until Captain James Cook, and the flurry of colonizing forces who followed after his well-deserved death at the hands of Indigenous Hawaiians, effectively began criminalizing not just homosexuality but queer identities altogether.

It's in the beautiful and ancient queer tradition of Hawai'i that Keanu Reeves has crafted an entire catalog of LGBTQ-friendly roles that have secured his place as a gay icon, regardless of his heterosexuality. In the following sections, we'll take a closer look at Keanu's queer and queer-coded roles.

My Own Private Idaho (1991)

Gay director Gus Van Sant's art film is one of the Keanu Reeves movies that receives a great deal of attention in academia, particularly around sexuality studies and queer representation. The vanguard of what was dubbed the "new queer cinema" of the 1990s, *My Own Private Idaho* was an absolute industry game-changer.[5] While Reeves and his costar River Phoenix were far from the first straight actors to play gay on-screen, the fact that they were so young and both such up-and-comers was a huge creative risk at the time that could have ended both of their careers. But they were fearless in committing to their roles as two young sex workers, and the resulting acclaim set the stage for more established actors to play gay in mainstream prestige dramas—like Tom Hanks in *Philadelphia* (1993), which won him an Academy Award for his portrayal of a gay man dying of HIV/AIDS. I draw an even clearer line between Reeves's and Phoenix's authentic portrayals and *Brokeback Mountain* (2005), which earned both Heath Ledger and Jake Gyllenhaal their first Oscar nominations for their portrayals of two closeted Wyoming cowboys in a decades-long love affair.[6]

But what's extra fascinating about *Idaho* that so many people tend to forget is the fact that Keanu Reeves's character, Scott Favor, isn't actually gay. He's a child of privilege essentially cosplaying as an unhoused sex worker whose primary clientele is gay men to scandalize his father, the mayor of Portland. As soon as Scott comes into his inheritance and his father dies, Scott reverts to type, abandoning all his hustler friends who had been counting on him to lift them out of poverty. On the other hand, Phoenix's Mike Waters is indeed gay, and his confession of love to Scott while on the road looking for Mike's long-missing mother is one of the most tender, beautiful, and heartbreaking moments ever put to screen. River Phoenix should've gotten a second Oscar nomination for his nuanced and absolutely engrossing performance.

And beyond Reeves and Phoenix's terrific work, *Idaho* has become a kind of time capsule that demonstrates the grittiness and hardship of life on the street for young gay men in the early 1990s. It's a struggle that continues today, but one that has evolved hugely with the advent of smartphones, the internet, and the surveillance state I discussed in chapter

12. The young men sex workers of *Idaho* have been abandoned, not just by their families but also by society at large, due to their sexuality, and they often blur the line between whether sex work is actually a choice for them or simply a necessity for survival. Though the particulars of street life may have changed, and the film itself may feel dated to newer audiences, that basic dynamic is just as true today.

Queer TV writer Conner Good (*Flowers in the Attic: The Origin*), a longtime *Idaho* fan, mused over a chat about what draws him back to the film, in particular Mike's recurring vision of a barn falling from the sky and crashing to earth. Good tells me, "I have a guttural reaction to it. I don't think it matters that it's not Mike's home. . . . It's an American frontier house. And it's something about the fragility of home, that's juxtaposed with the gay sex consummation of the opening blow-job scene. He ends up wayward and on the streets. I can still hear the sound of the wooden planks hitting and rolling across the road." Good also says, "Not to put too much rainbow icing on it, but I think the themes of the movie, its queerness, the hustlers—like, home is an even more fragile place when you experience same-sex desire. Not to mention same-sex love."

There's something about all of this that's particular to the gay male experience, and a queer woman like me can only partly access it through my own experiences. Hearing a young gay man like Good—who was born in 1993, two years after the film came out—discuss *Idaho's* importance three decades later in 2023 is a testament to this film's unique power, especially for queer folks.

Sweet November (2001)

Here's something fascinating I'll bet cash money that even the most dedicated Keanu Reeves fans didn't notice: his romantic drama *Sweet November* is a parallel narrative to *My Own Private Idaho*. First, Charlize Theron's Sara is a wealthy woman who has eschewed her money and family ties, inviting a new man to live with her each month as a trauma response to her terminal cancer. She's not exactly a sex worker in the same way that Scott Favor is in *Idaho*, but sex is part and parcel of what she offers these men for their dedicated month. Second, Sara is heavily reliant on the gay couple living downstairs, who moonlight as drag queens:

Chaz/Cherry and Brandon/Brandy, played by Jason Isaacs and Michael Rosenbaum, respectively, two more straight actors playing gay.

Ultimately, like Scott at the end of *Idaho*, Sara abandons her November companion Nelson (Reeves) and her gay community to return to her family estate and die in their care. Did Keanu and the rest of the *Sweet November* team realize they were doing an updated and less queer version of *My Own Private Idaho*? I'm not sure. But it's a connection that elevates *Sweet November* in so many beautiful, poignant, and heart-wrenching ways. Watch it again and you'll see. The two films make for a fascinating double feature.

Wolfboy (1984)

The overt queerness in Keanu's work didn't begin with *My Own Private Idaho*. In fact his status as a gay icon was seeded all the way back in 1984, when he was just twenty, with his role in the stage play *Wolfboy*. It's about two institutionalized young men who fall in love, one of whom believes himself to be a werewolf, and it involved Keanu in nothing but his underwear at one point, plus a number of love scenes. The only evidence of the latter is a series of steamy and sweaty production photos with Reeves and his costar Carl Marotte.[7] *Wolfboy* hasn't been staged that often since Keanu's run; there was a production in New Orleans in 2013, and a musical adaptation in London's West End in 2010.[8] The closest we may get to experiencing Reeves's version for ourselves is by reading playwright Brad Fraser's original script.*

Bram Stoker's Dracula (1992)

In Francis Ford Coppola's adaptation of Bram Stoker's classic horror novel, we meet the mysterious Count Dracula (Gary Oldman), whose hypersexual persona and literal bloodlust result in a number of terrifyingly erotic moments between the Transylvanian nobleman and English legal clerk Jonathan Harker (Reeves). Particularly memorable is the scene when Dracula watches Jonathan shaving and then, when a nervous Harker cuts himself, dramatically licks his blood off the razor. Later, Jonathan

---

* It's available in the collection *The Wolf Plays* (Edmonton, Alberta: NeWest, 1993).

wanders into a dangerous wing of the Dracula's castle and gets set upon by the count's three vampire "brides," who fondle him sexually as they bite various parts of his body. But Dracula appears in a rage and reminds them Jonathan is his and his alone, giving them a baby to feed on instead.

It's not just Dracula and Jonathan who give off homoerotic vibes: Jonathan's fiancée Mina (Winona Ryder) and her friend Lucy (Sadie Frost) kiss during a rainstorm after they've gotten tipsy together, highlighting a sexual undercurrent in their relationship that Bram Stoker only hints at in the book. Though in other ways Coppola's adaptation downplays the novel's queer coding, adding a heterosexual relationship between Dracula and Mina in a past life, he couldn't resist dramatizing the underlying queer subtext that drips from Stoker's novel.

Much Ado About Nothing (1993)

In "'There Is No Spoon,'" Julian Cha uses Keanu Reeves's role in the Shakespeare adaptation *Much Ado About Nothing* as an example of Hollywood's tendency to asexualize Asian men.[9] However, as much as I appreciate Cha's essay, I disagree. Reeves's villainous Don John oozes homoeroticism that absolutely sizzles through every shirtless and oiled scene he's in. We watch Don John get massaged by another man (his henchman Conrade, played by Richard Clifford), as he rages about his inability to hide what he truly feels. At one point he even holds Conrade's face in his hands like they are about to kiss. And when he finds out that young nobleman Claudio (Robert Sean Leonard) is engaged to be married, Keanu's performance suggests that Don John is jealous because he's in love with "the most exquisite Claudio," as Reeves's character describes him. Hence Don John's hugely disproportionate machinations against Claudio's betrothed, the innocent Hero (Kate Beckinsale), which almost get her murdered by her fiancé.

If you compare Reeves's turn as Don John to Vernon Dobtcheff's in the BBC's 1984 TV movie production, the difference is night and day. Dobtcheff's Don John is a quiet, soft-spoken psychopath, motivated only by the satisfaction it gives him to ruin lives. There are no homoerotic undertones in the least. Reeves's performance, on the other hand, is emotionally charged and highly eroticized, particularly in his singular, smoldering focus on Claudio himself. Another departure from traditional versions of *Much Ado* comes just minutes into the film, when everyone is bathing in preparation for the weekend's visitors and festivities. The full-frontal shots of all-male and all-female bathers only add to the homoerotic atmosphere, bolstering the reading of Don John as secretly in love with Claudio and in a jealous rage at his betrothal.

The *Matrix* Quadrilogy (1999–2021)

When *The Matrix* first came out in 1999, it absolutely exploded filmgoers' minds with its story, in which Reeves's Thomas Anderson discovers that the entire world is an illusion designed to control humankind and awakens to his physical body in the real world for the first time. But it wasn't until an interview with Netflix in 2020 that codirector Lilly Wachowski confirmed something that certain queer audiences had long suspected: that this brain-breaking story of awakening from an illusory life to a real one was intended to be an allegory for the transgender experience. She even mentioned that the story was originally meant to include literal trans representation in the character of Switch (Belinda McClory), who was initially conceived as being played by a woman inside the Matrix and by a man in the real world.[10] Lilly's confirmation made a lot of sense, given that she and her codirector sister Lana both came out as trans themselves years after the release of the first three *Matrix* films. The trans allegory adds amazing layers to an already extraordinary story.

Keanu himself may not have been aware of the allegory when he made the original trilogy, but when he learned about the Wachowskis' intentions, he was completely supportive. As he told Yahoo Entertainment in 2020, "I think *The Matrix* films are profound, and I think that allegorically, a lot of people in different versions of the film can speak to that. And for Lilly to come out and share that with us, I think is cool."[11]

At the time of this interview, Keanu was filming Lana Wachowski's solo effort *Matrix Resurrections* (2021). The last film in the quadrilogy was the culmination of the trans analogy, as the only openly queer installment in the series. *Resurrections* introduces us to a wizened, balding Thomas Anderson, who looks in the mirror and still sees his alter ego Neo. We also meet Tiffany, a middle-aged blonde woman, who looks in the mirror and sees Trinity (Carrie-Anne Moss). When they meet, they both recognize the hidden self under the mask they both feel forced to wear, and their connection is instant. They each see the other as they see themselves—a truth at the heart of the trans experience, beautifully put to screen.

Neo and Trinity were both killed at the end of *The Matrix Revolutions* (2003), but by the time of *Resurrections*, they've been revived by the machines who enslaved humanity. Meanwhile, as new generations of humans have continued to escape the Matrix and the machines' control, Trinity and Neo have become legendary figures in the real world. The resurrection of the fallen heroes solidifies their status at the head of a queer chosen family; though Neo and Trinity may never have had biological kids, they have an enormous collection of spiritual children who look up to them for guidance and so much more. So when the machine mastermind known as the Analyst (Neil Patrick Harris) tells Neo and Trinity he doesn't care if they "paint the sky with rainbows," it's an overtly queer reference that encapsulates the trans allegory of the entire franchise. The fact that Neo and Trinity will continue remaking the world into ethical iterations that center personal freedom and love—even if it's as futile as the Analyst claims—brings a level of optimism to this sci-fi franchise that up until the end of *Resurrections* had been a bleak cautionary tale of the dangers of technology and the power of the surveillance state.

With all this overt and covert queer textuality, it makes a lot of sense that the *Matrix* franchise has become an inspiration for queer communities in real life.[12] In 2019, Emily St. James published "How *The Matrix* Universalized a Trans Experience—and Helped Me Accept My Own," a love letter to the original film on its twentieth birthday that explores the various ways that *The Matrix* reflected and shaped the experiences of trans viewers like her, likening the events of the first film to the experience of being closeted as a trans person and eventually breaking free.[13]

And in 2021, after Lilly Wachowski confirmed that the *Matrix* franchise had been intended as a trans allegory all along, NPR published "'I, Too, Was Living a Double Life': Why Trans Fans Connect to 'The Matrix,'" by Connie Hanzhang Jin, a series of interviews with trans folks who all saw themselves reflected in the dual identities presented in the characters' Matrix and real-world selves.[14] One of the interviewees, Erin Reed, was just thirteen when she saw *The Matrix*, back in the days when getting online was a painstaking process involving a noisy modem. In a parallel to the original concept of Switch, Erin would come home from a school where everyone knew her as a boy and would spend hours chatting online under a woman's screen name, exploring the dimensions of her own femininity and transness. Like Erin, many of the other interviewees made this connection about the trans allegory long before Wachowski confirmed it. In an important note about the film, Jin writes, "Even now, over twenty years after its release, *The Matrix* still remains arguably the biggest piece of media ever made by trans creators. While more movies are starting to include trans characters and stories, many of them focus on or even define their trans characters by extreme tragedy or hardship. Others lean on offensive stereotypes." The *Matrix* films, on the other hand, foreground the possibility of a cathartic escape into a truer existence. With its fourth installment, *Resurrections*, this legacy of positive, trans-made media is intact and more important than ever.

The *John Wick* Series (2014–2023)

Of course, I can't end this section without reminding you of the queer reading of the *John Wick* franchise I developed in chapter 3, which explores the possibility that John Wick is a trans man as well as the many queer-coded characters who appear across the second, third, and fourth films. The character of the Adjudicator is openly nonbinary, played by enby actor Asia Kate Dillon. Akira actress Rina Sawayama is pansexual in real life, which raises the possibility that her Wickiverse character is as well. And other characters who can be read as queer coded for a variety of reasons include the Marquis (Bill Skarsgård) in his flashy bespoke suits, butch Katia (Natalia Tena) of the Ruska Roma, and quintessential leather daddy Klaus (Sven Marquardt).

These creative choices set *John Wick* apart, presenting a spectrum of gender without subjecting its queer characters to punching-down humor or homophobia the way many other action movies do. And all of the queer coding means that Keanu Reeves has starred in two blockbuster quadrilogies that incorporate trans-adjacent allegories and narratives, a fact that by itself sets Keanu's work apart from that of every other action star except Laurence Fishburne, who also starred in both *The Matrix* and *John Wick*.

Other Queer Representation

Even in the films where Keanu Reeves himself is not portraying a role that's queer or queer coded, his body of work is filled with other examples of queer representation. In *Freaked* (1993), when a mad scientist performs unsanctioned experiments on humans, turning them into all kinds of monsters and hybrids, Mr. T plays a man transformed into the Bearded Lady. In the end her transformation turns out to be the only consensual one: she had always wanted to be a woman. In a touching monologue she says, "When I first arrived here, I was nothing like I am now. I was confused—a walking contradiction, so full of questions. [. . .] But now I know who I am. I can say it to the world: 'Hey. This is me. I am woman. And I like me.'" It's a really beautiful moment of queer joy, gender euphoria, and self-acceptance in an otherwise bonkers satire about corporate and capitalist greed.

The heroine of *Even Cowgirls Get the Blues* (1993), a woman with giant thumbs who uses them to hitchhike around the USA, is pansexual. As messy as the film is (more on that in chapter 16), *Cowgirls* is ultimately a story about the attempted queer liberation of a lesbian-run dude ranch in the middle of the desert. Reeves actually represents the hetero portion of the narrative as the main character Sissy (Uma Thurman) looks to lose her virginity to a man. *Cowgirls* also features a trans modeling agent, the Countess, played by a delightful John Hurt, who handles the campy role with the expected finesse of a studied Shakespearean performer.

In the anorexia drama *To the Bone* (2017), one of the female patients of Dr. Beckham (Reeves) says, "Damn, Dr. Beck, you trying to turn me straight?!" when he shows up looking snazzier than usual. "That's a different program" is Dr. Beck's deadpan reply. This is a great moment for Keanu Reeves fans, because in real life there are a huge number of lesbians for whom Keanu is the only cis man they'd ever be interested in.

And in *Bill & Ted's Bogus Journey* (1991), not only is Death (William Sadler) comfortable in women's clothing during his time in Heaven, but also Bill and Ted's mentor Rufus (George Carlin) appears in drag as Ms. Wardroe, played by the legendary Pam Grier. Alex Winter shows up in drag as well—briefly, as his character Bill's creepy granny. And we can also read Bill and Ted's codependent friendship as aromantically or platonically queer. However, with all this sweet queer representation come three terrible moments of pure homophobia in the most unexpected of places. In *Bill & Ted's Excellent Adventure,* both Bill and Ted say the *other* f-word, the homophobic one, to each other after hugging and showing emotion. In *Bogus Journey,* their robot doubles brand them with the slur for expressing love, and the real duo later scream it at the devil himself as an insult. These three moments are brief but so ugly in the face of so much compassion and inclusion when it comes to queer communities. In fact, both *Excellent Adventure* and *Bogus Journey* now come with a warning about the homophobic slur, a move that both *Bill & Ted* stars, Reeves and Winter, have said they wholeheartedly support.[15]

Hetero Homoeroticism

Like the lesbians who are only attracted to Keanu Reeves, there are a hell of a lot of straight-identifying cis men who quite openly and happily admit that they have a crush on or are actually quite in love with this one particular man. For instance, Keanu superfan and straight dude Jordan Peele compares him to the adorable kitten who shares his name in the action comedy *Keanu* (2016): "The moment I had the idea to make him a kitten, he was Keanu."[16] And Reeves's *Street Kings* (2008) costar Hugh Laurie confessed during a press junket for the film, "Keanu Reeves is an icon. And I'm more than a little in love with him, I'll come right out and say that now," claiming tongue in cheek that he would leave unsigned love notes to Keanu around set.[17] And when it was announced that Reeves would appear in the 2020 video game *Cyberpunk 2077,* the denizens of online gaming forums—many of them men who are supposedly heterosexual—quickly became intensely curious as to whether his character would be romanceable.[18] (Unfortunately for them, he isn't.)

Similar moments of homoeroticism among purportedly straight characters can be found inside Keanu's films. In *Point Break* (1991), the bromance between undercover cop Johnny Utah (Reeves) and surfing bank robber Bodhi (Patrick Swayze) has homoerotic undertones: the two men share the same girlfriend in Lori Petty's Tyler, and their very intense connection eventually leads Johnny to allow Bodhi to end his life on his own terms. Swayze also toys with homoeroticism in the duo's previous collaboration, the hockey drama *Youngblood* (1986): his character Sutton fully kisses an official on the mouth as he tries to break up a brawl on the ice. Like Reeves, Patrick Swayze played with a variety of presentations of masculinity throughout his career, from sensitive dancer Johnny Castle in *Dirty Dancing* (1987) to a fight-ready bouncer in *Roadhouse* (1989), and it's poignant that the late Swayze's efforts to play with masculinity echo Reeves's own.

A comedically homoerotic moment occurs in a more recent Reeves project, the dark comedy *A Happening of Monumental Proportions* (2017), directed by actress Judy Greer. The double entendre of the title points, among other things, to the penis obsession of Reeves's character, Bob. He has just found out that his wife, Nadine (Jennifer Garner), is having an affair with her boss, Daniel Crawford (Common). When Bob finally confronts Daniel about the cheating, he shouts, "Pull out your cock!" in order to compare it to his own. It's a bananas moment in which the camera moves from Daniel's crotch to Bob's, as Daniel seems almost about to whip it out before deciding not to. This scene is not just bizarrely funny but also weirdly sexy given the two gorgeous men at its center, and it makes me hope for another team-up between Common and Keanu that could feature more of their great on-screen chemistry—with or without dick measuring.

A much darker homoerotic incident occurs in the diamond heist thriller *Siberia* (2018). It's the moment when Reeves's diamond smuggler Lucas Hill meets with Russian mobster Boris (Pasha D. Lychnikoff) to solidify a deal, only for Lucas's mistress Katya (Ana Ularu) to show up unexpectedly. Boris insists that his companion fellate Lucas while Katya fellates him, and at the moment of climax Boris requires Lucas to look into his eyes. This is how Boris requires sealing their sale of rare and elusive blue diamonds. Though the film cuts to the next scene before the culmination of the act, it's a moment of dark homoeroticism and homosociality that the rest of the narrative follows to its equally bleak ending.

Finally, the crime comedy series *Swedish Dicks* (2016–2018) follows Ingmar (Peter Stormare), a stuntman turned dysfunctional private investigator in Los Angeles who specializes in Hollywood cases. Ingmar's life is an absolute disaster, especially since his best friend and old stunt partner Tex (Reeves) died terribly in a stunt gone wrong. Ingmar often sees and talks to Tex's ghost, and in a sweet moment after Ingmar hires a new partner for his PI firm, Tex appears in a vision asking with a grin, "You cheating on me?" Ingmar is a very literal person, and it's a funny moment to watch him take so seriously this accusation from his dead friend, which suggests that he does feel like he's cheating on Tex by making a new friend at all.

What Would Keanu Do with Queerphobia?

There are several books about Keanu Reeves in the self-help vein—along with numerous online listicles—that repeatedly ask one question: What would Keanu do?[19] These texts attempt to extrapolate life lessons from Reeves's films and real-world statements, so naturally they're filled with advice centered around the importance of kindness and compassion. Yet even though queer themes have abounded in Reeves's work since the start of his career, not one single one draws lessons from Keanu's inclusivity when it comes to queer people and their representation on-screen.

But that inclusivity is certainly worth noting, since it's very much an anomaly in Hollywood. Most straight male movie stars worry about featuring too much positive queer representation in their films, for fear that people will speculate about their sexuality and their career will suffer. Keanu, on the other hand, seems to have no such fear; even when denying gay rumors, he'll commonly add, "But ya never know!"[20]

It's another in the long list of things that makes Keanu Reeves an extraordinary performer whose work is particularly meaningful, especially to LGBTQ+ people and communities around the world facing the disturbing and violent rise in homophobia. As I've mentioned, I'm writing this book in Florida, where anti-LGBTQ attitudes and legislation have prompted an exodus of queer families from the state, including famous ones like basketball player Dwyane Wade and his trans daughter Zaya, who feared for their safety.[21] So let me offer a new piece of advice to add to the lessons from Reeves's life and work: Be like Keanu and reject homophobia. Support queer communities around the world.

15

PERIOD PAINS

Keanu's Historic Fictions

PIGEONHOLED EARLY IN HIS CAREER as a 1980s Valley boy, Keanu Reeves set out to defy the stereotypes by playing characters from distant historical eras in films such as *Dangerous Liaisons, Bram Stoker's Dracula,* and *Much Ado About Nothing*—only to be targeted by critics for his perceived shortcomings in these period roles. The criticisms are so persistent that I've met people who parrot them without even having seen these films for themselves. But, as I'm sure you expected, I will argue that Keanu's cinematic forays into the past are greatly underrated—Keanu's stage training is obvious in these roles, as is his love of Shakespeare—and did indeed succeed, first and foremost, at breaking Reeves out of his previous typecasting.

Throughout this chapter, I'll not only get into why, with few exceptions, I disagree with the negative readings but also point out how these analyses of Reeves's period pieces, which cover a huge span of human history, have failed to acknowledge how meaningful it is for an actor of Keanu's racial and ethnic heritage to be represented in these historical contexts.

564 BCE: *Little Buddha*

As one of earliest period pieces in Keanu's catalog, 1993's *Little Buddha* harks back to 564 BCE and the birth of future Buddha Prince Siddhartha Gautama (Reeves) in ancient India—what is now Nepal. *Little Buddha* flits between that period and the present day, when a group of Tibetan monks exiled in Bhutan begin the search for the reincarnation of their master Lama Dorje (Geshe Tsultim Gyelsen). One of the potential candidates is a white boy named Jesse (Alex Wiesendanger) who lives in Seattle, where Lama Dorje spent the last years of his life. As Jesse and his parents Lisa (Bridget Fonda) and Dean (Chris Isaak) learn about Buddhism and Tibetan history, their journey takes them not just into the past but halfway around the world to determine if Jesse will become a monk himself.

This is one of the few films in Keanu's career for which I actually agree with the criticisms—and have a few of my own to add. First, even for 1993 it was wildly offensive to put an actor in brownface to play a South Asian man as they did with Reeves as Prince Siddhartha. Reeves's own heritage isn't remotely connected to that of Indian or Nepali Siddhartha, and it was an odd casting choice given so many (equally good-looking) race-appropriate Bollywood actors the filmmakers could've chosen from. In addition, Keanu's Desi accent is absolutely bogus, and by the end of the film he gives it up entirely for a version of the British one he served in *Bram Stoker's Dracula*. To Reeves's credit, though, aspects of his performance are raw and poignant, especially as Siddhartha struggles with his move toward enlightenment. Reeves's silent acting is a hundred percent on point here, and he is the *only* credit to this film.

Second, it is equally offensive to place a white family at the heart of a fundamentally South Asian story—this is peak Orientalism at play, whereby whiteness is seen as necessary to humanize an otherwise foreign story. In some ways worse, the young American boy does not in fact become a monk, ultimately returning with his family to their lives in Seattle. As Eve Mullen writes in "Orientalist Commercializations: Tibetan Buddhism in American Popular Film," "The notable lack of an effective denouement is indicative of the limits of our American fantasy of Shangri-La: Tibet as a distant, fantasy utopia is only a place in which to escape for a short time, and it is a place which must be kept distant for the fantasy to perpetuate."[1]

Further, as the story of this white family frames the film's adaptation of Prince Siddhartha Gautama's journey to enlightenment through meditation and deep introspection, it unwittingly reflects how the Buddha's journey has been co-opted by many real-life New Age spiritualities, turning Buddhism's notions of karma, dharma, and impermanence into consumer-driven ideologies and oxymoronic practices like competitive yoga.

But there's more. As mentioned in chapter 10, *Little Buddha* director Bernardo Bertolucci, along with actor Marlon Brando, have been implicated in turning a rape scene in their film *Last Tango in Paris* (1972) into a real-life sexual assault on Brando's costar Maria Schneider. While in theory it would seem almost sacrilegious that a sexual abuser would make a kind of art film about Buddhism, in fact Bertolucci's history mirrors the entrenched culture of abuse in Tibetan Buddhism, which is often glossed over due to the elevated rock-star status of the religion and its monks around the world. Buddhist supporters in the West often talk about Tibet before the Chinese occupation as if it was a perfect Shangri-la of enlightenment and compassion, when in fact the opposite is true.

Michael Parenti's 2003 essay "Friendly Feudalism: The Tibet Myth" exposes in terrifying detail the hierarchies of power that allowed Tibetan monks, lamas, and other religious leaders to effectively kidnap both boy and girl children from surrounding villages, who were used in ceremonies of ritual child sexual abuse and many other kinds of physical and psychological violence.[2] The *Guardian* and the *Daily Beast* have both written in-depth follow-ups to these grotesque revelations that entirely shatter the image, heavily promoted around the world, of pre-occupation Tibet as an enchanted paradise.[3] Eve Mullen's "Orientalist Commercializations" also provides a fantastic breakdown of the many myths of Tibet in the West promoted by *Little Buddha*, all of which continue to apply today, as Tibetan Buddhism maintains its status as a popular cause among white Americans in particular.[4]

But worst is the disgusting hypocrisy of many revered Buddhist leaders, who are not only grifters on par with a certain orange-tinged US president but sexual abusers and predators to boot. Among Reeves's costars in *Little Buddha* is Sogyal Rinpoche, a Tibetan Buddhist leader in Boulder, Colorado, who not only was accused of hoarding cash in a most un-Buddhist way but was also an accused rapist and sexual harasser who never answered for his financial or sex crimes before his death in 2019.[5]

Little Buddha is not available for streaming and DVDs are hard to come by, which in this case has turned out to be a good thing. The film has aged terribly—and that's saying a lot, since it was already way problematic back in the day.

1500s: *Much Ado About Nothing*

One of the things that bothers me inordinately to this day is the categorically unfair reviews of Keanu Reeves's performance in the Shakespeare adaptation *Much Ado About Nothing* (1993). Something I see again and again with criticisms of Reeves's work involves how often a film critic will transpose their (mis)perceptions of the actor onto his roles. Like *Vulture* writing about *Much Ado*, "Also on the Ridiculous List: Keanu Reeves, who uses only one expression for the entirety of the movie. Since he plays the villain, it is a scowl. Since it is Keanu Reeves, his scowl looks really confused."[6] From where I sit, Keanu Reeves's Don John isn't confused, he's absolutely smoldering with rage, popping up to commit dastardly deeds before lurking back into the shadows, his piercing eyes taking in everything as he plots away.

As I discussed in the previous chapter, I particularly love how Reeves's performance and Kenneth Branagh's direction add queer subtext to Shakespeare's story, portraying the villainous Don John as apparently in love with the young protagonist Claudio (Robert Sean Leonard). That twisted, toxic love is evident behind the rage that tightens Don John's beautiful features whenever he contemplates Claudio's blossoming romance with the sweet Hero (Kate Beckinsale). And Reeves's accent is nowhere near as bad as many viewers describe it. In fact, the person in *Much Ado* who should have been lambasted for his bizarre performance is Michael Keaton as an unhinged Dogberry, who borrows way too much from his role as Beetlejuice for a Shakespeare film. Keaton talks like a pirate with a muddled accent that is one part Irish, one part Scottish, and one part absolute nonsense.

But one of the most remarkable things about Reeves's presence in *Much Ado* is how it reflects the real-life history of Indigenous people from North America and the Pacific Islands like Hawai'i who lived in Europe between 1492 and 1800, some by choice but many by force.[7] Don John's brother in *Much Ado* is played by Denzel Washington, so we can savvy that Don Pedro's father is white and his mother is Black. If we read Don John as part Indigenous like Keanu himself, this could mean that their father either had an affair with a free Indigenous woman or assaulted an Indigenous maid or enslaved woman and decided to keep the son as his own. Situations like the latter were all too common among Indigenous women living in Europe at the time. Though the first known Pacific Islanders reached Europe in the 1700s, in 1613, just one year after the first documented performance of *Much Ado About Nothing*, Pocahontas herself was kidnapped from her family and tribe; three years later she was forced to move to England, where she died soon after.[8] These real-life details add important historical context to Reeves's presence in the film.

1700s: *47 Ronin*

In April 1701, a delegation from Kyoto was dispatched to the domain of Shogun Tokugawa Tsunayoshi at the behest of the emperor. Unfortunately, the lesser nobles sent to receive them were unfamiliar with court etiquette, and one in particular, Asano Naganori, did not offer a hefty enough gift to Lord Kira, who took it upon himself to verbally taunt the man to such a degree that Asano physically attacked him, a crime punishable by seppuku, or self-disembowelment. For an entire year after Asano carried out his punishment, his former samurai, now masterless warriors known as ronin, stewed in anger and resentment at the incident. Then one day forty-seven of them decided to collectively embark on a revenge rampage against Lord Kira. This vendetta ultimately ended in their own deaths by seppuku, but not before they presented Kira's head at Asano's grave.[9]

It is from this infamous historical moment of extreme bloodshed that Reeves's fantasy action tale *47 Ronin* (2013) is derived. It tells the story of a half-white, half-Japanese man named Kai (Reeves) who was orphaned and raised by the forest demons known as the Tengu before returning to the human world and becoming a samurai. Hollywood's version features not only demons but also monsters, giants, and a social-climbing witch who shape-shifts into a red fox and eventually a dragon. As with the reviews of Keanu's performance in *Much Ado About Notion*, the critics were not kind: "You will also see a baddie credited as 'Lovecraftian samurai,' and Reeves fighting back a blast of dragon-fire with an enchanted sword, and bird-men/monks attacking samurai in a forest temple. This sort of thing should be fun. Somehow it's not," wrote Simon Abrams of RogerEbert .com.[10] But this is what I don't understand, because as dramatic and disturbing as some of the themes and imagery are in this film, it actually *is* fun. The fight scenes are beyond grand. The action is well paced, and the characters are distinct. It's the first and only time Keanu Reeves has ever fought a dragon to date, and that shit is epic as fuck.

Which is not to say *47 Ronin* doesn't have its issues. The movie might have worked better in Japanese, even if that required recasting Keanu's role. But, in fact, the filmmakers apparently shot alternate Japanese-language versions of every scene, with Keanu himself even learning his lines in Japanese for those takes.[11] But this alternate cut has never been released—not even in Japan.[12] Such a pity. Keanu speaking Japanese would be value enough alone to revisit this more authentic-sounding version of the movie.

Another odd choice in the *47 Ronin* is how they chose a white man (Ron Bottitta) to narrate a film about Japan, offering statements like "Ancient feudal Japan, a land shrouded in mystery, forbidden to foreigners." Even referring to the setting as "ancient" when it takes place in the 1700s is weird, and the film certainly feels like it takes place at a much earlier time. All of this gives the story an implicitly Orientalist and racist bent, feeding into xenophobic stereotypes of Japan as a distant and exotic isle with strange people and customs, set apart in time and space from the rest of the world.

Strangely, none of these problematic issues even came up in critics' negative reviews. Still, they hated on it deeply enough that many filmgoers who might have enjoyed it skipped it altogether. It's actually one of my personal favorites of Reeves's catalog now. And for a fun double feature with historic relevance, check out Reeves narrating Steven Okazaki's fascinating 2015 documentary *Mifune: The Last Samurai*.

1760s: *Dangerous Liaisons*

Stephen Frears's *Dangerous Liaisons* (1988) takes place in prerevolutionary France and is based on Pierre Choderlos de Laclos's 1782 novel *Les liaisons dangereuses*, but Frears pushes the date back to the 1760s for stylistic reasons. We wouldn't have had all those fabulous wigs and gravity-defying bosom dresses had the adaptation been set in the less flamboyant 1780s.[13]

Reeves stars as nobleman Chevalier Raphael Danceny, and as with Don John in *Much Ado About Nothing*, Keanu's own Indigenous Hawaiian ancestry means that we can read Danceny as a mixed-race Indigenous man who inherited great wealth and thus is welcome among high society. I found it marvelous how the 2022 *Dangerous Liaisons* television remake on Starz in fact greatly diversified its cast and featured a number of Black and Brown characters who run the socioeconomic gamut from lords and ladies to the servant class, reflecting an underacknowledged reality of eighteenth-century Europe. I like to think they were inspired by Reeves's multiracial presence in Frears's version.

1897: *Bram Stoker's Dracula*

While Keanu's performance in *Bram Stoker's Dracula* (1993) has drawn some of the same complaints as his appearances in *Much Ado* and *Liaisons*, I'm going to spend some extra time digging into them, since his turn as Jonathan Harker in this film arguably serves as one of the biggest critical millstones weighing down the public perception of his acting ability. And you guessed it: by my analysis, the criticisms are wholly undeserved.

Let's start with Keanu's infamous British accent, which continues to get hated on all these decades later. Yes, Harker's accent is indeed rather stilted. But there's a simple explanation as to why: Jonathan Harker is not of the upper classes but works and lives among them. He's tried extraordinarily hard to mask his lower-class roots by affecting a posh accent, but he hasn't quite perfected it. His accent sets him apart from the aristocracy he serves—and he's not the only character whose way of speaking gives away their humble beginnings. Jonathan is a perfect match to his fiancée Mina Murray (Winona Ryder), a modest schoolteacher who now finds herself in the company of a wealthy gadabout, her friend Lucy Westenra

(Sadie Frost). Like Jonathan, Mina speaks with a rather forced accent, her phrasing often stilted, as she tries to match Lucy's effortless royalty.

Moreover, if we read Keanu's character as sharing his real-life Chinese/Indigenous heritage, Harker might have grown up abroad and English might not even be his first language—another reason why his speech might at times sound unpracticed. By the late 1800s, migration to Europe from both the Americas and the East was common, as were the stories of people with real-life backgrounds similar to the one I've proposed for Jonathan Harker. For instance, there was the British Chinese sailor James Robson, an orphan like Mina Harker in Stoker's original novel, who was brought to London by an English couple and served aboard a British sailing ship in the 1880s and '90s.[14] Barclay Price's *The Chinese in Britain: A History of Visitors and Settlers* explores in vivid detail the Chinese immigrants who began visiting and settling in London and thereabouts beginning in the early 1700s.[15] Unfortunately this reading of Francis Ford Coppola's film can only go so far, since he features no other people of color on-screen aside from Keanu.

Now that we've gone through several explanations for Reeves's accent, let's talk about something else you may have missed as you were being annoyed by how he speaks: his fantastic performance. As Jonathan Harker, Keanu's eyes are wildly expressive. You can see every thought and fear going through Harker's mind as his encounter with Count Dracula (Gary Oldman) goes to hell and beyond. This is one of Keanu's most underrated portrayals, controlled and focused. The character's torment and determination, especially after he realizes he's not getting out of Castle Dracula without a fight, remind me of his later, more highly regarded performances in *Speed* (1994), *Constantine* (2005), and *John Wick* (2014). There are similar shades of exhaustion—both physical and emotional—including momentary glimpses of resignation to a dark fate that quickly get replaced with anger and determination to survive.

Echoes of Keanu's beleaguered title characters in *Constantine* and *John Wick* are evident when Harker is chained in the bowels of the vampire's castle and being fed on by Dracula's beautiful monster brides, then finally musters up the last of his strength to scale the castle walls and flee to safety. This moment especially reminds me of the scene where John Constantine uses a dead woman's cat as a portal to hell, both resignedly

and resolutely putting his feet into a bucket of water and mentally pre-
paring for a journey as terrible as Harker's. And after Harker escapes
and the showdown with Dracula begins in earnest, I'm reminded of the
scene in *Speed* when Reeves's Jack Traven discovers that his partner
Harry (Jeff Daniels) has been murdered by the terrorist Howard Payne
(Dennis Hopper): Jack melts down with unbridled rage and despair and
Annie (Sandra Bullock) pleads with him to not lose hope. The dynamic
between Jonathan Harker and Dracula is similar to the one between Jack
Traven and Howard Payne; unlike the other vampire hunters, Jonathan
is supremely pissed off, as he should be considering Dracula's violence
against him was so very personal.

If we want to talk about ham-handed acting and an over-the-top
accent, look no further than another *Dracula* star: Anthony Hopkins as
Van Helsing, whose cackling absurdity often reminds me of Keaton's
Dogberry in *Much Ado About Nothing*. The weakest link in *Dracula* is
not Keanu Reeves.

1945: *A Walk in the Clouds*

Alfonso Arau's *A Walk in the Clouds* (1995) is a lush romantic drama
that follows WWII veteran Paul Sutton (Reeves) upon his return to the
Bay Area after fighting on the front lines for more than three years. On
his way to sell chocolates door-to-door, Paul runs into Victoria (Aitana
Sánchez-Gijón), a literature grad student who has been knocked up and
dumped by her professor. Paul steps in pretending to be her husband,
and finds himself enmeshed with Victoria and her charming Mexican
American family in many unexpected ways. Unlike all the previous films
discussed in this chapter, *A Walk in the Clouds* never received a deluge
of negative reviews and in fact seems to have only grown more beloved
over time. Granted, there is a great deal of cultural confusion in the
casting of the Mexican American characters: Sánchez-Gijón is of European heritage (Spanish and Italian), Victoria's father is played by Italian
actor Giancarlo Giannini, and her brother is Puerto Rican actor Freddy
Rodríguez. But *Clouds* is one of the few films in which legendary Mexican American actor Anthony Quinn actually plays a Mexican. He seems
to take particular delight in his role as Don Pedro Aragon, the kindly

patriarch of the family, and Quinn's scenes with Reeves are some of the highlights of this film.

Here, too, the narrative takes on fresh power when we view it through the lens of Keanu's Chinese and Hawaiian heritage. According to the US Army Center of Military History, there were roughly thirteen hundred Chinese Americans from Hawai'i enlisted in the US military at the start of World War II. Many of these were multiracial Chinese–Indigenous Hawaiians, like Keanu and his ancestors.[16] And the National Museum of the American Indian notes that after the attack on Pearl Harbor in 1941, up to 10 percent of Indigenous populations from the mainland joined the military to fight for the USA.[17] We rarely see their stories represented on-screen, so casting Keanu Reeves as a multiracial WWII vet is a much-needed example, even if nobody has identified it as one until now. It's also worth noting that Reeves's Paul Sutton never knew his parents and grew up in an orphanage. Could this have been because at the time of his birth interracial relationships were actually illegal? This possibility adds a new level of tragedy to Paul's already heartbreaking story.

The other underappreciated facet of real-life history that *A Walk in the Clouds* reflects is the longtime presence of Mexican Americans as the owners and managers of vineyards in Napa Valley, like the Aragons. For example, the Robledo family began tending fields in the US in the 1940s as migrant workers, established their own Napa vineyard in 1984, and went on to create a wine label that's currently one of the best in California.[18] It has even been served at the White House.[19] Unlike the Aragon family, however, the Robledos didn't come from old money in Mexico but rather worked their way up in the spirit of that often-problematic American Dream we discussed in chapter 11.

A Walk in the Clouds also reflects a darker side of history, when Quinn's Pedro Aragon discusses the first Pedro Aragon, who came over from Spain in the 1600s and settled in Mexico. What this story glosses over is the fact that Mexico had been colonized by the Spanish—a violent process that involved illegal land grabs, slavery, and genocide. Even if Don Pedro the First wasn't a murderer himself, to establish his family in the "New World" he benefited from that violence, which cleared space for him to build a life unencumbered.

1946: *The Last Time I Committed Suicide*

Even though *The Last Time I Committed Suicide* (1997) is set only a year after *A Walk in the Clouds*, the America the two films present couldn't be more different. *Suicide* follows rakish muse of the Beat poets Neal Cassady through a variety of exploits, particularly those involving young women. The film was released to middling reviews from critics, most of whom appreciated how the film's tone captures this particular postwar American moment as it foreshadows the adventures of the Beat generation that was still years away.[20]

The film is based on what's now known as the Joan Anderson Letter, a real-life missive Cassady wrote to Jack Kerouac, in which his girlfriend Joan's suicide attempt and emergency C-section serve as the jumping-off point for a narrative of his exploits with women. The letter's style would soon be emulated by Kerouac and the rest of the Beat poets to global and historic acclaim.[21] Though the letter was believed to be lost until 2014, *Suicide* closely follows the details of the only known excerpt at the time. Reeves's character, Harry, is one of the few divergences from the source material. In Cassady's letter, his "younger blood-brother" Bill is the barfly who entices Neal to overstay and overdrink, leading to key events like Neal's eventual arrest for statutory rape. In the film, Bill has become Harry, a much older thirty-two- or thirty-three-year-old man living a stunted adolescence at the pool hall. In a collection of seedy characters from Cassady's letter, Harry's characterization is highly exaggerated on-screen, a role Keanu tackles with gusto.

Reeves's Chinese and Indigenous heritage complicates this film in some interesting ways, albeit in the negative. Harry hangs out with people at least a dozen years his junior. He has no discernible job. He is obsessed with high-school girls and actively pursues them. And he serves as a consistent bad influence on an already kooky Neal, in particular when one drink turns into three dozen. Asian men don't necessarily face a negative stereotype about drinking other than not being able to hold their liquor—at one point Harry has a prolonged and graphic bout of puking after drinking too much eggnog. But it's a different story entirely for Indigenous men, with the "drunk Indian" stereotype persisting from long before 1946 till today. But even though they don't mention it, it seems clear Reeves is playing white here, considering the racial segregation that marked the era and the fact that Bill Tomson, the real Cassady's "blood-brother" on whom Harry appears to be based, was unequivocally white. This film is a rare case in which it may be better to just let the whitewashing stand rather than challenge it.

1951: *Tune in Tomorrow*

Keanu Reeves has starred in seventy-eight movies to date, and sadly a number of his films from the 1980s are no longer easily available on DVD and are absent from streaming services altogether. One of these is *Tune in Tomorrow* (1990), a wild romp set in 1951 New Orleans that follows a recent divorcée, Julia (Barbara Hershey), who falls in love with her much younger nephew by marriage, Martin (Reeves). Their drama goes meta when curmudgeonly radio show writer Pedro Carmichael (Peter Falk) begins inserting details from their real-life romance into the serial melodrama he's broadcasting that has audiences rapt. It's such a fun film, with great costumes and set design and a story-within-a-story that plays out in surprising and hilarious ways. But unfortunately for my analysis in this chapter, Keanu's character is unambiguously white—his parents are played by white actors Paul Austin and Mary Joy—so we must forgo any possibility of historical Asian and Indigenous representation here. Still, it's a period piece that's perfect for modern audiences, making it a shame it's never been available to stream.

Bonus: *Bill & Ted's Excellent Adventure*

The main characters' jaunts through time do not make *Bill & Ted's Excellent Adventure* (1989) a period piece by any stretch of the imagination—a fact that allows the sci-fi comedy to escape the kind of sociocultural scrutiny I've given the other films in this chapter—but we should still talk about the historical figures whose most heinous deeds are glossed over for the sake of comedy.

Sigmund Freud (Rod Loomis) is presented as a series of jokes about psychoanalysis and the fact that he's a "geek." But there's nothing funny about how the real Freud's bizarre theories of penis envy and hysteria led to so many women being institutionalized. In fact, if we turn his theories onto him, we find an individual with a penis obsession bordering on fetishistic that he projected onto women in particular, who as a group he truly seemed to hate. Feminist Freudian revisionists have done some fantastic work refuting his theories, even if there's a grain of truth in some of his less sexist ideas—like the fictional Freud's analysis of Ted's father issues.

Similarly, Billy the Kid (Dan Shor) is a gunslinger who cheats at cards, and Genghis Khan (Al Leong) is a guy with anger issues, but in real life the former was a murderous outlaw, and the latter a brutal warlord and colonizer whose acts of violence against massive numbers of human beings were so extreme we still talk about them today. Not to mention "So-crates Johnson" (Tony Steedman), who comes across as wise and lovable, while in real life Socrates represented a Greek society that was shaped by slavery, a caste system, and institutionalized sexual abuse of young male students by their teachers—a norm we would now call pedophilia. All of this reflects a perspective on history that is all too common, where unpleasant truths are glossed over and problematic or complicated figures are presented in straightforwardly positive terms.

That's seen most clearly in the way our history valorizes Abraham Lincoln, who as played by Robert V. Barron is positioned as a hero in *Excellent Adventure* as well. Yes, Lincoln signed the Emancipation Proclamation on January 1, 1863, which led to the dissolution of slavery as a dominant social contract in the USA. But it's rather more complicated than just this. First, just because he signed the thing doesn't mean that all enslaved people were instantly freed. The proclamation applied only to the states currently at war with the Union, and the holiday Juneteenth exists because it took until June 19, 1865—more than two years later—for enslaved people in the last Confederate state, Texas, to even find out that they were no longer other people's property by law. And while Lincoln's initial proclamation kicked off the events that ultimately freed Black Americans from enforced bondage, just days earlier, in December 1862, he personally approved the largest mass execution in American history, in which thirty-eight Indigenous Dakota men were hanged in what amounts to a kangaroo court of justice.[22] Most heinous actions, indeed, even if they were made under extreme duress.

Of course, *Excellent Adventure* is an exercise in absurdity and caricature. And not all the ways it tweaks the historical record are to its
detriment—it always makes me happy to see Joan of Arc (Jane Wied-
lin) get a brief moment to let loose and dance before she's returned to
fifteenth-century France to be burned at the stake. But we can still take a
moment to recognize the nuances of actual history in a broader context.

One of the most beautiful and meaningful aspects of Keanu's work
on-screen is how it provides for just such moments of recognition. Simply by bringing his own Hawaiian and Chinese heritage to his period
pieces, he provides a fresh historical perspective, encouraging us to finally
acknowledge the longstanding presence and immense social and cultural
contributions of Asian and Indigenous folks across Europe and North
America.

16

EMBRACING HIS
MEDIOCRE NOTHINGNESS

Keanu's Cinematic Stumbles
According to Critics

FOR SOMEONE SO BELOVED AS A PERSON, Keanu Reeves receives a shocking lack of grace when it comes to his performances. It's arguably one of the most toxic aspects of audiences' parasocial relationship with him: he's often perceived as actually being the cheerful dimwit he's played in movies like *Bill & Ted's Excellent Adventure*, instead of a talented actor who's especially good at portraying such roles. And this perception has been fueled by the dismissive attitude of most film critics, who over the years have often failed to see the art—or anything good at all—in many of Keanu's movies. In the preceding chapters, I've argued that Keanu's work deserves to be taken more seriously, looking at the themes that run through his films and thinking about what drew him to each role. Now I want to take a closer look at Reeves's worst-reviewed films from that same perspective.

Collating data from popular film databases like IMDb and Rotten Tomatoes and entertainment magazines like *Vulture*, *GQ*, *Screen Rant*, and *Looper*, I found that the general consensus of critics is that Keanu's worst films are *The Watcher, 47 Ronin, Even Cowgirls Get the Blues,* and *Replicas.*[1] Other films that were on the worst-of lists of least two of those sites include *Feeling Minnesota, Exposed, Generation Um . . . , Little Buddha, Siberia, Johnny Mnemonic,* and *Sweet November.* I discussed the problems with two of these movies, *Little Buddha* and *47 Ronin,* in the previous chapter, so I won't revisit them here. But for the rest, I'll dive into the terrible reviews and offer my own take—which often differs from the critics' and takes issue with many of their specific criticisms. And I'll offer some alternative and intersectional perspectives that may help you better appreciate many of these films in future rewatches.

The Watcher (2000)

We start with one of the few instances where I completely agree with the critics' negative reviews: Chuck Klosterman of the *Akron Beacon Journal* wrote, "What's ultimately most frustrating about *The Watcher* is the way it takes a scenario that's genuinely frightening and makes it seem implausible," and Lisa Schwarzbaum wrote for *Entertainment Weekly,* "Multiple candles may be a universal symbol in movies (and rock videos) for romance and spirituality. But they're useless in illuminating the deadness of *The Watcher.*"[2] In this film, Reeves stars as David Allen Griffin, who enjoys kidnapping, torturing, and murdering young women with dark hair. After nearly getting caught by FBI agent Joel Campbell (James Spader), Griffin goes underground for a short time before resurfacing to embroil Campbell in a fresh cat-and-mouse game.

When I saw the movie on its initial release, my first thought was that something was throwing off Keanu's performance. It seemed so forced, and Keanu appeared obviously miserable, that I worried maybe he was ill. It would be years before I'd learn that he was essentially coerced into making the movie by a former friend who forged his signature on the contract. To avoid a prolonged legal battle, Keanu did the work.[3] But his performance serves as a veiled protest, as we see the one time in his career that Reeves phones it in. The actor himself notes, "I hate that movie. It's terrible. It's a disaster."[4]

And it's not just Reeves that's off in this film. The script is atrocious. Directorial choices are bizarre, including a certain slow-motion camera technique that was so popular in the 1990s and early 2000s, presenting images in a kind of visual stutter through fog, that hasn't aged well in the era of high definition. The best thing I can say about it is that while Reeves's character is a serial killer of women, at least he isn't a rapist, and the murder scenes are kept mostly off camera.

If you're looking for a movie that shows what *The Watcher* could have been, check out Reeves's directorial debut *The Man of Tai Chi* (2013) for his chilling portrayal of a serial killer posing as a businessman.

Even Cowgirls Get the Blues (1993)

Based on the bestselling novel by Tom Robbins, *Even Cowgirls Get the Blues* is the story of Sissy Hankshaw (Uma Thurman), a girl with freakishly huge thumbs that she uses to hitchhike all over the United States. Her journeys on the road connect her with a wild assortment of characters, including a transgender modeling agent known only as the Countess (John Hurt) as well as Bonanza Jellybean (Rain Phoenix) and her cowgirl crew at the Rubber Rose Ranch.

Director Gus Van Sant's film attempts in some ways to serve as the girl-power version of his previous feature, the critically acclaimed *My Own Private Idaho* (1991), but the results were widely derided by critics. *Vulture* referred to *Cowgirls* decades later as "Gus Van Sant's famously terrible adaptation of Tom Robbins's novel," adding that it "never gets the tone even close to right, and all sorts of amazing actors are stranded and flailing around."[5] While this is an accurate description of the film, what's bizarre to me is that the criticisms of the film don't mention the blatant racism and racial insensitivity throughout.

They start with the main character, Sissy, who claims Indigenous ancestry but is played by white actor Uma Thurman. Reeves himself plays a "full-blooded Indian" in worse brownface than *Little Buddha*. And while his narcolepsy is a touching tribute to the late River Phoenix's character Mike Waters in *Idaho* (*Cowgirls* is even dedicated to River), that's about all good we can say about Keanu's Julian Gitche.

Worse is a character named "the Chink" played by Pat Morita, which is true to Robbins's 1976 novel but didn't come across well on-screen in 1993—and certainly doesn't today. Even though the story does acknowledge that "the Chink" is actually a Japanese American mystic, the commentary on the "All Look Same" phenomenon facing Asian Americans is wholly lost amid this film's other blunders, like weird pacing, awkward writing, and uneven performances.

I do love the story of the Rubber Rose Ranch, particularly Lorraine Bracco as bullwhip-wielding cowgirl Delores Del Ruby—a powerhouse performance that didn't get any of the flowers it should have—but it remains bananas to me that no other film critic has mentioned the racism that runs through the narrative the same way that Sissy's thumbs carry her across America. I can overlook all the other stylistic issues, uneven performances, and awkward writing. But the anti-Indigenous and anti-Asian racism is what I find unforgivable.

Replicas (2018)

"Equal parts plot holes and unintentional laughs, *Replicas* is a ponderously lame sci-fi outing that isn't even bad enough to be so bad it's good." That's the critical consensus according to review aggregator site Rotten Tomatoes. And this summary is galaxies kinder than the opinions of most of the individual critics; of the dozens of reviews cataloged on the site, only 9 percent are positive.[6] But it's the positive reviews that resonate with me—like Steve Biodrowski of *Hollywood Gothique*, who wrote, "*Replicas* is hardly the apex of cerebral cinema, and it doesn't fully explore its interesting premise, but even the attempt it laudable, especially when wrapped up in an engaging emotional package."[7]

It's this "emotional package" I especially appreciate—how the film defies the typical cold-blooded logic of this kind of sci-fi thriller. *Replicas* follows robotics engineer William Foster (Reeves), who has been developing a process to transfer human consciousness into cybernetic bodies. While the technology is not yet perfected, William forces his efforts into overdrive when his wife and children are killed in a car accident and he realizes he might be able to bring them back as cyborgs. It's unusual to see a "mad scientist" character who's motivated not by revenge or anger but by a deep love for his family and a desperation to tamp down his extreme grief. The scenes where a mourning William is forced to decide which one of his three children he will have to permanently let go of—only three cybernetic bodies are available to his family of four—are beautifully performed by Reeves, who tends to be most emotionally raw in moments of familial grief like these. It's also really refreshing to see comedian Thomas Middleditch in a more dramatic role as William's assistant Ed; he brings a lot of pathos to the screen.

Yes, there are hokey aspects to the plot, with a villain who's a caricature rather than a three-dimensional character. But this film isn't nearly as dreadful as the critics make it seem. Its bleak ending is particularly memorable, as it turns out the lifesaving technology William has developed will be marketed predominantly to wealthy people who want to live forever rather than shared for the good of all. The ending is extremely true to life, which ultimately elevates the entire project.

Feeling Minnesota (1996)

Jjaks Clayton (Reeves) returns home from a stint in prison for robbery to find that his brother Sam (Vincent D'Onofrio) is about to marry a sex worker named Freddie (Cameron Diaz) who has been sold to Sam by her pimp Red (Delroy Lindo). When Freddie decides to seduce Jjaks on her wedding day and run away with him, a chaotic chase ensues across the country, punctuated by bouts of extreme violence that include Sam shooting Freddie and Jjaks leaving her for dead in the woods. It's a lot.

The biggest problem with *Feeling Minnesota* is its pacing and editing, which end up making the movie feel closer to two hours and forty-five minutes long, when in fact it only runs an hour and thirty-nine minutes. But most critics had more extensive complaints. In *Variety*, Emanuel Levy wrote, "Almost everything in and about . . . Steven Baigelman's disappointing directorial debut . . . is irritatingly derivative: the secondhand plot, the small-time characters and, above all, the limited, movie-ish vision." He criticized the "lackluster acting" and said of Keanu's performance in particular, "Reeves is back to the amorphous style that marked his goofy, spacey portrayals in the '80s."[8]

Is this Reeves's best film? No. But is it as bad as all that? Also nope.

As for the performances, Reeves and D'Onofrio have fantastic chemistry as the estranged brothers, and there's something poignant about their toxic relationship. Even as they spend most of the movie taking turns punching each other out, including in the dick, it's clear that both men are desperate for family love and connection, but they can't break out of their multigenerational cycles of twisted masculinity. The movie was mislabeled as a romantic dark comedy, but reclassifying it as a crime drama might help viewers reconceive it in a more positive light.

Exposed (2016)

Originally titled *Daughter of God*, *Exposed* was meant to weave together several parallel storylines: a Latinx family's unfortunate run-ins with corrupt law enforcement in New York City, a murder mystery about a crooked cop's death, and a young woman's traumatic past involving sexual violence. However, executives at the film's distributor, Lionsgate, meddled with the original cut by writer-director Gee Malik Linton, reediting the story to center Keanu Reeves's character Detective Galban.

Consequently, Linton insisted on giving up his director's credit—the film is credited to his pseudonym "Declan Dale"—and the movie ended up with multiple story threads that don't ever properly come together, like some failed imitation of a Steven Soderbergh film.[9] Only fragmented hints remain of Linton's original plans, and anyone who has seen director Gaspar Noé's devastating *Irréversible* (2002) will be able to guess at least one of the plot twists, as *Exposed* straight-up grabs from that horror movie to flesh out its uneven storylines.

This is another case where I agree with most of the criticism the film has received. "The confused, heel-dragging mystery drama *Exposed* suggests an especially dour, arty episode of *Law & Order: SVU*, minus any reasons to keep watching," the *AV Club* wrote, under the apt headline EXPOSED ASKS WHETHER IT'S POSSIBLE TO YAWN FOR 102 MINUTES STRAIGHT.[10] And *Flickering Myth* snarked, "To call *Exposed* one of the worst movies of the year would be insulting to the other terrible releases that have come out and will come out during the remainder of the year."[11]

The only positive thing I have to say about *Exposed* is that it's another Keanu Reeves film that is strongly anti-copaganda, exposing the truly heinous crimes that cops often get away with unless citizens take matters into their own hands. Keanu has a beautifully raw moment as his character opens a birthday card from the son he abandoned and breaks down in grief. Reeves's performance shows him at his most vulnerable here, but it gets lost amid the confusing narrative. I wish we'd had the opportunity to witness Linton's own vision of the film, as opposed to the hodgepodge version that executive meddling got us.

For a glimpse of what the movie should have been, see Paula Lee's article for *Salon* that compared *Exposed* to *Daughter of God* after Linton sent Lee a copy of his original cut.[12] It's a stark contrast indeed: Filmed mostly in Spanish, *Daughter of God* centers on traumatized young Isabel (Ana de Armas), who's Peruvian, and the multiethnic Black and Brown communities among which she lives in Washington Heights; the murder of the cop is peripheral to Isabel's story. But *Exposed* is a predominantly English-language police procedural that focuses on Keanu Reeves's Detective Galban investigating his partner's murder, while unfolding Isabel's story concurrently as a secondary plot. Even if *Daughter of God* wasn't perfectly executed, as Lee notes in her article, I'm going to bet it would have received better reviews across the board.

Generation Um . . . (2012)

Where *Exposed* wants to be a meaty Soderberghian psychodrama, Mark Mann's *Generation Um . . .* actually gets closer to the mark with this indie drama inspired by Soderbergh's *Sex, Lies, and Videotape* (1989). Yet the movie currently has a brutal 0 percent positive reviews on Rotten Tomatoes.[13] *GQ* called *Generation Um . . .* "A mumblecore wannabe with the astute observation that millennials are superficial—never heard *that* one before."[14] I, on the other hand, find it a weirdly compelling story. Following John (Reeves) and his two much-younger, manic, drug-addled companions Violet (Bojana Novakovic) and Mia (Adelaide Clemens) over the course of twenty-four hours, *Generation Um . . .* calls back to some of the early 1990s independent films like Kevin Smith's *Clerks*, minus the humor. It also prefigures several of Keanu's more highly regarded films from later in the 2010s: on the surface the plot seems to mirror *Knock Knock* (2015), with Reeves playing against two much younger, disturbed women. But a closer reading calls to mind *The Neon Demon* (2016), as it portrays a society that elevates women for their beauty and then thanks them by eating them up.

The film ends with an eye-opening twist, revealing that Violet and Mia are actually sex workers and John is their driver, requiring a second viewing to recontextualize everything that came before. While so much is presented without comment and without judgment in this movie—including the young women's sexual escapades and John's kleptomania (the latter of which turns into a hilarious foot chase through Manhattan, foreshadowing many moments in *John Wick*)—the ending most certainly illustrates how blurry the line of consent can be when it comes to choosing sex work as a profession. While Violet and Mia enjoy making big money for a few hours of work, we see how dangerous it can be when they are alone in groups of rowdy, entitled men who want what they want when they want it. Do Violet and Mia have good work nights? Probably. But at least from what we can glean, they've been on a bad streak for some time and have been compensating with extreme drug abuse and drinking, while Mia appears to be in a dissociative state for much of the story.

Is this one of Keanu's best films? No. But it definitely doesn't deserve that 0 percent rating on *Rotten Tomatoes*. *Generation Um . . .* is much better, and also much more heart-wrenchingly tragic in many ways, on a second watch. By now I've seen it several times, and with every fresh viewing Novakovic's and Clemens's performances move me to tears. They both beautifully portray the complicated mess of compensating for long-term trauma, and in particular sexual trauma. This film really needs a reexamination.

Siberia (2018)

"Icily inhospitable to compelling performances or a sensible narrative, *Siberia* offers audiences a harsh and seemingly interminable exile from entertainment," reads the Rotten Tomatoes critics consensus for Matthew Ross's romantic thriller *Siberia*.[15] I wonder if the fact that half of the film is in Russian with English subtitles prompted such negative responses, because in my estimation, to use the parlance of our times: this movie fucks. It features a series of intensely intimate and graphic sex scenes that hark back to the days of *Basic Instinct* (1992). *Siberia* is the quintessential international erotic thriller of the 1990s, with a 2018 high-definition edge that cuts in some intriguing ways.

Lucas Hill (Reeves) is a diamond dealer turned smuggler whose contact in Russia has gone dark while in the possession of some rare blue diamonds. As Lucas tries to solve the mystery of his missing partner and the coveted stones, he finds out his wife Gabby (Molly Ringwald) has been cheating on him, so he decides to have an affair with a much younger bartender, Katya (Ana Ularu), that eventually turns into something more. But when you have Russian mobsters in the mix, there will be blood. This film's ending is as bleak as its titular setting.

I'm actually surprised there was no discourse about the cunnilingus in *Siberia* the way there was after Ryan Gosling and Michelle Williams's "controversial" scene in the romantic drama *Blue Valentine* (2010). *Siberia* actually features a similar but much longer scene featuring Reeves and Ularu—the first and so far the only time Keanu goes down on a woman in any of his films. I don't know about you, but I think that's an event worth celebrating. I also particularly appreciate the stunningly horrifying ending, which is inevitable but still quietly devastating. *Siberia* is what *John Wick* would be if it were realistic rather than an action fantasy, and the echoes between the two add fresh depth to *Siberia*.

Johnny Mnemonic (1995)

It never fails to blow my nerd brain that the cyberpunk classic *Johnny Mnemonic*—which, as I discussed in chapter 12, proved fabulously predictive about the plight of service workers in the digital age—remains so unpopular with both critics and audiences. It doesn't have *Generation Um . . .*'s 0 percent rating on Rotten Tomatoes. But a 20 percent rating among critics based on forty reviews is still shockingly low, with critics like Roger Ebert writing in 1995, "'Johnny Mnemonic' is one of the great goofy gestures of recent cinema, a movie that doesn't deserve one nanosecond of serious analysis but has a kind of idiotic grandeur that makes you almost forgive it."[16] Set in an imaginary 2021, the plot follows a data courier named Johnny who has overloaded the wet-wired data port in his brain to make enough money to retire from this highly dangerous and physically taxing job. On his journey to deliver the data that's slowly killing him, he discovers that the information is the cure to Nerve Attenuation Syndrome (NAS), the side effect of addiction to the variety of technology humans depend on.

OK, yeah, I will concede that *Mnemonic* is extremely dated in many ways, especially now that we've passed the actual year of its setting. Like, if you have the advanced tech to put a data chip in a person's brain, why do the codes to unlock it have to be sent by fax machine? Why is everyone in an interconnected digital future still recording video on VHS tapes? But these inadvertent anachronisms aside, literally the week I began writing this chapter (May 26, 2023) racist billionaire Elon Musk's company Neuralink received the go-ahead for human trials of his own brain-chip product that almost exactly mirrors what the wet-wired implants do in *Mnemonic*.[17] And while the seizures and other physical side effects of NAS are much more dramatic, technology addiction is a growing problem in the modern world, and seems to be one of the few things that affects the very young and very old in similar ways.[18]

Without *Johnny Mnemonic*, based on William Gibson's highly prescient short story (where the dolphin character makes a lot more sense than it does in the movie), we wouldn't have the *Matrix* series and many other cyberpunk classics. As Roxana Hadadi wrote when she revisited the film in 2020 for *Crooked Marquee*, "*Johnny Mnemonic* is no *Matrix*; its world-building lacks the specifically nuanced grit. . . . [but] the ideas Gibson thrust forward furthered the cyberpunk conversation onscreen for years to come."[19] The recent rediscovery of *Mnemonic* has also included a gorgeous black-and-white version for the film's twenty-fifth anniversary that accentuates the film's important themes as it overrides the hokier aspects like outdated CGI that haven't aged as well.[20]

Sweet November (2001)

"Schmaltzy and manipulative, *Sweet November* suffers from an implausible plot and non-existent chemistry between its leads," reads the critics consensus on Rotten Tomatoes about Keanu Reeves and Charlize Theron's second film together (after 1997's *The Devil's Advocate*), Pat O'Connor's *Sweet November*. While there might be a mismatch in performances here, between Theron's unevenly characterized manic pixie dream girl and Reeves's depressed businessman masquerading as a workaholic, there is still a lot to appreciate that deserves more than its 15 percent rating on Rotten Tomatoes.[21]

Most important, as I discussed in chapter 14, *Sweet November* is something of a hetero version of *My Own Private Idaho*, and it features some lovely queer representation in Sara's gay drag queen neighbors Chaz/Cherry (Jason Isaacs) and Brandon/Brandy (Michael Rosenbaum)—in spite of the fact both actors are straight playing gay. Like Reeves's Scott Favor in *Idaho*, Theron's Sara Deever has abandoned her family money and relies on the queer community of San Francisco, as well as her monthly boyfriend, to give her life meaning and purpose before she abandons them all to return home to die of her terminal cancer. This connection to *Idaho* elevates *Sweet November* in some beautiful and heartbreaking ways, and as a result I can't bring myself to offer any hate.

The ending of *Sweet November* is also deeply beautiful and authentic, reflecting the real-life truth that love isn't capable of doing all the heavy lifting that's expected of it, especially in romantic dramedies. A conclusion like that isn't manipulative. It's lovely. And Keanu Reeves sings. Automatic win in my book.

Shining Greater Than Any

"The man who embraces his mediocre nothingness shines greater than any," Keanu Reeves says as the over-the-top version of himself in *Always Be My Maybe* (2019), and it's a sentiment that connects many of these worst-of films—worst according to critics other than me. Even at their most supposedly mediocre, Keanu's films still offer intriguing characters, interesting plots, and soulful performances from Reeves in particular. If these are movies you've only watched once or skipped altogether due to their reputations, I recommend checking them out and seeing whether my suggested reinterpretations help some of these movies find long-overdue redemption.

17

YES, I CAN-ADA

Keanu Reeves's Extraordinary Comedic Talent

WITH THE PURELY SUBJECTIVE NATURE OF COMEDY, what's funny to one person might not be funny to the next. Case in point: me. I'm not a fan of the comedy genre in general; I often find jokes offensive, especially those that punch down at people with less power or privilege. But when it comes to Keanu Reeves, his comedies are in fact my favorites—even films like *A Happening of Monumental Proportions* (2017), which was critically panned yet cracks me up without fail thanks to Keanu's perfectly delivered through-line of dick jokes. I also cry laughing at his dozen or so straight-faced zingers as the voice of Batman in the animated movie *DC League of Super-Pets* (2022). And *The SpongeBob Movie: Sponge on the Run* (2020) is for me a full-on ab workout as I belly laugh through every one of Keanu's scenes as Sage, the disgruntled spirit guide of two hapless sea creatures.

Beyond my own personal taste, which is admittedly unorthodox, Keanu Reeves's films are positively littered with comedic moments and one-liner zingers, whether the movie in question is action, science fiction, or even drama. And yet, probably because Keanu is best known for his roles in these noncomedic genres, he gets very little credit for his stupendous comedy work—with only a few exceptions. He has been celebrated for his comedic performances in *Always Be My Maybe* (2019) and the *Bill & Ted* franchise, as well as his iconic deadpan line deliveries in action films like *Speed* (1994) and the *Matrix* franchise. Since these are some of the few comedic outputs we can (mostly) all agree are objectively funny, I'm breaking tradition with my usual practice elsewhere in the book: instead of focusing on Reeves's less acclaimed works, this chapter will take a quick dive into his most beloved comedic films and performances to find out what it is that makes him such an extraordinary comedic talent.

The Keanu Reeves Theory of Self-Referential Humor

The weekend the rom-com *Always Be My Maybe* came out on Netflix in May 2019, I received a flurry of texts and messages from friends telling me to watch it immediately before its surprises got spoiled. That should have been a hint at what was to come, but I was going through a really difficult time and it didn't occur to me what the surprises might be—even as the film unfolded and the female lead, Ali Wong's Sasha Tran, teases the exciting new love interest she met at a film industry wrap party. Then Sasha's guy makes his first appearance: cut to Keanu Reeves entering in slow motion, playing himself. I was so surprised I actually burst into tears. My tears turned to laughter as Vivian Bang's character Jenny also begins crying in earnest after meeting this turbocharged version of Keanu. My own personal meta moment. But this kind of meta humor is a hallmark of Reeves's comedy: though Keanu is known as an action star first and foremost, his comedy roles often poke fun at that self-serious reputation.

In *Maybe*, for instance, Reeves fully commits to playing the alpha male celebrity asshole version of himself. This Keanu Squared frequently references his own work, noting that residuals from his "hit movie *Speed*" paid for their $6,400 dinner, and that the stunt coordinator for *John Wick* invented the drinking game Icebreaker, "Like Truth or Dare, but a little more apocalyptic." He also spouts off a list of Chinese dignitaries, sports glasses without lenses he's wearing for a role, and smashes a vase of flowers over his own head. But there's also a cleverly embedded joke here for super-nerd fans of the *Matrix* and philosopher Jean Baudrillard: Keanu Reeves is literally presenting a simulacrum of himself within the simulation that is the movie. Meta cyberphilosophy meets comedy in the best way possible.

This Baudrillardian dynamic isn't limited to *Always Be My Maybe*. It extends to the final film in Reeves's time travel action comedy franchise, *Bill & Ted Face the Music* (2020), in which Keanu calls back to several of his earlier roles, at one point mimicking the hand gesture in *The Matrix* (1999) that stops Agent Smith's hail of bullets, and in another responding with John Wick's trademark "Yeah." And of course we shouldn't forget about Reeves's action-figure stuntman Duke Caboom in *Toy Story 4* (2019), who overcomes a crisis of confidence by exclaiming, "Yes, I CAN-ada!" and then makes an impossible motorcycle jump—a sweet nod to the famous bus jump in *Speed*, the motorcycle stunts in the *Matrix* series, and Keanu's own Canadian heritage.

And it's not just his films that Keanu's comedy references. He also spoofs internet myths about himself, like the meme that is constantly making the rounds about Keanu being immortal. Alex Winter's short 2016 film *Anyone Can Quantum*, about a chess match between actor Paul Rudd and physicist Stephen Hawking, starts with narration by the present-day Keanu Reeves backed by a *Matrix*-like musical score. Rudd soon receives e-mails from Keanu's future self seven hundred years in the future, which present-day Keanu finds plausible because "I don't age."

This sort of self-parody, especially the willingness to embrace both silly internet memes and unflattering stereotypes about asshole celebrities, reflects a total lack of pretense and ego on Keanu's part—meaning that his humbleness is a key ingredient in the potion that makes his comedic magic.

Superiority Theory, Incongruity Theory, Disposition Theory, and the *Bill & Ted*-verse

Since comedy is such an amorphous concept, it surprised the hell out of me to discover that there are an entire host of theories of comedy dating back to the fourth century BCE. The very first theory of humor, asking the question of why we laugh, was developed by the ancient Greek philosopher Plato, and his *superiority theory* functions on the notion that we laugh *at* someone because we feel superior to them—ergo, comedy and malice go hand in hand.[1] This is the kind of comedy that relies on schadenfreude, with observers laughing at people because they delight in their misfortune. And there's quite a lot of that in one of Keanu's most beloved comedy franchises, the *Bill & Ted* trilogy. So much of what makes the main characters funny is the fact that these dim-witted goofballs are nothing like what we would perceive ourselves to be, nor do they react the way we would to their incredible journeys through space and time. We laugh at them because they are the joke.

But that doesn't totally explain *Bill & Ted*'s enduring appeal. Schadenfreude-based comedy may have been popular in 1989 when the series began, but today audiences are more sensitive to such punching-down humor. To explain how the series has maintained its comedic appeal all these decades later, we must zoom from ancient Greece and Plato to eighteenth-century Scottish poet-philosopher James Beattie. Beattie proposed the *incongruity theory* of comedy, which posits that something can be funny because it defies our expectations in some way or has within it an inherent contradiction, sometimes in the form of plays on words or sarcasm.[2] Like "What's black and white and read all over? A newspaper." Incongruity theory underlies the comedy of a setup followed by an unexpected punch line, and *Bill & Ted* is brimming with these kinds of jokes. More than that, in the three *Bill & Ted* films we watch a variety of historical figures transposed into time periods that are not theirs, exploring the humor inherent in these incongruities of time and culture. Beattie's theory also extends to gallows humor, where something as grim as death is faced with a surprising lack of seriousness; examples abound in both *Bogus Journey* (1991) and *Face the Music* (2020), as the characters spend extended amounts of time dead and in hell yet find ways to take it in stride, make jokes, and magnanimously maintain their upbeat spirits amid some most gnarly of challenges. In many ways, this is the polar opposite of superiority theory. We are laughing because the characters have ended up being far more noble and pragmatic than we might be in their shoes.

Bill & Ted also reflects a more recent framework for comedy known as *disposition theory*. It was formulated in the 1970s as a direct response to the superiority theory of humor, adding important nuance. Disposition theory proposes that feelings of superiority only trigger a humor response to the extent that we are negatively disposed to the person or group being disparaged. Like, we don't enjoy watching bad things happen to people we like, but we *do* take pleasure in seeing bad things happen to folks we don't like.[3] When it comes to Bill and Ted, we may be laughing at them at first as we watch them bumble their way through their lives. But before long we reach a point in the story where their undeniable charm and sweetness win us over. This is when, disposition theory would argue, the humor of feeling superior should diminish. But we never stop finding the characters funny, because now we're laughing *with* them, in a touching reversal of self-positioning. Thanks to both Reeves's and costar Alex Winter's all-in performances as Bill and Ted—which really flex in *Face the Music* as the two actors play a variety of versions of their original characters—the humor in these films will remain timeless standouts.

The Art of the Deadpan

One of the most popular and widespread comedic theories, first introduced by Lord Shaftesbury in the early eighteenth century, has special relevance to Keanu's *non*-comedy movies. *Relief theory* proposes that humor is a means of releasing pent-up emotions, both positive and negative, through laughter.[4] This is exactly how the most memorable comedic moments in Keanu's high-octane action films tend to function.

For instance, *Speed* spins out funny one-liners on a much faster timer than the bombs of Howard Payne (Dennis Hopper). One of the opening jokes punctures a tense hostage situation, in which a group of office workers are trapped in an elevator rigged to plummet thirty floors: "Is there anything else that'll keep this elevator from falling?" SWAT officer Harry (Jeff Daniels) asks his partner Jack Traven (Reeves). Jack's quippy response is "The basement." And in the harrowing final battle between Jack and bomber Howard Payne, when Payne insists that he'll win because he's smarter, Jack quips, "Yeah, but I'm taller," as he decapitates the would-be mass murderer. I can't even imagine how much more stressful an experience *Speed* would be without these frequent moments of levity, which land perfectly thanks to Keanu's exceptional comedic timing. I also love how there is no punching-down humor in the film either; all of the jokes are situational and humane, and there isn't a racial or misogynistic slur in the entire film. That's rare for an action film—and practically unheard-of for one from the early 1990s.

The same dry humor is also foundational code in the *Matrix* quadrilogy. Most recently, as Neo is being chased by Agent Smith's goons in *The Matrix Resurrections* (2021), an ally asks if he can use his long-dormant powers of flight to escape. The music swells dramatically, Neo bends toward the ground, then reaches skyward . . . and only succeeds in jumping a few feet into the air. "Yeah. That's not happening," he deadpans. Reeves infuses this particularly tense moment with perfect comedic delivery that gives us a brief break from the action to emotionally reset and laugh. But Reeves has been doing this in the *Matrix* franchise since the very first film. Who can forget his wry delivery of "I know kung fu" after hundreds of new skills are uploaded directly into his brain? It's another perfect example of the relief theory of humor at work, giving us a moment to reset and prepare for the higher levels of tension that are sure to come.

And Keanu is an absolute master of this deadpan delivery. There are dozens of examples of it across his entire film catalog of seventy-eight movies to date. And in nearly all of his non-comedy projects there is at least one moment of levity that is so keenly and dryly presented it becomes a standout. With only a handful of exceptions, like nihilistic *The Neon Demon* (2016) and all-around hot mess *The Watcher* (2000), you can pick any Keanu Reeves movie from the filmography at the end of this book and be sure to find a nugget of Keanu comedy gold that's been overlooked by audiences and critics alike.

A King of Comedy

Keanu Reeves's flawless comedic timing is something that's virtually impossible to learn, and I'd argue that it's his strongest skill as an actor—and his most underappreciated. It's what gives him the versatility to embody such an enormous spectrum of roles, while maintaining a total lack of self-importance that allows him to lean right into a good old fashioned dick joke—let me once again plug Reeves's hilarious dark comedy *A Happening of Monumental Proportions*—sometimes for no other reason than because it's really fucking silly. And he is certainly not averse to making himself the butt of the joke.

I haven't reminded you in a while of the fact that Keanu reads all kinds of scripts and chooses his roles carefully out of hundreds that are on the table. Keeping that in mind, Keanu's commitment to silliness and self-deprecation is particularly noteworthy. It's not a choice his movie star contemporaries, or even generations of actors since, have often embraced; most of them let their sense of self-importance and desire to protect their celebrity reputation become more important than really giving themselves over to a role or a good joke. Keanu Reeves is already widely lauded as one of the world's greatest action stars and most romantic of leading men. But it's long overdue for him to be recognized as a king of comedy as well.

18

WHOA. YEAH. DUDE

Keanu Reeves's Art of the Monosyllable

"I AM NOT OF MANY WORDS," Keanu Reeves's Don John says by way of introduction in Kenneth Branagh's *Much Ado About Nothing* (1993). Many commentators apply the same characterization to Reeves the performer as well—often as a criticism. But it's actually a testament to Keanu's expressive face and silent acting ability that he doesn't always need dialogue to get his point across. For instance, in the whopping 169-minute—69, dudes!—runtime of *John Wick: Chapter 4* (2023), Reeves speaks a grand total of only 380 words.[1] Putting this into context: in the publishing world, the industry standard for one page of printed text is about 250 words—meaning all of Wick's dialogue amounts to less than a page and a half.

Whoa, indeed.

Having met Mr. Reeves briefly in person and watched him perform with his band Dogstar, I can confirm his charisma and stage presence are as truly remarkable off-screen as on. And it really would have been something to see him perform onstage in *Hamlet* back in the '90s. (I'll take a closer look at Keanu's music and stage work in chapter 20.) However, since the metric for "serious" acting often rests on a performer's skill at delivering lengthy monologues and explosive lines of dialogue, Reeves's nonverbal talents are regularly overlooked and even denigrated. Zach Galifianakis pokes fun at this particular view of Keanu when interviewing him for the talk show spoof *Between Two Ferns: The Movie* (2019). He asks Reeves, "On a scale of one to a hundred, how many words do you know? [. . .] Do you know fifty words? Do you know seventy-five words? Do you know eighteen words?" Keanu demonstrates zero words with a tired sigh, and Galifianakis moves on.

But a more fitting reference from Keanu's filmography might be to the character of Station in *Bill & Ted's Bogus Journey* (1991). This alien creature, voiced by Frank Welker, is the preeminent scientific genius of the universe, and similar to Groot in the *Guardians of the Galaxy* films, he speaks only his own name. Reeves's Ted "Theodore" Logan refers to him as "the dude who can make one word mean anything"—which could also describe Keanu's own trademark talent. By now the word "whoa" is as much a part of Keanu's signature as his middle-parted shoulder-length hair, his patchy beard, and his minimalist outfits that often include a favorite pair of jeans and boots. From *Bill & Ted*'s "whoas" of shock to *The Matrix*'s "whoa" of wonder as Neo watches Morpheus make an impossible jump, this one word has become an auditory tattoo, one that I can't help but associate with Keanu no matter where I hear it. And filmmakers who work with him have certainly leaned into the word's ubiquity: as Duke Caboom in *Toy Story 4*, Reeves caps the last scene involving the "lost toys" with a "whoa" after Bunny (Jordan Peele) claims to be able to shoot lasers out of his eyes. Like "dude," which peppered Reeves's dialogue throughout the '80s and '90s especially, "whoa" is immediately associated with Keanu Reeves.

But where Reeves is in fact singular in the art of the monosyllable is in the fact that he's possibly the only actor who can make the word "yeah" sound like an entire dictionary depending on the context. Across four films in the *John Wick* franchise, Reeves's "yeahs" run the gamut from resigned to heartbroken, exhausted to frustrated, and furious to absolutely terrifying and you should run away immediately. The result is a powerful minimalism that pairs and contrasts beautifully with the movies' high-octane action.

Similarly, in one of Reeves's less-discussed films, the disturbing legal drama *The Whole Truth* (2016), Keanu has a scene with Gugu Mbatha-Raw where he replies "yeah" several different ways, each holding a unique meaning that we understand solely through his inflection and facial expressions. From despair, to anger, to frustration, to agreement, this exchange is an artful moment within an otherwise prototypical legal drama. It reminds me of the infamous "Fuck" scene from *The Wire* (2002–2008), where detectives McNulty (Dominic West) and Bunk (Wendell Pierce) analyze a crime scene for four full minutes using only variations on the word "fuck" as dialogue, said with every single nuance possible.

Coming from Keanu, even a single monosyllabic utterance can mean so much. In *Generation Um : . . ,* Reeves's John gives a long "umm," as he tries to figure out what to say into a video camera he stole and now uses to help himself process the people and world around him. The movie got its name from this moment, and it's an "umm" that to me reads differently every time I watch the film. Sometimes it's confusion. Another time sadness. The last time I watched this film the sound was filled with loneliness. Keanu is a master of loaded subtext, just through vocal patterns.

Yet some film critics characterize Keanu's monosyllabic deliveries as "vacuous" and empty, devoid of emotion and pathos, and pull out that hateful adjective "stiff," which stalks Reeves like the monster in *It Follows*.[2] Other critics with deeper insight into his work, like Angelica Jade Bastién, instead comment on his "transfixing stillness," and how "Keanu Reeves missed his calling as a silent film actor."[3] These are the analyses that take into account Reeves's extensive stage training and love of Shakespeare, as well as his generosity as a performer that makes space for his costars to shine in tandem. In *They Shouldn't Have Killed His Dog, John Wick* writer Derek Kolstad says, "Keanu and Bob Odenkirk . . . are among the few actors who, when you work with them on a screenplay, they're more in tune with everything that they're *not* saying and doing than what they are. So they don't want *more* dialogue, they want less. They want more character and for it to be truly unspoken."[4]

Keanu's acting MO will never favor the monologue-heavy, award-baiting, often self-centering performances that are the signature of peers such as Robert Downey Jr., Daniel Day-Lewis, and Michael Keaton, who rely on these moments as the core of their portrayals. Even other actors known for their on-screen stoicism, like Clint Eastwood and Tommy Lee Jones, still have their big monologue moments, which end up feeling out of character in the context of all the quiet that came before. Reeves could totally pull off those kinds of monologues if he wanted to. In contrast, actors more in the style of Day-Lewis and Downey would struggle with the on-screen stillness Bastién describes, which Keanu manages effortlessly.

I agree with Bastién that Keanu Reeves would have been right at home working with a silent film great like Buster Keaton or Charlie Chaplin, a performer who understood the power of what was unspoken and used his body and expressive face to communicate accordingly. Each man's physicality and voiceless charisma would have brought out the best in the other. We even have a Buster Keaton–esque moment in *Hardball* (2001), when Reeves's character visits the classroom of the kids he's been coaching at baseball to pay off his gambling debts, hoping to impress their teacher as a responsible businessman. He shows up to the class wearing an ill-fitting suit and too-short trousers, and proceeds to spill his briefcase everywhere. He then makes a big, silly show of gathering himself up, which is endearing to the classroom of children as well as us in the audience.

But as good as Keanu is with such wordless and nearly wordless moments, when I was researching this book and investigating theories of brevity in both science and art, I was surprised to learn that psychologically speaking, fewer words don't necessarily facilitate better understanding. In fact, a 2020 article in *Psychology Today* outlined seven key reasons why brevity can lead to a failure in communication, the main one of which is that it leaves too much open for interpretation, and thus can be used to promote misinformation or even problematic stereotypes.[5] While this article uses political slogans as its examples of "brief expressions," I suddenly understood why there is such a huge gulf between writers like Bastién and me and almost every other film critic. Keanu Reeves's moments of brevity are being weaponized against him, promoting the false narrative that he's a bad actor and reducing him to the stereotype of Valley boy Ted. But to those who resist the easy narratives and stereotyping, Keanu's brevity as a performer can be interpreted in more generous and expansive ways.

This brings us back to the World tarot card that defines this portion of the book—a card of openness and expansion. Where many see nothing in Keanu's monosyllabic moments, others see entire universes. As I process these nuances, a new hypothesis comes into focus: Brevity might not be the best and most effective form of communication generally. But in the specific case of Keanu Reeves, his monosyllables are orchestras, and his silences speak galaxies of emotions. You just have to calibrate yourself to hear and see them.

19

CHICKS DIG SCARS

Complicating Keanu Reeves's Underdog Sports Tales

FROM THE HAMILTON MUSTANGS of *Youngblood* to the Washington Sentinels of *The Replacements*, underdog sports stories have been a recurring theme in Keanu Reeves's movies. It's not surprising; legends of the underdog are popular not just in sports history but in history in general. In fact, a 2005 dissertation by Nadav Goldschmied at the University of South Florida explores the influence of the "underdog effect," outlining the variety of ways humans are prone to root for the person least likely to win.[1]

What's actually fascinating about Keanu Reeves's David-versus-Goliath sports stories is that there are a relatively small number of them, compared to other megastars like Dwayne Johnson who regularly frame their characters as the least likely to win even as they show off superhero physiques and larger-than-life personas from the get-go. Is Reeves himself aware—consciously or subconsciously—that his real-life status as a Hollywood megastar makes him an unlikely candidate to play underdogs, hence how rarely he's done it? It's an interesting choice regardless.

Just as interesting are the nuances of the few underdog sports tales Reeves has chosen to participate in. In this chapter, we'll take a closer look at those stories, which often complicate the all-too-typical narrative of the underdog.

San Dimas Football Rules

It's ironic that a Canadian actor like Keanu Reeves has on several occasions played that most iconically American of roles: the football hero. He plays a star quarterback in *The Brotherhood of Justice* (1986) and *Point Break* (1991), and as we've discussed in previous chapters, the dramatic tension comes from more than his characters being scrappy underdogs. Derek in *Brotherhood of Justice* is a wannabe leader overcompensating for his absent parents, who leads his fellow high school students into vigilantism and violence. And through the lens of Keanu's Indigenous Hawaiian and Asian heritage, undercover FBI agent Johnny Utah in *Point Break* can be seen as owing his mastery of code-switching to his experiences as an underrepresented minority in the upper echelons of college football.

And, of course, in sports films like *Point Break* where Reeves's multiracial identity is in play within the story, it also serves as a tribute to the underappreciated real-life sports stars of Asian and Hawaiian descent. Here in Florida, our local team the Miami Dolphins has a new Hawaiian Samoan quarterback, Tua Tagovailoa, who of course reminded me of Reeves's Shane Falco in *The Replacements* (2000).[2] That film, along with *Hardball* (2001), are later Keanu sports pictures that add interesting complications to Keanu's work in the genre; each film will get its own section later in the chapter.

Blood and Hockey Pucks

But first, before Keanu Reeves's films associated him with American football, he was actually on track to be a real-life professional ice hockey player. And that's how he got his first big-screen film role—albeit a very small one—playing goofy French Canadian hockey player Heaver in director Peter Markle's 1986 film *Youngblood*. Also starring Patrick Swayze and Rob Lowe, the movie follows Dean Youngblood (Lowe), a young farmer from the Midwest who shoots his shot to get on a professional hockey team in Vancouver. While *Youngblood* is a fairly standard sports film, a few things stand out all these decades later. The first is how the alternate options for this group of young men include working on family farms or in mills, mines, and factories: the working-class roots of the sport are extremely evident here, offering a snapshot of life in the 1980s.

Also related to the '80s setting is the specter of the HIV/AIDS crisis and the threat of blood-borne infection, which looms unspoken in the background. The hockey action portrayed in the film is incredibly bloody: in one of Dean's first plays on the ice, he gets smashed in the face by an aggressive foe, leaving a huge wound above his eyebrow; the team doctor sews it without Novocain, giving Dean a prominent facial scar before he's even played a full game. It's disturbing to see the players covered in blood, routinely spitting blood on the ice and each other. Of course, at the time, HIV/AIDS was still widely considered a disease that only affected gay men, so many straight folks were unaware of the threat. In fact, Bill Goldsworthy, an NHL player who retired in 1979, ended up dying of AIDS-related complications in 1995, attributing his infection to years of unprotected sex with women.[3] While there have been no studies on HIV transmission via sports injuries like the ones we see in hockey, it does put a dark edge on these games and this film in particular.

One thing hasn't changed since 1986, though, and that's the level of extreme violence in the sport, which in a horrifying sequence of events leads to Swayze's character, Sutton, getting blindsided and cracking his skull open on the ice. More tragically, Sutton was so close to making a step up in his career that would have offered a much bigger salary and more future security, before the injury that almost ended his life finished off his ice hockey career. While hockey players certainly have more and better padding these days, injuries continue to be as horrific as Sutton's— and veteran hockey players continue to be infamous for not having any of their own teeth left.

Youngblood wouldn't be Reeves's only sports movie in 1986. One of Keanu's next dramas was Paul Lynch's gymnastics drama *Flying* (a.k.a. *Teenage Dream*), in which his character, Tommy, takes a backseat to support the star player. Robin (Olivia D'Abo) was a star gymnast* until the car accident that killed her father and smashed up her knee. As she struggles

---

* Yes, gymnastics is a sport.

to grieve as well as heal and train to get herself back in the game, her mother's abusive new husband makes life a living hell for her. Then her mother also passes, and Robin finds herself almost on her own. Tommy steps in, alongside Robin's best friend Carly (Jessica Steen), to support Robin—who wins the championship after a fabulous floor routine that garners perfect 10s. Shout-out to all the other gals who, like me, tried their damnedest back in the day to replicate Robin's flawless performance. And kudos to Keanu for being willing, even this early in his career, to play roles that demonstrate how to be a most excellent boyfriend and partner. It's rare for someone who was a sports star himself to embrace playing a supporting role in a sports film, and it shows how quickly Keanu demonstrated the ability to break molds with his choices.

Gangs and Gambling Addictions

Reeves plays a messier role as Conor O'Neill in 2001's *Hardball*, a fairly typical sports fable about a down-on-his-luck gambler who finds himself coaching baseball for underserved Black children at the ABLA housing project in Chicago. Based on a nonfiction book by Daniel Coyle, in its original format it's one of many examples of a white savior narrative whereby a benevolent white person comes into a situation to save individuals or communities of color. But by casting a multiracial star like Keanu as Conor and not specifying his on-screen heritage, *Hardball* instead can be read as a story about interracial allyship. The film presents teamwork and sports as a potential escape from not just poverty but also social pressures like gang involvement and gun violence—an important message at the time that today, a couple decades later, is approaching cliché. We have seen these hard-luck-to-championship "inner city" stories a little too much, and while it's mostly done tastefully here, a huge number of plot points in the film really needed a Black writer who could capture the nuances of life in a housing project like ABLA, including the historical roots of exactly how these communities came to be so marginalized in the first place.

Its complicated racial politics aside, *Hardball* is also a tale about gambling addiction and how sports have been weaponized by capitalist greed. The movie opens with the audience learning that Conor isn't just in for several thousand dollars with at least two bookies, he's even taken out bets on his dead father's account to feed his compulsion. It's an even more relevant concern today: as more US states have legalized various forms of betting, especially online, sports betting has become a multibillion-dollar industry and rates of gambling addiction have skyrocketed. While Conor engages in the illegal kind of sports betting, even the legal kind has been reported to cause huge upticks in bankruptcy, depression, and even suicide when bets don't go the gambler's way.[4] Legalization seems to have made the problem worse.

By the end, *Hardball* provides a small reversal of these all-too-common real-life stories. Conor O'Neill has gotten himself out of debt, there's no longer a hit on him, and he has a job as a school sports coach. Unlike other sports tales where the coach saves the players, in *Hardball* they end up saving him—yet another way in which it is not a standard white savior narrative.

Scabs Are Not Heroes

Director Howard Deutch's 2000 film *The Replacements* closes with the Wallflowers' cover of David Bowie's "Heroes," the music swelling as a football team of ragtag, underdog replacement players pulls off a win to take the Washington Sentinels into the playoffs, just in time for the regular players to end their strike. But as heroic as the ending makes these players look, they are actually the villains in the story: they crossed a union picket line to take the striking players' jobs. They're called "scabs" for a reason.

Workers' unions are a fundamental and underappreciated part of the landscape of American history. Some of the earliest unionizing efforts date back to the mid-1800s, when women workers fought for equal pay and much more. In the nearly two centuries since, labor unions have brought modern society things like the five-day workweek, overtime pay, worker's compensation, health benefits, the end of child labor, and humane working conditions. Essentially anything you can think of that would protect an employee from exploitation by business owners has been brought to you by some form of union action.[5] This is why when a union goes on strike, you're not supposed to cross the picket line. The improvements they fight for will likely benefit not only their own immediate working conditions but workers in general, for generations to come.

The Replacements does its best to minimize the importance of union organizing by framing the striking NFL players as greedy millionaires who want to raise the $8 million cap on their salaries. And yeah, in the story it's true. Striking player Martel (Brett Cullen) and his teammates are gaming the system, and their one-dimensional characters do make it all about the rich getting richer for not doing anything extra. In fact, the owner of the Washington Sentinels, Mr. O'Neil (Jack Warden), straight-up says he would rather have "a team of poor nobodies who play to win, not a bunch of bitchy millionaires." The replacement players headed by Reeves's Shane Falco are certainly not getting even close to a proper NFL salary for their four vital games. And they do it all for the love of the game—which is extremely convenient for the NFL owners and investors who only rake in more cash by underpaying men willing to cross a picket line. The film also glosses over the fact that the team's cheerleaders, certainly not millionaires, are also out on strike—why else would head cheerleader Annabelle (Brooke Langton) be auditioning a replacement cheer squad?[6] Worse still, The Replacements even features a scene where Coach McGinty (Gene Hackman) puts glue on a replacement player's hands so he can catch a touchdown. That's not just being a scab, that's straight cheating, which should have disqualified the team altogether.

But thankfully, in real life Keanu Reeves is a Screen Actors Guild member and has a history of honoring labor strikes—which is sadly not always the case for powerful figures in Hollywood. I wrote an early draft of this chapter during the Writers Guild of America (WGA) strike of 2023, during which stories broke about executives hiring scab writers for a variety of projects, such as the long-running General Hospital.[7] Even Keanu's Babes in Toyland costar Drew Barrymore returned to her talk show before caving to WGA pressure to also shut down.[8]

Setting aside its anti-union perspective, The Replacements does have a few redeeming qualities. One is that although it's based on the real-life replacement squad fielded during the 1987 NFL players strike by the team now known as the Washington Commanders—the one that until 2020 was named after a racial slur for Indigenous Americans—the production didn't use a corresponding slur in the movie, renaming the beleaguered team the Sentinels instead. In this respect, at least, The Replacements was twenty years ahead of its time in choosing a more humane and culturally sensitive moniker.

The Replacements also shines when it comes to representation of certain marginalized groups within the NFL. I've already discussed how Reeves's own identity reflects the league's precious few Asian and Indigenous Hawaiian players. But it also highlights other underrepresented groups: deaf players, sumo wrestlers turned 'ballers, and Brits playing American football. Did you know there have only been a handful of hearing-impaired NFL players in its history, including Larry Brown (1969–1976), Bonnie Sloan (1973), Kenny Walker (1991–1992), Flozell Adams (1998–2010), and Derrick Coleman (2013–2018)?[9] In 2022 an amateur sumo wrestler, Hidetora Hanada, played one American football game, proving that even without experience he could absolutely dominate.[10] As of December 2023, Hanada was a defensive lineman for Colorado State on a football scholarship; his player's jersey even features his name in Japanese.[11] And there were six British players in the NFL as of 2023, including Julian Okwara, Efe Obada, David Ojabo, Graham Gano, Jamie Gillan, and Jermaine Eluemunor.[12] Do they smoke on the pitch like Nigel (Rhys Ifans) in Replacements? I hope not.

But there's a more common NFL demographic that The Replacements only hints at, via replacement player Wilkinson (Michael Jace), a convicted felon. This is actually a frighteningly common background for NFL players: there are dozens of them both charged with and convicted of crimes ranging in severity from fraud to sexual assault, domestic violence, and more.[13] That aspect is not funny at all.

On- and Off-Screen Scars

One moment in The Replacements has entered the pantheon of memorable Keanu Reeves quotes. As Shane Falco says to his team just before the end of the big game, "Pain heals. Chicks dig scars. Glory lasts forever."

There is no shortage of scars in this and other sports narratives. But while we're on the topic, let's go back to Keanu Reeves's own massive belly scar from his near-death motorcycle accident in 1988, which is rarely covered up in his films. In fact, we see it prominently in many of his movies, including Hardball and The Replacements. In Brennan Moline's insightful

"Keanu Reeves' Body as a Battleground," Moline has fascinating ideas about how Keanu's real-life scar informs his fictional characters, bringing an inherent Keanu-ness to his roles that adds to his unique charm as a performer.[14] The belly scar is so Keanu that in *Bill & Ted's Bogus Journey* (1991), the production team even included it on the prosthetic belly of the Evil Ted robot, and the animators of *A Scanner Darkly* (2006) made sure to include it on Reeves's rotoscoped body.

As I was rewatching Reeves's entire catalog while writing this book, I noticed something striking: The first time we see his abdomen in a movie is 1988's *The Prince of Pennsylvania*, and it is scar free. When we see his abs again a year later in 1989's *Parenthood*, Reeves has a fierce, red, and raw scar that runs from the middle of his chest to past his underwear line. It looks angry as hell and really brings home how bad that real-life accident must have been. And in keeping with Moline's insights, Keanu's scar lends dimension to his character, since Tod himself is a drag racer and motorcycle rider who could gotten the scar in much the same way as the actor who plays him. Toward the end of *Parenthood*, Tod even gets into a horrific accident on-screen, after which he spits in despair, "That's a good job for me. Crash dummy." Here, too, Keanu's real-life accident adds weight to the on-screen drama—while also feeding into the persistent myth that Keanu is not a talented actor and performer but simply playing himself.

In the present day, however, it's not just the belly scar that defines Keanu Reeves's particular brand of physicality. The now-veteran actor has fresh scars, the provenances of which I'm unsure about, though some of them are probably also related to motorcycle riding or martial arts training. In *Bill & Ted Face the Music* (2020), the thing that surprised me the most about seeing a clean-shaven Keanu for the first time in years was just how many scars now line his face. What has baby-face Ted been doing within the story to get all those scars? Jackassery, most likely. This takes Moline's theory about Reeves's physicality to an even deeper place, where Keanu's own body is creating backstories for his characters that never need to be explained on-screen. Seeing the scars is more than enough. Where many of his peers would plastic surgery their scars away to maintain an unblemished image of themselves, Keanu Reeves embraces his own humanity by leaving his scars intact. And yeah, it's not just chicks who dig them.

Stuntmen and Swedish Dicks

Another way that Keanu is committed to the physical reality that other stars work hard to conceal is in his affection for the stuntpeople who risk their own bodies to make his sports and action films look real and exciting. Since Keanu himself has been well known for doing many of his own stunts since the late 1990s, it's unsurprising that he feels a connection to the colleagues who've made it their career,* and it was probably only a matter of time before Reeves played a stuntman himself: Tex, the late partner of stuntman turned PI Ingmar (Peter Stormare) in the crime comedy series *Swedish Dicks* (2016–2018).

Real-life stuntman Chad Stahelski first met Keanu as his stunt double on *The Matrix* (1999), and the two became friends and longtime collaborators. Stahelski worked with Reeves on the three subsequent *Matrix* films, as well as *The Replacements* and *The Gift* in 2000 and *Constantine* in 2005. That same year, he was even Keanu's stunt double in the non-action drama *Thumbsucker*. When Keanu made his directorial debut with *The Man of Tai Chi* in 2013, he brought Stahelski aboard as the movie's martial arts choreographer, and after Reeves brought him the screenplay for *John Wick* to get his advice, Stahelski ended up directing Keanu in all four films in the franchise.[15]

Weirdly, on the day I started diving into Stahelski's on-set history with Reeves, news broke that Stahelski has been lobbying the Academy Awards for a category honoring stunt performers, telling *Variety* that these discussions had made "made real movement forward to making this happen."[16] This is welcome news, since in many ways it feels like few folks in Hollywood take the work of stuntpeople as seriously as it should be taken, given the huge risks they take with their bodies and lives. Few, that is, other than Keanu Reeves. On *John Wick: Chapter 4* (2023), not only did Reeves hand out personalized T-shirts to the film's dozens of stunt performers that noted how many times each performer had been killed on-screen, but he also presented his four-person stunt crew with personalized Rolexes to thank them for their hard work.[17] This wasn't the

---

* One of those people, believe it or not, is *Jackass* frontman Johnny Knoxville, who doubled for Keanu on *Bram Stoker's Dracula* (1992).

first time either. Notably, Reeves gifted Harley-Davidsons to the stunt crew of *The Matrix Reloaded* (2003) back in the day, for all their tireless help making the actors on-screen look awesome.[18] These are just a few of the ways that Keanu has shown his appreciation for the *real* athletic underdogs of Hollywood.

20

SOMEWHERE BETWEEN
THE POWER LINES
AND PALM TREES

Keanu Reeves Transcending
the Silver Screen

As OPEN ENDED AND HARD to define as the notion of creativity might be, there is a wealth of sociocultural analysis about its origins and key components as they're reflected not just in the arts but also in scientific and other technical fields that demand out-of-the-box thinking to produce new concepts, theories, or even concrete products. In the second edition of the *Encyclopedia of Creativity*, a marvelously enormous tome that gets into the nitty-gritty of what defines creativity across fields, one particular chapter stood out to me in relation to Keanu Reeves's creative output: R. J. Sternberg and J. C. Kaufman's "Intelligence (as Related to Creativity)," which emphasizes the important ways that intellectual abilities contribute to creativity, giving rise to the "synthetic ability" that enables a person to see things in a new way and recombine them into valuable new ideas.[1]

Why focus on this chapter in the encyclopedia out of dozens? Mainly because all these decades into Keanu's career, a mistaken reputation continues to follow Reeves that he's somehow not intelligent. For instance, in a 2023 *Wired* interview about *John Wick: Chapter 4*, the interviewer was legitimately shocked to discover that Keanu has well-informed and articulate opinions about advances in AI and corporate greed.[2] Through Sternberg and Kaufman's lens, the intelligence of an extraordinarily creative soul like Keanu shouldn't come as a surprise. And, on the other hand, it should be just as unsurprising that an artist as thoughtful as Keanu doesn't limit his artistic outputs to only acting on-screen. The fact that he's achieved a great deal of success in these off-screen ventures is telling in and of itself—even though I often worry that the man doesn't get enough sleep.

Theater

Reeves didn't get the acting bug from movies to begin with; he got it from performing onstage. He was in a production of Arthur Miller's *The Crucible* when he was in high school,[3] and early in his career he was drawn to theater in a huge way, culminating in a professional production of the homoerotic thriller *Wolfboy* in 1984, which began shaping him into the queer icon he is today. Even after he became a star, the stage continued to beckon: in 1995, Reeves turned down 20th Century Fox's offer to reprise the role of Jack Traven in *Speed 2* to star in *Hamlet* at the Manitoba Theatre Centre in Winnipeg—which landed him on a Fox blacklist that lasted for more than a decade, before his bankability as a star overrode the studio's resentment and he was cast in *The Day the Earth Stood Still* (2008).[4] Truthfully, it's a choice a lot of us would've made after seeing the script for *Speed 2*, with its unlikely plot of a cruise liner that can't slow down.

For those of us who have never had the chance to see Keanu onstage, *Playbill* reported in August 2024 that Keanu and his *Bill & Ted* and *Freaked* costar Alex Winter would be headlining a Broadway production of the Samuel Beckett stage classic *Waiting For Godot* for the 2025–2026 season.[5] A most excellent development.

Dogstar

It's not just theater that draws Keanu Reeves to the stage. During the 1990s, Keanu traveled with the band Dogstar as their bass player; they even opened for David Bowie in 1995. Cofounded by Reeves and pianist turned drummer Rob Mailhouse, and featuring Bret Domrose on lead vocals and guitar, the rock band appears in two films: the satirical Hollywood exposé *Ellie Parker* (2005) and the unlikely-female-friendship motorcycle road trip drama *Me and Will* (1999). Dogstar earned a certain amount of commercial success with their EP *Quattro Formaggi* (1996) and albums *Our Little Visionary* (1996) and *Happy Ending* (2000), but unfortunately not enough to break into the charts before the group disbanded in 2002. In 2023 the band reunited onstage for the first time in over two decades to perform at the BottleRock Napa Valley festival, garnering great reviews and announcing plans for an upcoming album. Their US and Japan reunion tour later that year sold out almost immediately.

Keanu Reeves isn't the only one in the band with a broad creative spirit. Mailhouse is a gifted actor himself, having starred, for example, in the iconic *Seinfeld* episode "The Beard" (1995) as Elaine's gay love interest, Robert, who she attempts—and fails—to turn straight. (This moment is in fact echoed in *Ellie Parker*, as Naomi Watts's Ellie sleeps with Chris, played by Scott Coffey, only for him to reveal the encounter made him realize he's gay.) Mailhouse is also the infamous businessman in the harrowing elevator scene in *Speed* (1994), uttering the terrifyingly hilarious line "Jesus. Bob, which button did you push?" after the elevator plummets several stories and lurches to a stop. During an interview with Dogstar on *The Allison Hagendorf Show*, we learned that Mailhouse's creative talents extend to the kitchen, where he chefs it up regularly and keeps himself on his toes with cooking classes.[6]

Lead singer Bret Domrose is no creative slouch either, as he writes Dogstar's music and lyrics and plays a variety of different guitars. During Allison Hagendorf's interview, Domrose discussed the huge number of instruments he experimented with as he helped create the rich sound of Dogstar's new album, *Somewhere Between the Power Lines and Palm Trees*, which was released in October 2023. And in the years Dogstar was on hiatus, Domrose shifted gears into composing music for film and television, and even ended up with an original song, "Second Chance," on the soundtrack for Keanu's film *The Replacements* (2000). He also has an amusing moment in *Ellie Parker* where he goes home with Ellie's best friend—who had been trying to land Keanu in their earlier scenes together.

As a fan of the band since the '90s, I finally had my opportunity to see them perform, once in Denver during the initial reunion tour in 2023 and twice in Northern California during their 2024 Summer Vacation Tour. Their individual creative energy and group synergy were undeniable, as was Keanu's pure joy onstage. Makes me wonder why they ever broke up to begin with.

ARCH Motorcycles

A lifelong motorcycle aficionado, in 2011 Reeves cofounded ARCH Motorcycles with Gard Hollinger. The company creates bespoke machines, marrying Keanu's design sense and his personal love for riding bikes. Like another iconic motorcycle brand, Harley-Davidson, ARCH bikes are made in the USA, which is a welcome change from all the outsourcing that happens with so many other automotive vehicles in the country.

My personal experience with motorcycles is limited to this one time that I was roofied at a rave in Goa, India, my senior year of high school, the winter of 1996. I was about to get into a taxi back to the hotel, an act that would have surely resulted in me being eventually found dead in a rice paddy, if I was found at all. But a gallant and sober friend strapped me to his back on his dirt bike and got me to my room safely. As I was in and out of consciousness on the rumbling bike, the only thing I remember is a feeling of absolute terror as the landscape rushed past my face. I've never been on a motorcycle again. So reading reviews of ARCH's products has been a fun exercise in imagination. For example, the *Robb Report* calls their second "café-racer-inspired" motorcycle a "chortling brute that's light on its feet," a description so intriguing it almost makes me want to try riding one.[7] Almost. Bike EXIF calls ARCH's KRGT-1 "bonkers" in a good way, somehow without that term referring to its $128,000 price tag.[8]

While these bikes are certainly not for folks in lower income brackets— they seem to start at around $85,000 for a non-custom motorcycle—the reviews suggest that they're safe and sturdy products, which is definitely not something to scoff at when we take into account how devastating motorcycle accidents can be. I mean, just ask Keanu Reeves himself how he got that scar on his abdomen.

To see Reeves himself riding one of his company's creations, look no further than the 2018 Super Bowl ad for Squarespace that has Keanu doing some decidedly Duke Caboom–esque stunts on an ARCH bike.[9]

In 2022 ARCH announced they are also considering designing an electric bike, which would just be cool, really.[10] It's clear that the company isn't just a vanity project for Reeves. It's a passion project. It obviously means enough to him that longtime collaborator Lana Wachowski inserted a cute nod to Keanu's company into *The Matrix Resurrections* (2021), in which Trinity has her own motorcycle shop where she customizes bikes, seemingly for other women riders. How can anyone forget Trinity's most epic of motorcycle chases in *Matrix Reloaded* (2003)? That narrative thread into Keanu Reeves's own life and side business is beautiful in a most cyberpunk way.

Publishing

Over the course of his life as a public figure, Reeves has made no secret of his great love of reading. It's how the actor, who famously never finished high school, developed the wide breadth of knowledge that *Wired* interviewer found so astonishing. So it makes perfect sense that Reeves would also dabble in publishing, alongside his life partner, artist Alexandra Grant. Their first collaboration, 2001's *Ode to Happiness*, is a darkly funny commentary on the challenges of adulthood, with text written by Reeves and artwork and lettering by Grant. Marketed as "a grown-up's picture book, a charming reminder not to take oneself too seriously,"[11] *Ode to Happiness*'s text includes lines like "I draw a hot sorrow bath" and "I wash my hair with regret shampoo."[12] This limited print run sold out almost instantly, and one of the only copies now available for sale on Amazon.com goes for the bargain price of $3,999.99.[13] And Keanu's second collaboration with Grant, 2016's *Shadows*, is a collection of poems and photographs of Reeves's silhouette in negative, which also sold out immediately and remains out of print.[14] Most recently, in 2017, Reeves and

Grant founded their own publishing company, X Artists' Books, which produces high-end art books.[15]

As publishing has been going well for Reeves, he's now expanded into graphic novels. In 2021 he cowrote his first comic, *BRZRKR*, an ultraviolent tale of Unute, or B, a godlike "child of lightning" who is used by modern governments as an unkillable mercenary but begins grappling with his past deeds as guilt propels him toward redemption. This *John Wick*–esque tale with more ancient twists and ancestral evils is written by Reeves and Matt Kindt, with art by Ron Garney and color by Bill Crabtree. There are also plans for a film adaptation, with Keanu himself set to star as B.

Also set in the *BRZRKR* universe is 2024's *The Book of Elsewhere*, Keanu's hauntingly beautiful novel collaboration with "weird fiction" author China Miéville. *Elsewhere* dives deep into Unute's eighty-thousand-year history, telling his story from the perspective of family, lovers, and victims. What struck me most about this novel is its focus on themes that also run through Keanu's *John Wick* and *Matrix* films: isolation and loneliness as forces that drive characters to seek connection or annihilation—or both. The novel also focuses on questions of mortality, as we witness the immortal Unute's deep desire for death. And as Unute makes his way through centuries of changes on earth, *Elsewhere* features descents into hell both literal and metaphorical, like much of Keanu's on-screen work. While extremely gory and often veering into intense grotesqueries, B's story is heartbreaking, and when it's eventually put to screen with Reeves in the starring role, I suspect it will end up being an unexpected tearjerker. Meanwhile, the success of Keanu's first novel makes me hope he writes more, in or out of the *BRZRKR* universe.

Video Games

And while it's still experienced on a screen, we shouldn't overlook Keanu's first appearance in an original video game property: in 2020 he voiced and provided motion capture for cybernetic mercenary Johnny Silverhand in *Cyberpunk 2077*. (His only previous video game work was nearly twenty years earlier, when he voiced the character of Neo in the 2003 *Matrix* tie-in game *Enter the Matrix*.) While the dystopian hellscape of Silverhand's future world certainly draws a great deal of inspiration from Reeves's own catalog, especially *Johnny Mnemonic* and *The Matrix*, the blockbuster game provided an entirely new realm of cyberspace for Keanu to occupy.

Cyberpunk has also opened the door for a great deal of academic theory around the ideas of posthumanism, transhumanism, and how the digital avatars that represent players inside a video game are socially constructed, not just personally created by players.[16] Michał Kłosiński's "Ghosts and Mirrors: Devourment by the Other in *Cyberpunk 2077*" unpacks how the game allows players to virtually experience social and cultural otherness through its dramatization of psychosis, while Alice Fox's "The (Possible) Future of Cyborg Healthcare: Depictions of Disability in *Cyberpunk 2077*" discusses how the game helps to normalize disability.[17] Fox points out that real-life humans with disabilities are often stigmatized socially and culturally, while characters with comparable disabilities are almost deified in *Cyberpunk*. In this way, Fox notes, the game offers a rough blueprint for mainstreaming disabilities in the real world.

As usual, it's not *just* a video game, it's become its own kind of organism, thanks at least in part to Keanu's role in drawing critical attention to the work.

Whiskey

"For relaxing times, make it Suntory time," intones Bill Murray's self-referential character, aging movie star Bob Harris, in *Lost in Translation* (2003). It's a moment of art imitating life in another way as well, as real-life celebrities from Sammy Davis Jr. to Matt Dillon have been doing ads for the luxury Japanese whiskey from the House of Suntory for decades. And while many of Keanu Reeves's side hustles are unconventional for Hollywood superstars, in this respect he follows the crowd, having been a Suntory spokesman since the days of *Point Break* (1991). (This is yet another way that Reeves is an invisible presence hanging over *Lost in Translation*, in addition to serving as the imaginary costar of Anna Faris's starlet character Kelly, who gushes about working with him.)

When Suntory celebrated its one-hundred-year anniversary in 2023, it released a short film by *Translation* director Sofia Coppola that includes a collage of previous Suntory ads and celebrity endorsements, and new footage starring Keanu himself.[18] Though Reeves joins a long line of celebrities who have endorsed their favorite liquors, he hasn't followed the lead of those like his costars Sarah Jessica Parker (*Life Under Water*) and Dan Aykroyd (*Feeling Minnesota*) who've created their own liquor brands. At least, not yet.

Synthetic Ability

Even as Keanu Reeves works to transcend his illustrious reputation on the silver screen, he's become a human conduit for metatextuality as these outside pursuits tend to follow him back into his on-screen roles. From riding motorcycles (*The Matrix, Chain Reaction, To the Bone*), to playing bass and other instruments (*Permanent Record*, the *Bill & Ted* franchise, the *Matrix* films), to appearing onstage in a theater production (*Henry's Crime*), and even to John Wick drinking a handle of Suntory in *Chapter 4*,[19] Reeves shows us the breadth and depth of his extensive creative talents as they extend through the screen and beyond.

Ultimately these off-screen ventures provide concrete examples of Keanu Reeves's "synthetic ability," his capacity for expressing himself creatively in a myriad of ways. His high level of accomplishment across so many different fields defies the common misconception that he's a cheerful dolt who somehow lucked into being good at movie stardom. This misconception is probably enabled by the fact that many of Keanu's other creative ventures aren't necessarily accessible to the greater public in the way his movies are. But that same lack of accessibility likely provides the necessary buffer for a superstar like Reeves to do other things he loves, without the risk that the public's overwhelming attention might cloud or complicate these more intimate examples of his creative expression.

21

DUST IN THE WIND

The Imaginary Philosophies
of Keanu Reeves

"THE ONLY STARS THAT MATTER are the ones you look at when you dream," the heightened Keanu-playing-Keanu version of the actor intones in the rom-com *Always Be My Maybe* (2019), fueling a starstruck fan's ardor while admonishing her at the same time. This tongue-in-cheek Keanu Squared reflects the real-life Reeves's reputation among fans as something of a beloved Zen master. Thanks to his spiritually and philosophically minded characters and films, from Ted "Theodore" Logan's messages of "Be excellent to each other" and "All we are is dust in the wind, dude" to *The Matrix*'s multitude of metaphysical concepts (literally millions of words have been written both online and in print that explore the philosophy of the *Matrix* franchise),[1] Keanu has attained a Buddha-like status. Which is funny, because he actually played the Enlightened One in Bernardo Bertolucci's *Little Buddha* (1993).

But his reputation also derives from the endless supply of *fake* quotes attributed to Keanu online and in print, including plenty of pithy neo-Buddhist (see what I did there?) sound bites. I discussed this phenomenon in chapter 12, so this is just a quick reminder of the many well-known statements like "You're a badass with a heart of an angel" that I've found no evidence anywhere Keanu actually said. And since books like Chris Barsanti's *What Would Keanu Do?* and James King's *Be More Keanu* don't cite any of their sources, it's impossible to trace where these fake quotes originated. But what's bizarre about these books and websites spreading fake information about our favorite guy is that they actively overlook the considerable advice for living actually uttered by Reeves in many of his less-talked-about films. So let's dive into those.

Are you in a comfortable seated position?

Deep breath in through your nose. Long slow breath out through your mouth.

Ready? Let's feast.

On Trauma, Grief, and Healing

Written and directed by Marti Noxon based on her own experiences struggling with an eating disorder, *To the Bone* (2017) was met with a world of controversy, with mental health professionals and those recovering from this illness pointing out the ways it glamorizes anorexia.[2] While those are legitimate criticisms of the film, one aspect of *To the Bone* resonates with both truth and insight: the counseling sessions with Keanu's Dr. Beckham, affectionately known by his patients as Dr. Beck. As someone who has gone through intensive trauma therapy myself, I find that Dr. Beck's sessions ring very true, and he doles out some actionable advice not just for folks with eating disorders. His wisdom bombs include:

- "Fault and blame have no place here, only how you wanna live moving forward. Who you wanna be."
- "Bad things are going to happen. That's not negotiable. What is, is how you deal with it."
- "Yeah, that's bullshit. That voice that says you can't. Every time you hear that voice I want you to tell it to fuck off: *Fuck off, voice!*"

Many of us struggle with this kind of doubt, what RuPaul on *Drag Race* memorably calls the "inner saboteur." Dr. Beck's advice provides the perfect solution: you need to tell that self-sabotaging voice to fuck right off.

Later, when Dr. Beck's patient Ellen/Eli (Lily Collins) complains about therapy and healing in general, saying "I just don't see the point," he replies:

> There is no point. Or at least big picture, we don't get to know what it is. [. . .] I can't reassure you. This idea you have that there's a way to be safe, it's childish and cowardly. It stops you from experiencing anything, including anything good. [. . .] Stop waiting for life to be easy. Stop hoping for somebody to save you. You don't need another person lying to you.

He ends with the kicker that a lot of people don't want to hear: "Face some hard facts and you could have an incredible life."

Some of these are lines I've heard in my own therapy sessions long before I saw this movie, and they are certainly words to heal by. Because so much of therapy is hearing things you don't want to hear. That many of us are waiting for someone to give us the solution to our own problems, hoping that someone else will save us, when ultimately we are the only ones with the power to make choices to save ourselves and change our reality from wounded to healing.

Similarly, in Mike Mills's *Thumbsucker* (2005), Reeves plays orthodontist Perry Lyman, who has a fascination with Eastern philosophy that he brings into his practice. When faced with teenage patient Justin (Lou Taylor Pucci) and his thumb-sucking problem that's messing up his life in a variety of ways, Dr. Lyman takes it upon himself to help, explaining to Justin, "All of us carry a certain weight. A weight we don't recognize. Some of us have heavy loads. [. . .] A force from inside. We don't know its name, but it makes us do things. Things we don't like to admit." After a hypnosis session that makes Justin's thumb taste like echinacea, Justin goes into a psychological free fall until he finally addresses the roots of his compulsion and makes peace with his strange parents. By the close of *Thumbsucker*, we find out Dr. Lyman has been on a corresponding journey of his own that began out of guilt and ends with him saying, "I've rewritten my whole philosophy of life. Found new answers to my questions. [. . .] There's no try, there's only do." Though he apparently borrowed part of his new philosophy from Yoda, it's actually good advice. There's a huge difference between attempting and actually doing something, and if you want real change you have to make concrete steps toward your goals, not just say you're going to.

And what's extraordinary about Keanu's character is that he learns. Adults often act like they are static beings, with fossilized personalities. But Dr. Lyman shows that adults have as much capacity for change, development, and growth as kids. It just takes adults more work. Dr. Lyman's ultimate conclusion is "The trick is living without an answer. I think." We can see this same wisdom in what Reeves says as Siddhartha in *Little Buddha* as he begins his path to enlightenment: "To learn is to change." And even in *Swedish Dicks* (2016–2018) when Reeves's Tex Johnson says, "We all have to find our place in the universe."

And in healer roles like Dr. Lyman and Dr. Beck, Reeves also harks back to his teen suicide drama *Permanent Record* (1988) and the song lyrics his character, Chris, writes about the trauma of his friend's suicide, beginning with the lines "Your friends may lie / The truth can come from strangers." If ever there was an endorsement for therapy in ten words, this is it. Oftentimes an outsider perspective is exactly what we need to heal, and Drs. Beck and Lyman both attest to it.

But Tex from *Swedish Dicks* offers an important counterpoint, telling his former stunt partner Ingmar (Peter Stormare), "Being in here [in prison] makes you think of what's important in life. Friends are important." After the COVID-19 pandemic and, for many people, years of social isolation, folks have been reminded of the importance of community—not just online but in person. This is what Tex is talking about when he says that friends are important. And when Tex's buddy Axel (Johan Glans) is about to get hitched, Tex offers advice as a man who's been married a whopping six times: "Listen. [. . .] Listen to your wife." Why isn't *this* a Keanu statement that's gone viral? It's arguably the best advice any heterosexual man can get. Instead of making up silly fake quotes from Keanu, put this one in memes and on T-shirts.

On Spirituality

As Sage the sage in *The SpongeBob Movie: Sponge on the Run* (2020), Keanu is a floating head inside a ball of tumbleweed—and a surprisingly insightful fount of spiritual wisdom. Sage drops nuggets like "Beware, young seekers. All is distortion," and "The coin was just a symbol. The courage you seek is inside you, not in the coin. And it will come to you in your hour of need." What's true about therapy is true about spiritual growth as well: more often than not we already have the answers that we are looking for, we just don't like those answers and want someone to give us different ones. We grow by accepting even the things we don't want to hear.

But what's remarkable about Sage is that even though he's supposed to be an enlightened spiritual adviser, we see him actively grapple with very human emotions as he deals with the obtuse titular character. At their first meeting, SpongeBob leaps into action prematurely, leaving Sage to shout after him, "I didn't give you your challenge!" Sage breathes deep and reminds himself, "Patience, Sage. Patience." As the story continues, the Zen-adjacent character has moments of pure rage and even toys with the notion of self-harm, telling SpongeBob and his friend Patrick, "Seriously, it's hard enough being stuck in a tumbleweed. [. . .] But dealing with you two makes me want to light myself on fire." Because even the most enlightened of beings will have moments that challenge their inner peace, and watching Sage struggle with these in the form of a Keanu-faced tumbleweed is weirdly poetic and powerful. Everyone gets angry, everyone loses their patience, even spirit guides, even Keanu Reeves.

Years earlier, in 1988's *The Prince of Pennsylvania*, Keanu's Rupert Marshetta gets loaded and waxes philosophical in a way Sage in particular would appreciate. "We, like Socrates, we're not appreciated in our time. [. . .] Well, nobody likes Socrates because he spoke the truth. They made him drink hemlock for it. [. . .] We offend the common rabble with our truth. We are the truth! [. . .] Yuckiness is truth." Rupert is right. Ignoring the difficult and ugly parts of life does not a full life make, and herein lies the essential conflict between Rupert and his overbearing father, who would rather whitewash life and pretend than accept the ugliness in front of him. Growing up means accepting that there is good and bad, and our own role in creating this entire spectrum of experiences in our own lives. Rupert's father cannot reconcile his decisions with the terrible life he has, but by the end Rupert is not going down that same path.

True maturity also means reconciling spirituality and sexuality, as Keanu Reeves's character demonstrates in *The Private Lives of Pippa Lee*

(2009). Chris Nadeau had been on the track to join a Jesuit seminary but was rejected. When asked more about his loss of faith and ongoing obsession with world religions and philosophy, he says, "I just stopped believing God was a mystery you could nail down with one book." There's a beautiful, wordless moment between Chris and Pippa (Robin Wright) after her husband's death that presents the act of orgasm as a prayer, a spiritual release, and even the doorway to a variety of enlightenments. This sort of reconciliation is echoed in *Parenthood* (1989), when Tod (Reeves) learns that his teenage brother-in-law Garry (Joaquin Phoenix) has been compulsively masturbating. Tod sits with him and explains masturbation is perfectly normal, and sexuality isn't something that needs to be kept secret: "I told him, 'That's what little dudes do. We've all done it.'" It's wildly forward thinking for a film that came out in the 1980s. In some communities, it's ahead of its time even now. You can be both a spiritual person and a sexual person—the two are not mutually exclusive—and in fact a healthy dose of both only makes for a more balanced individual.

On Environmental and Social Justice

The collective gospel of Keanu Reeves's career extends beyond the personal to matters of global importance. "I came to save the Earth," says Reeves's alien Klaatu in *The Day the Earth Stood Still* (2008), speaking to the activism that grows increasingly important as climate change escalates. And Alex Winter's environmentalism satire *Freaked* (1993) offers evergreen advice for any kind of activist, when Julie (Megan Ward) says of Keanu's character, "Ortiz taught me to channel my anger for the common good."

The flip side of that attitude is expressed by Bob Arctor (Reeves) in *A Scanner Darkly* (2006), who says, "The most dangerous kind of person is the one who's afraid of his own shadow." It reflects how real-life reactionaries harness people's fear and paranoia to impede social progress—like the right-wing and white nationalist groups who convince people that marginalized communities are to blame for the white man's woes.

Sage from *SpongeBob*, meanwhile, offers a warning about the dangers of capitalism, overconsumption, and greed: "If you aren't careful the Lost City will draw you into her fickle embrace, blind you with her dazzling distractions, and tempt you with her fleeting games of chance. Whatever you do, don't be led astray, don't lose focus, and don't forget why you came here." Though SpongeBob and Patrick's seduction by the roller coasters and pizza of the Lost City of Atlantic City is an absurdist fictional version of this phenomenon, it reflects how easy it is to get sucked into the excesses of consumerism.

Be Like Keanu?

One of Reeves's most beloved characters, John Wick, offers few words of wisdom. In fact, as mentioned in chapter 18, he's a man of few words at all. The kernels of insight to be found within the franchise come from other characters, like *Chapter 4*'s the Harbinger (Clancy Brown), who advises that "a man's ambition should never exceed his worth," and the Marquis (Bill Skarsgård), who warns that "a man without purpose is nothing." Still, the ultimate philosophical message of *John Wick* comes down not to words but to John's own actions, which illustrate the pointlessness of this kind of revenge rampage.

John Wick kills over four hundred people—for what? To die in the end with nothing solved. Nothing won. Nothing gained. His beloved wife is still gone. The High Table rebuilds without him. A new mass murderer will rise through the ranks, plucked from the stolen orphans they traffic across the planet. This isn't an aspirational story. Ultimately, John Wick is no hero. Love was never enough to redeem him. Nor was revenge. Only a peace he would never know. Do not be like John Wick.

Do not be like Keanu Reeves either. Be yourself. Unless you're an asshole. Then, yeah, learn from Keanu. After all, he's the one who said, in response to Stephen Colbert's question about what happens to us after we die, "I know that the ones who love us will miss us."[3]

In the end, maybe what's most compelling about the on-screen philosophies of Keanu Reeves and his characters is how, whether in a block-buster action movie or a little-known indie film, they offer an expansive thoughtfulness that unites fans of all kinds behind messages of hope and affirmation: Be kind to yourself. Heal your traumas. Be good to others. Take care of the planet. Work as a team toward a greater good. Don't be a dick.

And with such a plethora of actual great, thought-provoking quotes to pull from, my hope is that people will stop making up fake ones and putting them in his mouth. Not only is it rude, but it violates Reeves's agency as an actor and a human being. It's seriously uncool. With that, as Reeves's character says to SpongeBob at the culmination of their quest: "Sage out."

22

PRESENTING A UNIFIED CRITICAL REEVES THEORY

Keanu Is a Cinematic Treasure

"THIS ROAD WILL NEVER END," Keanu's costar River Phoenix says as Mike Waters in *My Own Private Idaho* (1991). "It probably goes all around the world." Twenty-two chapters later, and this line effectively sums up Keanu Reeves's social and cultural impact—how his art and creativity have left indelible marks on art and society across the globe.

To help identify those imprints, the previous chapters have relied on two important analytical methods. The first is *critical theory*, which attempts to explore the various historical and other conditions that underlie and shape human perceptions, with an ultimate goal of striving for equity. If critical theory does not combat oppression and oppressive practices directly, then its goal is to call them out and present fresh possibilities for a more inclusive world. The second is *critical race theory*, an extension of critical theory that has become a huge part of right-wing scare tactics in recent years. It focuses on the various intersections of race and/or ethnicity and how they shape social inclusion—or exclusion—in order to level the playing field for those most marginalized.[1] Through the book, you've seen how both of these approaches to Keanu Reeves's movies, television series, and other artistic endeavors not only reveal deeper themes within his work but also connect them to underappreciated historical truths and scientific research, from the diversity of early modern Europe to psychological theories of brevity.

In pursuit of a unified Critical Reeves Theory, let's review the major points.

1. Reset Your Preconceived Notions

First, audiences and critics alike need to ditch their preconceived notions of who Keanu Reeves is on-screen to fully grasp the scope of his talents as a performer. Keanu has long been stereotyped as the hapless himbo he portrayed in the *Bill & Ted* franchise, but that's just one of many widely different characters Reeves has played, and reducing all of them to Ted "Theodore" Logan deprives us of the opportunity to engage with everything else Reeves has to offer as an actor.

In fact, let's just put the himbo stereotype to rest right now: Out of seventy-eight movies at the time of writing, Keanu Reeves has only played doofuses in seven of them: *Youngblood* (1986), *The Night Before* (1988), *Parenthood* (1989), *I Love You To Death* (1990), and the three *Bill & Ted* movies (1989, 1991, 2020)—which is a grand total of only 9 percent of his entire catalog. Even though he often gets accused of it, Reeves is categorically not bringing that Valley boy energy into unrelated narratives—in particular when it comes to his period pieces, which become fascinating windows into a variety of historical moments when we consider them in light of his Asian and Indigenous Hawaiian ancestry.

Another common misinterpretation sees Keanu Reeves not as a stereotypical himbo but as nothing at all—a blank slate onto which each viewer can project themselves. Instead, I would encourage viewers to make *themselves* the blank slate, letting go of the stereotypes and assumptions and taking in each Keanu performance on its own terms. It's possible that this new perspective will align with the alternate takes I've presented, especially when it comes to Reeves's most maligned projects.

2. Asian and Indigenous Hawaiian Heritage

Taking into account Keanu's Asian and Indigenous Hawaiian identity is crucial to a full understanding of his work. In movies like *Point Break* (1991) and *Bram Stoker's Dracula* (1992), assuming that Reeves's character shares his heritage allows us to find fascinating parallels with real-life folks of a similar background throughout world history and in the modern world—people who are too seldom discussed in history textbooks or current public discourse. For instance, Reeves playing an Asian/Indigenous sports star brings some vital representation to a small but mighty community of players like Kevin Mawae and John Henry Wise who don't get a lot of recognition.

Yes, this sort of analysis can be complicated when Reeves plays a whitewashed character or a role outside of his own race and ethnicity. But even when he seems to be playing a white character, as in *Street Kings* (2008), the racial possibilities are still important to consider, as many in Asian communities may attempt to pass as white or align themselves with whiteness in a variety of ways. Just look at the many South Asian right-wingers like Vivek Ramaswamy and Nikki Haley who spout racist talking points without even a hint of irony in efforts to ingratiate themselves within white power structures.

And let's not forget the deep dives we did into the ways Reeves serves as a multiracial messiah on-screen, and the variety of issues this brings up—both positive and negative.

3. Challenging Masculinity

Keanu Reeves also constantly plays with masculinity in ways that challenge the stereotypes pushed by most other male action heroes and movie stars. Reeves has never bulked up like other action stars, retaining his distinctive slim physique even as he too does many of his own stunts. And keeping with his lithe frame, when fighting larger opponents Reeves's character will often go into taboo territory by kicking, punching, or even shooting other men in the crotch, below-the-belt behavior that very few of his colleagues would ever do for fear of disturbing their carefully cultivated hypermasculinity.

He also smashes toxic masculine tropes in the number of times he gets beat up or even dies by the end of his action films—and how often he's saved by women, who are treated not as sex objects but three-dimensional characters and equals. Reeves stands against toxic masculinity in real life as well, showing respect to women costars and fans, and he's one of the few Hollywood stars who has not been accused of any sexual misconduct during the #MeToo movement.

Keanu Reeves is also an LGBTQ+ ally, having embraced his status as a queer icon on-screen, while many of his peers have done the opposite out of fear of being considered gay.

4. Ethical Leading Man

Keanu's characters often come into a narrative with a great deal of respect for women. His characters often give the women characters room to express and explore their own sexualities; it's surprising how often Keanu Reeves is topped by his leading ladies. His movies aren't cavalier about age differences, so on-screen romances with age-appropriate women far outnumber those with much younger women. And when there is a huge age discrepancy, with only three exceptions (*Replicas*, *47 Ronin*, and *Bill & Ted Face the Music*), there is a plot-based reason, often one that speaks to the imbalance of power in these kinds of relationships. Unlike the films of many popular leading men, which normalize or even glorify the "older male lead and much younger love interest" dynamic, Keanu's movies tend to highlight the phenomenon's violence and toxicity.

Reeves has also never been shy about being the younger man, and in these roles he challenges the notion that middle-aged women aren't attractive or sexy, giving ageism a nice middle finger in half a dozen projects. Reeves also defies Hollywood's presumption that love stories should center on white people by default; simply by playing a romantic lead as a multiracial Asian/Indigenous man, he provides groundbreaking representation for these communities. Further, in a significant number of his narratives, he doesn't end up with the girl or has no love interest at all, smashing expectations for an actor with his good looks and charm.

However, while all of this is awesome, Reeves has never had a Black or curvy love interest, and the only darker-complected love interest in his career was the inimitable Sarita Choudhury in *Generation Um . . . .* Keanu Reeves's romantic characters might be groundbreaking for many reasons, but he hasn't yet broken out of Hollywood's anti-Black and fatphobic paradigms. He still has time, though, and I hold out hope.

5. Archetypes and Recurring Themes

Another key aspect that makes Keanu Reeves such a globally appreciated performer are the recurring themes in his work that in many ways are archetypal and universal. For example, Reeves's regular journeys into hell and other underworlds, both metaphorical and actual, resonate with audiences everywhere. So too does a particular emotional hell that serves as a narrative thread throughout his filmography: the theme of difficult father relationships.

But amid the familiar paradigms, Reeves is also drawn to out-of-the-box narratives that challenge the status quo, like the staggering number of anti-copaganda narratives in his catalog. Especially for an action star, the prevalence of cop-critical stories is a major thing that sets him apart from colleagues who have made their careers on stories glorifying the police and state-sponsored violence in general.

Since the start of his career in the mid-1980s, Reeves has chosen projects that spotlight the ongoing epidemic of gender-based violence, never shying away from portraying the horrors of rape, domestic violence, child abuse, and the like. Also since the mid-'80s, Reeves's films have exposed the myth of the American Dream. These sorts of stories, which Keanu continues to be drawn to even as a superstar who has his personal pick of any role that interests him,* give his work a vital social justice bent that helps both his Hollywood blockbusters and his lesser-known smaller movies stand the test of time. In addition, beginning with *Johnny Mnemonic*

---

* Many of these recurring themes even carry over into films Keanu produces but doesn't star in, like the 2019 drama *Already Gone*, which features an abusive stepfather, a sixteen-year-old boy in love with a twentysomething woman being abused by said stepfather, and eventually a surrogate dad / older brother figure. *Already Gone* also features many visual motifs from Reeves's own films, including stolen cars, an epic foot chase scene, and a moment at a playground when Robinson (Tyler Dean Flores) stands on a huge white-outlined map of the US, just as Reeves does at the beginning of *A Walk in the Clouds* (1995).

in 1995, Reeves has starred in and produced a number of surprisingly pre-scient films about the perils of technology, from advancements in artificial intelligence to the threat of the surveillance state and more. However, the one aspect where Reeves is in unfortunate lockstep with peers is in the way his films help to normalize gun violence—a problem in the USA in particular, where mass shootings and other gun crimes continue to ter-rorize citizens on a daily basis.

But given all the distinctive themes that seem to interest Keanu, you may be able to use this book to predict what kinds of movies he has in the pipeline. They will likely explore the same basic ground represented by the tarot cards of the Emperor, the Devil, and the World.

6. The Keanu Reeves Cinematic Universe

Keanu Reeves is so ubiquitous, with a presence so preternaturally tran-scendent, that his movies often comment on one another and on Keanu himself. This is evident in Reeves's mastery of self-referential comedy, and in the other callbacks and visual echoes that abound throughout his cata-log. When these metatextual moments are viewed together, they outline a Keanu Reeves Cinematic Universe, in which Keanu seems to exist as a pop culture icon even within the fictional universes where he plays a character.

What this means, oddly enough, is that sometimes Keanu's own charac-ters appear to know about Keanu Reeves the actor and the previous movies he's been in. For example, when Ted "Theodore" Logan raises his arm in a "stop" motion in *Bill & Ted Face the Music* (2020), we can read this as Ted being inspired by Neo stopping bullets in *The Matrix* (1999). And when the title character of *John Wick: Chapter 3* (2019) requests, "Guns. Lots of guns," we can interpret it as John also having seen *The Matrix* and mak-ing a rare and nerdy joke. On the other hand, when Reeves's Henry Torne in *Henry's Crime* (2010) says, "No guns, somebody could get hurt," the character could be thinking about Neo's oft-quoted line and the subsequent bloodbaths, which Henry with his tender heart would like to avoid. We can even read Neo's first and most iconic "Whoa" at Morpheus's rooftop jump in the original *Matrix* as in-universe reference to the Valley boy "Whoas" of *Bill & Ted's Excellent Adventure* (1989), which would've been a pop culture staple for a decade at the time of the Matrix's simulated 1999.

This is unlike the way other artists such as David Lynch make use of metatextual moments; they employ Brechtian theatrical principles to highlight the artificiality of drama, deliberately distancing the audience from his art by reminding them that they are spectators rather than participants in the story.[2] But when Keanu's movies break the fourth wall, they instead draw us further into Keanu's cinematic universe with shared moments of recognition. It's not just Keanu who's in on the metatextual jokes—we all are. This serves not just as an implicit acknowledgment that we as the audience are actually here, watching him, but as Keanu's nod of gratitude to us for doing so. It goes a long way toward explaining why so many people feel a kinship with Reeves, not just for his individual roles or generally as an actor, but as a person.

7. The Keanu Reeves School of Minimalist Performance

A Critical Reeves Theory must also highlight how Keanu's performances are often far more nuanced than he's given credit for, including adapting his handedness from role to role. One of his most underappreciated abilities is his ability to convey so much with so few words, which is often mistaken for vacuousness or stiffness.

Critics and viewers are also misled by contradictory aspects of Keanu's public persona. He's considered a role model to young people due to his kindness and chill personality, but at the same time he's been a cigarette smoker for decades both on- and off-screen, and as mentioned earlier in the chapter, his work often normalizes gun violence. In addition, Reeves's reputation as a sort of chill Zen master is completely at odds with his workaholic history. Until the COVID-19 pandemic and actor and writer strikes slowed Hollywood production to a crawl in the early 2020s, Reeves had only six years in his thirty-plus-year career in which he released no films (1987, 1998, 2002, 2004, 2007, 2011) and five years with only one film (1992, 1994, 2009, 2010, 2014), but fourteen years with three or more projects released back-to-back (1986, 1988, 1990, 1991, 1993, 2000, 2003, 2005, 2006, 2016, 2017, 2018, 2019, 2020). If we didn't know he was all too human, we'd think this man was a machine for how hard he works.

8. Critical Thinking and Critical Theory in Action

The notion of a Critical Reeves Theory is a kind of quantum physics, in the same way that I've argued Keanu himself is. On the one hand, it's a tongue-in-cheek term, meant to elicit a nerdy chuckle with the play on words. But on the other hand, the critical theory and critical race theory I've relied on to analyze Reeves's work are very real—and at the moment very contentious. I write from Florida, where the governor has declared a war on these concepts and the reality they reflect: he's instituted a ban on books with "sexualized content" in schools (one that initially included the works of Shakespeare!), rewritten the Black history curriculum to suggest that slavery was beneficial to the enslaved, sought to erase queer people from daily life, criminalized trans folks, and so much more.

My hope is that this book will help to promote the ideas and ideals that people like Florida's governor have tried to bury. It's my version of cultural commentary as social justice activism—a cordial invitation to bring critical thinking and analysis into your everyday life, not just with Keanu Reeves's movies but with all kinds of cultural productions. I hope it inspires you to look past the surface of visual media and unpack the hidden nuances, whether they be overlooked historical and cultural realities, queer subtext, feminist content, or abolitionist ideas. You'll find such nuances in every corner of the culture—but rarely so clearly and consistently as in the work of the incomparable Keanu Reeves. If you were stranded on a desert island with only Keanu's catalog, you'd have plenty to keep your mind occupied for years.

From comedy to drama to action and horror and everything in between, Reeves's extraordinary catalog absolutely stands the test of time—and rewards those who make the effort to appreciate his work more deeply. There's a reason why *Bill & Ted Face the Music* ends with dozens of fan-made videos in which people from all across the globe dance and play along with the long-promised song that will unite the universe.[3] Because Keanu's creative road really does go all around the world. Keanu Reeves himself might not be immortal, but his art certainly is.

FILMOGRAPHY

1984

Hangin' In (TV series): Teen Client

1985

Night Heat (TV series), episodes "Crossfire" and "Necessary Force": Mugger / Thug #1
Letting Go (TV movie): Stereo Teen #1
One Step Away (short): Ron Petrie

1986

Youngblood: Heaver
Act of Vengeance (TV movie): Buddy Martin (as Keannu Reeves)
The Magical World of Disney (TV series), movie *Young Again*: Michael Riley, age seventeen
Flying, a.k.a. *Teenage Dream*: Tommy Warneki
The Brotherhood of Justice: Derek
River's Edge: Matt
Under the Influence (TV movie): Eddie Talbot
Babes in Toyland (TV movie): Jack Fenton / Jack-Be-Nimble

1987

Trying Times (TV series), episode "Moving Day": Joey

1988

The Night Before: Winston Connelly
Permanent Record: Chris Townsend
The Prince of Pennsylvania: Rupert Marshetta
Dangerous Liaisons: Le Chevalier Raphael Danceny

1989

Bill & Ted's Excellent Adventure: Ted "Theodore" Logan
American Playhouse (TV series), short *Life Under Water*: Kip
Parenthood: Tod
The Tracey Ullman Show (TV series), episode "Two Lost Souls": Jesse Walker

1990

I Love You to Death: Marlon
Tune in Tomorrow: Martin Loader
Bill & Ted's Excellent Adventures (TV series), 13 episodes: Ted "Theodore" Logan (voice)

1991

Providence: Eric
Point Break: Johnny Utah
Bill & Ted's Bogus Journey: Ted "Theodore" Logan
My Own Private Idaho: Scott Favor

1992

Bram Stoker's Dracula: Jonathan Harker

1993

Freaked: Ortiz the Dawg Boy (uncredited)
Much Ado About Nothing: Don John

Even Cowgirls Get the Blues: Julian Gitche
Little Buddha: Prince Siddhartha

1994

Speed: Officer Jack Traven

1995

Johnny Mnemonic: Johnny Mnemonic
A Walk in the Clouds: Paul Sutton

1996

Chain Reaction: Eddie Kasalivich
Feeling Minnesota: Jjaks Clayton

1997

The Last Time I Committed Suicide: Harry
The Devil's Advocate: Kevin Lomax

1999

The Matrix: Neo
Action (TV series), episode "Pilot": Keanu Reeves
Me and Will: Himself (Dogstar)

2000

The Replacements: Shane Falco
The Watcher: David Allen Griffin
The Gift: Donnie Barksdale

2001

Sweet November: Nelson Moss
Hardball: Conor O'Neill

2003

The Animatrix, short "Kid's Story": Neo (voice)
The Matrix Reloaded: Neo
Enter the Matrix (video game): Neo (voice)
The Matrix Revolutions: Neo
Something's Gotta Give: Dr. Julian Mercer

2005

Ellie Parker: Himself (Dogstar)
Thumbsucker: Dr. Perry Lyman
Constantine: John Constantine
Echo (short): Narcissus

2006

A Scanner Darkly: Bob Arctor
The Lake House: Alex Wyler
The Great Warming (documentary): Narrator

2008

Street Kings: Detective Tom Ludlow
The Day the Earth Stood Still: Klaatu

2009

The Private Lives of Pippa Lee: Chris Nadeau

2010

Henry's Crime: Henry Torne

2012

Generation Um . . . : John
Side by Side (documentary): Host (also producer)

2013

Man of Tai Chi: Donaka Mark (also director)
47 Ronin: Kai
Extreme Pursuit (short): Mr. D (prequel to *Man of Tai Chi*)

2014

John Wick: John Wick

2015

Knock Knock: Evan Webber (also executive producer)
Interrogations Gone Wrong (TV series), episode "Keanu Reeves Arrested, Interrogated, and Really Pissed Off": Keanu Reeves
Deep Web: The Untold Story of Bitcoin and the Silk Road (documentary): Narrator
Mifune: The Last Samurai (documentary): Narrator

2016

Exposed: Detective Scott Galban (also producer)
Anyone Can Quantum (short): Narrator / Keanu Reeves (voice)
Keanu: Keanu (voice)
The Whole Truth: Richard Ramsay
The Neon Demon: Hank
The Bad Batch: The Dream
Quantum Is Calling (TV short): The One (voice)
The Film Prayer (short): Narrator
Swedish Dicks (TV series), 6 episodes: Tex

2017

To the Bone: Dr. William Beckham
John Wick: Chapter 2: John Wick
A Happening of Monumental Proportions: Bob
SPF-18: Himself
Swedish Dicks (TV series), 2 episodes: Tex

2018

Siberia: Lucas Hill (also producer)
Destination Wedding: Frank
Replicas: William Foster (also producer)
Swedish Dicks (TV series), 5 episodes: Tex

2019

John Wick: Chapter 3—Parabellum: John Wick
Always Be My Maybe: Keanu Reeves
Toy Story 4: Duke Caboom (voice)
Between Two Ferns: The Movie: Keanu Reeves
Already Gone (executive producer)

2020

The SpongeBob Movie: Sponge on the Run: Sage
Bill & Ted Face the Music: Ted "Theodore" Logan
Cyberpunk 2077 (video game): Johnny Silverhand
A World of Calm (TV series), episode "Living Among Trees": Narrator

2021

The Matrix Awakens: An Unreal Engine 5 Experience (video game): Neo
The Matrix Resurrections: Neo / Thomas Anderson

2022

DC League of Super-Pets: Batman

2023

John Wick: Chapter 4: John Wick (also executive producer)
Cyberpunk 2077: Phantom Liberty (video game): Johnny Silverhand

NOTES

1. What's So Great About Keanu? Reeves in the Collective Consciousness

1. Robin Heiminge, "Does Exhaustivity Require Linguistic Processing? An Exhaustive Research" (thesis, University of Groningen Faculty of Science and Engineering, Netherlands, 2020), https://fse.studenttheses.ub.rug.nl/21789/1/Robin_H_Thesis_upload_version.pdf.

2. Janet Weeks, "Film Teacher's Excellent Venture Dissects Work of Keanu Reeves," *Chicago Tribune*, April 2, 1994, https://www.chicagotribune.com/news/ct-xpm-1994-04-02-9404020087-story.html.

3. "About Us," Whoa Is (Not) Me, accessed February 21, 2024, http://www.whoaisnotme.net/about.htm.

4. Larry Fitzmaurice, "Nicolas Winding Refn on the Joys of Vinyl and the Transcendent Keanu Reeves," *Vulture*, June 5, 2015, https://www.vulture.com/2015/06/nicolas-winding-refn-on-keanu-and-crate-digging.html.

5. Angelica Jade Bastién, "The Grace of Keanu Reeves," *Bright Wall/Dark Room*, April 21, 2016, https://www.brightwalldarkroom.com/2016/04/21/the-grace-of-keanu-reeves.

6. Film Crit Hulk, "Keanu Reeves and What We Consider 'Good Acting,'" *Observer*, September 10, 2018, https://observer.com/2018/09/film-crit-hulk-keanu-reeves-and-good-acting.

7. Search results for "Keanu Reeves," *Journal of Celebrity Studies*, accessed February 21, 2024, https://www.tandfonline.com/action/doSearch?AllField=%22Keanu+Reeves%22&SeriesKey=rcel20.

8. Renée Middlemost, "The Incredible, Ageless Reeves: Aging Celebrity, Aging Fans, and Nostalgia," *Celebrity Studies* 13, no. 2 (April 17, 2022): 228–243, https://doi.org/10.1080/19392397.2022.2063404.

9. Renée Middlemost, "Introduction to the Special Issue: Keanu Reeves as Palimpsest," *Journal of Celebrity Studies* 13, no. 2 (2022): 137–142: https://www.tandfonline.com/doi/full/10.1080/19392397.2022.2063394.

10. Tanya Horeck, "'Too Good for This World': Keanu Reeves, God of the Internet," *Celebrity Studies* 13, no. 2 (April 22, 2022): 143–158, https://doi.org/10.1080/19392397.2022.2063395.

11. For background on parasocial relationships, see Yang Xu, Mariek Vanden Abeele, Mingyi Hou, and Marjolijn Antheunis, "Do Parasocial Relationships with Micro- and Mainstream Celebrities Differ? An Empirical Study Testing Four Attributes of the Parasocial Relationship," *Celebrity Studies* 14, no. 3 (2023): 366–386, https://doi.org/10.1080/19392397.2021.2006730.

12. Keanu Reeves Is Immortal, https://www.keanuisimmortal.com/.

13. Justin Curto, "Jacob Tremblay Says He Was 'Harnessing Keanu Reeves' in 'The Matrix' for a 'Good Boys' Scene," *People*, August 15, 2019, https://people.com/movies/jacob-tremblay-keanu-reeves-the-matrix-good-boys.

14. "20 Years of 'The Matrix': 5 Times Bollywood Got Inspired by It," News18, March 31, 2019, https://www.news18.com/news/movies/20-years-of-the-matrix-5-times-bollywood-got-inspired-by-it-2083183.html.

15. Bradley Russell, "The 20 Best Matrix References in Other Movies and TV Shows," *Total Film*, December 21, 2021, https://www.gamesradar.com/best-matrix-references-in-other-movies-shows.

16. Stuart Jeffries, "Žižek, the Matrix and 9/11," Verso Books official blog, October 27, 2021, https://www.versobooks.com/blogs/5180-zizek-the-matrix-and-9-11.

17. Mark Rowlands, "Keanu's Cartesian Meditations," *Think* 3, no. 7 (Summer 2004): 71–75, https://doi.org/10.1017/S1477175600000841; William Irwin, ed., *The Matrix and Philosophy: Welcome to the Desert of the Real* (Chicago: Open Court, 2022).

18. "Connections," *Bill & Ted's Excellent Adventure*, IMDb, accessed March 26, 2024, https://m.imdb.com/title/tt0096928/movieconnections; "Connections," *Bill & Ted's Bogus Journey*, accessed March 26, 2024, https://m.imdb.com/title/tt0101452/movieconnections/.

19. Eric Diaz, "The '80s Pop Culture Easter Eggs in Stranger Things 4," Nerdist, July 6, 2022, https://nerdist.com/article/stranger-things-4-pop-culture-easter-eggs/.

20. Natalie Finn, "These 23 Secrets About *Point Break* Are a Total State of Mind," E! News, July 12, 2021, https://www.eonline.com/news/1287348/these-23 -secrets-about-point-break-are-a-total-state-of-mind.

21. "Christopher Nolan Reveals How 11 Classic Films Inspired 'Dunkirk,'" *IndieWire*, May 25, 2017, https://www.indiewire.com/gallery/dunkirk-christopher-nolan -films-inspired/dunkirk-2017/.

22. Meriah Doty, "The Story Behind Key and Peele's 'Keanu': How the Kitten Got Its Name," *Wrap*, April 29, 2016, https://www.thewrap.com/the -story-behind-key-and-peeles-keanu-how-the-kitten-got-its-name-meriah -doty/; Anna Klassen, "How Keanu Reeves Inspired 'Keanu,'" *Bustle*, April 28, 2016, https://www.bustle.com/articles/157337-how-keanu-reeves -inspired-keanu-according-to-key-peele.

23. Amy Kaufman, "How Filmmakers Got Keanu Reeves to Voice a Cat in 'Keanu,'" *Providence (RI) Journal*, April 28, 2016, https://www .providencejournal.com/story/entertainment/movies/2016/04/29/how -filmmakers-got-keanu-reeves-to-voice-cat-in-keanu/31072069007/.

24. Phil Yu (@angryasianman), "I don't know if this is the best single punch in film history, but this is certainly the best single about a punch in film history," Twitter/X, July 4, 2022, 11:37 AM, https://twitter.com/angryasianman /status/1543997523219529728.

25. Keanu Reeves, Rob Mailhouse, and Bret Domrose, interview by Allison Hagendorf, YouTube, July 21, 2023, https://www.youtube.com/watch?v =LaLpGTtbwlM.

26. Shenja van der Graaf, "Much Ado About Keanu Reeves: The Drama of Ageing in Online Fandom," in *The Ashgate Research Companion to Fan Cultures*, ed. Linda Duits, Koos Zwaan, and Stijn Reijnders (London: Routledge, 2014), available at SSRN, https://papers.ssrn.com/sol3/papers .cfm?abstract_id=2178482.

27. Corridor, "Keanu Reeves Stops A ROBBERY!," YouTube, July 13, 2019, https://www.youtube.com/watch?v=3dBiNGuflJw; Corridor Crew, "How We Faked Keanu Reeves Stopping a Robbery," YouTube, July 14, 2019, https:// www.youtube.com/watch?v=IzEFnbZ0Zd4.

28. Nick Romano, "Keanu Reeves Road Trips with a Bunch of Plane Passengers After Flight Makes Emergency Landing," *Entertainment Weekly*, March 26, 2019, https://ew.com/celebrity/2019/03/26/keanu-reeves-flight-bus-ride/.

29. Michael Shnayerson, "Young and Restless," *Vanity Fair*, August 1995, https://archive.vanityfair.com/article/share/f2cd9db8-0d0a-4ee0-a5e1-deb619442a33.

30. Qasim Hasnain, "John Wick: 10 Hidden Things About The Main Character Everyone Missed," *Screen Rant*, March 3, 2020, https://screenrant.com/john-wick-hidden-details-main-character-missed/; Jennifer Vineyard, "The Matrix's Stunt Coordinators and Choreographers Reveal How the Iconic Fight Scenes Were Made," Syfy, March 25, 2019, https://www.syfy.com/syfy-wire/the-matrixs-stunt-coordinators-and-choreographers-reveal-how-the-iconic-fight-scenes-were.

31. Larissa Zageris and Kitty Curran, *For Your Consideration: Keanu Reeves* (Philadelphia: Quirk, 2019), 52–53.

32. Bastién, "Grace of Keanu Reeves," https://www.brightwalldarkroom.com/2016/04/21/the-grace-of-keanu-reeves/.

2. I Saved Your Life, Bro: Johnny Utah as Shape-Shifter

1. "It's Make or Break" (featurette), *Point Break*, special ed. DVD (20th Century Fox, 2006).

2. Finn, "23 Secrets About *Point Break*," https://www.eonline.com/news/1287348/these-23-secrets-about-point-break-are-a-total-state-of-mind.

3. Natalie Finn, "Keanu Reeves: Patrick Swayze Lived Life, Jumped Out of Planes 'With an Open Heart,'" E! News, September 15, 2009, https://www.eonline.com/news/144403/keanu-reeves-patrick-swayze-lived-life-jumped-out-of-planes-with-an-open-heart.

4. Roger Ebert, review of *Point Break*, *Chicago Sun-Times*, July 12, 1991, https://www.rogerebert.com/reviews/point-break-1991.

5. Richard Corliss, "Cinema: Board Stiff," *Time*, July 22, 1991, https://content.time.com/time/subscriber/article/0,33009,973430,00.html.

6. Owen Gleiberman, review of *Point Break*, *Entertainment Weekly*, July 26, 1991, https://ew.com/article/1991/07/26/point-break-3/.

7. Hal Hinson, review of *Point Break*, *Washington Post*, July 12, 1991, https://www.washingtonpost.com/wp-srv/style/longterm/movies/videos/pointbreak_rhinson_a13f81.htm.

8. Peter Travers, review of *Point Break*, *Rolling Stone*, July 12, 1991, https://www .rollingstone.com/tv-movies/tv-movie-reviews/point-break-248363/.

9. April Wolfe, "Revisiting Hours: 'Point Break' Is the Greatest Female-Gaze Action Movie Ever," *Rolling Stone*, August 31, 2018, https://www.rollingstone .com/movies/movie-features/stream-this-movie-point-break-717570/.

10. Dan Jackson, "14 Reasons 'Point Break' Is Still an Action Masterpiece," Thrillist, December 29, 2015, https://www.thrillist.com/entertainment/nation /point-break-remake-review-point-break-1991-comparison.

11. "Point Break Live!," CELLspace, 2009, http://www.cellspace.org/new /node/125 (site discontinued).

12. Janet Maslin, "Surf's Up for F.B.I. in Bigelow's 'Point Break," *New York Times*, July 12, 1991, https://www.nytimes.com/1991/07/12/movies/review -film-surf-s-up-for-fbi-in-bigelow-s-point-break.html.

13. Bastién, "Grace of Keanu Reeves," https://www.brightwalldarkroom. com/2016/04/21/the-grace-of-keanu-reeves.

14. See, e.g., Marc Shapiro, *Keanu Reeves' Excellent Adventure: An Unauthorized Biography* (Riverdale, NY: Riverdale Avenue, 2020), preface, digital ed.

15. "Kevin Mawae 'Humbled' to Be First Native Hawaiian Inducted into Pro Football Hall of Fame," KHON2, August 4, 2019, https://www.khon2.com /sports/kevin-mawae-humbled-to-be-first-native-hawaiian-inducted-into -pro-football-hall-of-fame/.

16. Catherine Cruz and Sophia McCullough, "The Story of John Henry Wise, the First Native Hawaiian College Football Player in 1892," Hawai'i Public Radio, February 28, 2022, https://www.hawaiipublicradio.org/the -conversation/2022-02-28/the-story-of-john-henry-wise-the-first-native -hawaiian-college-football-player-in-1892.

17. "9 Best NFL Players Born In Hawaii," *Cloud Nine Magazine*, January 31, 2021, https://cloudninemagazine.com/25-best-nfl-players-born-in-hawaii/.

18. Bradley Geiser, "The Most Famous Asian NFL Players of All Time," Sportscasting, November 17, 2019, https://www.sportscasting.com/the-most -famous-asian-nfl-players-of-all-time/ (page discontinued).

19. Farris Gunning, "Asians in the NFL: Why Aren't There More Asians Playing Football?," Bleacher Report, January 6, 2009, https://bleacherreport.com /articles/107693-asians-in-the-nfl-why-arent-there-more-asians-playing -football.

3. Baba Yaga or a Man: A Queer Reading of *John Wick*

1. Sabrina Maddeaux, "Please. John Wick Is the Only Action Movie That Doesn't Compromise," *National Post*, July 25, 2021, https://nationalpost.com /opinion/sabrina-maddeaux-please-john-wick-is-the-only-action-movie -that-doesnt-compromise.

2. Sezin Koehler, "The Real-Life Inspirations Behind Everything in the John Wick Universe," *Looper*, March 20, 2023, https://www.looper.com/243310 /the-real-life-inspirations-behind-everything-in-the-john-wick-universe/.

3. David Fear, "In Praise of 'John Wick,' the Last Great American Action-Movie Franchise," *Rolling Stone*, May 16, 2019, https://www.rollingstone.com/movies /movie-features/john-wick-the-last-great-american-action-movie-franchise -832310/.

4. Angelica Jade Bastién, "Why Keanu Reeves Is Such an Unusual (and Great) Action Star," *Vulture*, February 17, 2017, https://www.vulture.com/2017/02 /keanu-reeves-is-our-greatest-action-star.html.

5. Koehler, "Real-Life Inspirations," https://www.looper.com/243310 /the-real-life-inspirations-behind-everything-in-the-john-wick-universe/.

6. Georgy Manaev, "How John Wick Got Baba Yaga Completely Wrong," *Russia Beyond*, May 31, 2019, https://www.rbth.com/arts/330441-how -john-wick-got-baba-yaga-wrong.

7. Sezin Koehler, "John Wick's Entire Backstory Explained," *Looper*, March 20, 2023, https://www.looper.com/196168/john-wicks-entire-backstory-explained/.

8. Yaron Matras, *I Met Lucky People* (London: Allen Lane, 2014).

9. Lucie Fremlova, *Queer Roma* (Milton Park, Abingdon, Oxon, UK: Routledge, 2022).

10. Madeline Potter (@madeline_cct), "I've not actually seen John Wick yet . . . ," Twitter/X, April 17, 2023, 3:11 PM, https://twitter.com/madeline_cct /status/1648056722198769666.

11. Taisia Kitaiskaia, "Baba Yaga Will Answer Your Questions About Life, Love, and Belonging," Literary Hub, October 28, 2020, https://lithub.com /baba-yaga-will-answer-your-questions-about-life-love-and-belonging/.

12. Marissa Clifford, "The Enduring Allure of Baba Yaga, an Ancient Swamp Witch Who Loves to Eat People," *Vice*, November 3, 2017, https://www.vice

.com/en/article/evbbjj/the-enduring-allure-of-baba-yaga-an-ancient-swamp
-witch-who-loves-to-eat-people.

13. George Pierpoint, "Is 'Bisexual Lighting' a New Cinematic Phenomenon?,"
    BBC, April 21, 2018, https://www.bbc.com/news/entertainment-arts-43765856.

14. Eric Francisco, "'John Wick: Chapter 3': Including a Non-Binary Charac-
    ter Was a 'No-Brainer,'" Inverse, May 18, 2019, https://www.inverse.com
    /article/55839-john-wick-chapter-3-parabellum-asia-kate-dillon-first-non
    -binary-character.

15. Kat Moon, "Rina Sawayama Is Fighting for Inclusion, One Song at a Time,"
    Time, October 13, 2021, https://time.com/6103208/rina-sawayama-next
    -generation-leaders.

16. Ann C. Hall, "John Wick: Keanu Reeves's Epic Adventure," Heroism Sci-
    ence 7, no. 2 (2022): 1–19, https://scholarship.richmond.edu/cgi/viewcontent
    .cgi?article=1049&context=heroism-science.

17. Simon Bacon, "'But Now, Yeah, I'm Thinking I'm Back': The All-Consuming
    Gothic Nostalgia in the John Wick Franchise," in Gothic Nostalgia: The Uses
    of Toxic Memory in 21st Century Popular Culture, ed. Simon Bacon and
    Katarzyna Bronk-Bacon (Cham, Switzerland: Palgrave Macmillan, 2024),
    197–209.

18. Laura Westengard, "Queer Gothic Literature and Culture," in Twentieth-
    Century Gothic: An Edinburgh Companion, ed. Sorcha Ní Fhlainn and Ber-
    nice M. Murphy (Edinburgh: Edinburgh University Press, 2022), 259–260.

19. B. Moline, "Keanu Reeves' Body as Battleground," Celebrity Studies 13, no. 2
    (2022): 185–199, https://doi.org/10.1080/19392397.2022.2063399.

4. Pop Quiz, Hotshot: Re(eves)imagining the Action Hero

1. Edward Gross and Mark A. Altman, They Shouldn't Have Killed His Dog:
   The Complete Uncensored Ass-Kicking Oral History of John Wick, Gun Fu,
   and the New Age of Action (New York: St. Martin's, 2022), 79.

2. James Hibberd, "How a Keanu Reeves Suggestion Saved the Script for
   'Speed,'" Hollywood Reporter, August 29, 2023.

3. Julian Cha, "'There Is No Spoon': Transnationalism and the Coding of
   Race/Ethnicity in the Science-Fiction/Fantasy Cinema of Keanu Reeves,"

Studies in Popular Culture 35, no. 1 (2012): 47–69, http://www.jstor.org/stable/23416365.

4. Rob Mayo, review of *Masculinity in Contemporary Science Fiction Cinema: Cyborgs, Troopers and Other Men of the Future* by Marianne Kac-Vergne, *Foundation* 48, no. 134 (2019): 107–110, https://www.proquest.com/openview/f41171009c7a33952f74025208251084/1?pq-origsite=gscholar&cbl=636386.

5. Jeanne Hamming, "The *Feminine* 'Nature' of Masculine Desire in the Age of Cinematic Techno-Transcendence," *Journal of Popular Film and Television* 35, no. 4 (2008): 146–153, https://doi.org/10.3200/JPFT.35.4.146-153.

6. Brian Brutlag, "Bodies in Pods: Masculine Domination, Sexuality, and Love in *The Matrix* Franchise," in *Global Perspectives on the Liminality of the Supernatural: From Animus to Zombi*, ed. Rebecca Gibson and James M. VanderVeen (Lanham, MD: Lexington Books, 2022), 129–140.

7. Tony Myers, *Slavoj Žižek* (London: Routledge, 2003), 1.

8. Moline, "Keanu Reeves' Body as Battleground," https://doi.org/10.1080/19392397.2022.2063399.

9. Brian Davids, "'John Wick' Director Chad Stahelski on the Scene He Fought For," *Hollywood Reporter*, May 17, 2019, https://www.hollywoodreporter.com/movies/movie-news/keanu-reeves-pushed-studio-violent-john-wick-3-scene-1211258/.

10. David Griffin, "John Wick 4: Director Chad Stahelski Talks Keanu's Nunchuck Skills and Ghost of Tsushima Movie," *IGN*, November 10, 2022, https://www.ign.com/articles/john-wick-4-ghost-of-tsushima-interview.

11. A. Rochaun Meadows-Fernandez, *Investigating Institutional Racism* (New York: Enslow, 2019), 37.

12. Janie Boschma, Curt Merrill, and John Murphy-Teixidor, "Mass Shootings in the US Fast Facts," CNN.com, accessed September 26, 2024, https://www.cnn.com/us/mass-shootings-fast-facts/index.html.

13. Roxane Dunbar-Ortiz, *Loaded: A Disarming History of the Second Amendment* (San Francisco: City Lights, 2018).

14. Sezin Koehler, "Why White Male Shooters Are Often Called 'Lone Wolves,'" *Teen Vogue*, April 9, 2018, https://www.teenvogue.com/story/why-white-male-shooters-are-often-called-lone-wolves.

5. I (Still) Know Kung Fu: Claiming an Asian Identity

1. Rachel DeSantis, "Why Ali Wong Cast Keanu Reeves (as Himself!) in Netflix Rom-Com 'Always Be My Maybe,'" *People*, June 3, 2019, https://people.com /tv/why-ali-wong-cast-keanu-reeves-always-be-my-maybe/.

2. Camilla Fojas, Rudy P. Guevarra, and Nitasha Tamar Sharma, eds., *Beyond Ethnicity: New Politics of Race in Hawaiʻi* (Honolulu: University of Hawaii Press, 2018).

3. Mayo, review of *Masculinity in Contemporary Science Fiction Cinema* by Kac-Vergne, https://www.proquest.com/openview/f41171009c7a33952f7402 5208251084/1?pq-origsite=gscholar&cbl=636386.

4. Ricky Lee Allen, "Wake Up, Neo: White Identity, Hegemony, and Consciousness in 'The Matrix,'" *Counterpoints* 209 (2002): 104–125, http://www.jstor .org/stable/42979490; Sang-Keun Yoo, "Speculative Orientalism: Zen and Tao in American New Wave Science Fiction" (PhD diss., University of California, Riverside, 2022); Hee-Jung Serenity Joo, "Oriental Style and Asian Chic: The Politics of Racial Visibility in Film and Fashion," *American Studies* 52, no. 1 (2012): 153–162, http://www.jstor.org/stable/41809573.

5. Robert Horton, "Nonconformist: Bernardo Bertolucci's 'Little Buddha,'" *Film Comment* 30, no. 4 (1994): 26–28, http://www.jstor.org/stable/43456458; Eve Mullen, "Orientalist Commercializations: Tibetan Buddhism in American Popular Film," *Journal of Religion & Film* 2, no. 2 (October 1998), https:// digitalcommons.unomaha.edu/cgi/viewcontent.cgi?article=1852&context=jrf.

6. Chrishandra Sebastiampillai, "Crazy Rich Eurasians: White Enough to Be Acceptable, Asian Enough to Be an Asset," *Celebrity Studies* 12, no. 2 (2021): 219–233, https://doi.org/10.1080/19392397.2021.1912166.

7. LeiLani Nishime, *Undercover Asian: Multiracial Asian Americans in Visual Culture* (Urbana: University of Illinois Press, 2014), 85.

8. Gerald Sim, *The Subject of Film and Race: Retheorizing Politics, Ideology, and Cinema* (New York: Bloomsbury, 2014), 153.

9. Emilly Prado, *Examining Assimilation* (New York: Enslow, 2019).

10. For an example of this commentary directed at Keanu, see Carrie Rickey, "Keanu Reeves: Quiet Power," *Greensboro (NC) News and Record*, June 17, 1994, https://greensboro.com/keanu-reeves-quiet-power/article_e2ae55b1 -40f3-5dde-bc1e-8de9e8e64b23.html/.

11. Fred Topel, "TIFF 2013: Keanu Reeves on Man of Tai Chi," CraveOnline, September 12, 2013, http://www.craveonline.com/film/interviews/569539 -tiff-2013-keanu-reeves-on-man-of-tai-chi/2 (site discontinued).

12. Joi-Marie McKenzie, "Keanu Reeves Is a Proud Person of Color, but Doesn't Want to Be 'a Spokesperson,'" *Essence*, December 6, 2020, https:// www.essence.com/entertainment/keanu-reeves-person-of-color-doesnt -want-to-be-a-spokesperson/.

13. Diep Tran, "Keanu Reeves, Priyanka Chopra on 'The Matrix,' Respecting Asian Cultures in Filmmaking," NBC News, December 17, 2021, https://www .nbcnews.com/news/asian-america/keanu-reeves-priyanka-chopra-matrix -respecting-asian-cultures-filmmaki-rcna9079.

14. Megan C. Hills, "What Keanu Reeves Taught Me About White-Passing Privilege," *Standard*, September 5, 2020, https://www.standard.co.uk/insider /celebrity/keanu-reeves-chinese-hawaiian-asian-heritage-white-passing -a4539726.html.

6. He Is the One: Keanu Reeves as the Multiracial Messiah

1. Nadra Nittle, *Recognizing Microaggressions* (New York: Enslow, 2019).

2. "Where We Live Affects Our Bias Against Mixed-Race Individuals," Association for Psychological Science, March 15, 2016, https://www.psychologicalscience .org/news/releases/where-we-live-affects-our-bias-against-mixed-race -individuals.html.

3. "Where We Live Affects Our Bias Against Mixed-Race Individuals, Psychology Study Finds," New York University, press release, March 14, 2016, https://www.nyu.edu/about/news-publications/news/2016/march /where-we-live-affects-our-bias-against-mixed-race-individuals-psychology -study-finds.html.

4. Kristal Brent Zook, "How the Brain Processes Mixed-Race Faces," *ZORA*, September 23, 2019, https://zora.medium.com/how-the-brain-processes -mixed-race-faces-fc83b242f08e; Alexandros Orphanides, "Why Mixed-Race Americans Will Not Save the Country," NPR, March 8, 2017, https:// www.npr.org/sections/codeswitch/2017/03/08/519010491/why-mixed -race-americans-will-not-save-the-country.

5. Sana Siddiqui, "Critical Social Work with Mixed-Race Individuals: Implications for Anti-Racist and Anti-Oppressive Practice," *Canadian Social Work Review* 28, no. 2 (2011): 255–272, http://www.jstor.org/stable/41669946; Diana T. Sanchez, Sarah E. Gaither, Analia F. Albuja, and Zoey Eddy, "How Policies Can Address Multiracial Stigma," *Policy Insights from the Behavioral and Brain Sciences* 7, no. 2 (2020): 115–122, https://doi.org/10.1177/2372732220943906; Celeste Vaughan Curington, Ken-Hou Lin, and Jennifer Hickes Lundquist, "Positioning Multiraciality in Cyberspace: Treatment of Multiracial Daters in an Online Dating Website," *American Sociological Review* 80, no. 4 (2015):764–788, https://doi.org/10.1177/0003122415591268.

6. Tanya Horeck "'Too Good for This World': Keanu Reeves, God of the Internet," *Celebrity Studies* 13, no. 2 (2022): 143–158, https://doi.org/10.1080/19392397.2022.2063395.

7. Anton Karl Kozlovic, "The Cinematic Christ-Figure," *Furrow* 55, no. 1 (2004): 26–30, http://www.jstor.org/stable/27664881.

8. "Jesus Keanu," Know Your Meme, accessed April 12, 2024, https://knowyourmeme.com/photos/1639232-keanu-reeves.

9. Jack Garner, "'Buddha' Ends Trip from Marxism to Mysticism," *Democrat and Chronicle* (Rochester, NY), June 17, 1994.

10. Sim, *Subject of Film and Race*, 165–166.

11. Jeff Karnicky, "Keanu Rhizome," *Symplokē* 6, no. 1/2 (1998): 135–144, http://www.jstor.org/stable/40550428.

12. Will Harris, *Mixed-Race Superman: Keanu, Obama, and Multiracial Experience* (Brooklyn, NY: Melville House, 2019).

13. Cha, "'There Is No Spoon,'" http://www.jstor.org/stable/23416365.

14. Lisa Nakamura, "Race in the Construct, or the Construction of Race: New Media and Old Identities in 'The Matrix,'" in *Domain Errors! A Cyberfeminist Handbook of Tactics*, ed. Michelle Wright, Maria Fernandez, and Faith Wilding (New York: Autonomedia, 2003), 63–78.

15. Brutlag, "Bodies in Pods," 129–140.

16. Amjad M. Hussain, "Religion, Film and Post-modernism: The Matrix, a Case Study," in *Sinema ve Din*, ed. Bilal Yorulmaz et al. (Istanbul: Değerler Eğitimi Merkezi, 2015), 1199–1209.

17. LeiLani Nishime, "Guilty Pleasures: Keanu Reeves, Superman, and Racial Outing," in *East Main Street: Asian American Popular Culture*, ed. Shilpa Dave, LeiLani Nishime, and Tasha Oren (New York: New York University Press, 2005), 273–291.

18. C. Richard King and David J. Leonard, "Racing the Matrix: Variations on White Supremacy in Responses to the Film Trilogy," *Cultural Studies ↔ Critical Methodologies* 6, no. 3 (2006): 354–369, https://doi.org/10.1177/1532708606288638.

19. Brette D. W. Kristoff, "Contextualzing Trumpism: Understanding Race, Gender, Religiosity, and Resistance in Post-Truth Society" (master's thesis, University of Saskatchewan, 2023), https://harvest.usask.ca/server/api/core/bitstreams/5e52f161-2e1d-42d9-b771-2f8acddf60f0/content.

20. Laura M. Holson, "Keanu Reeves Is Whatever You Want Him to Be," *New York Times*, July 3, 2019, https://www.nytimes.com/2019/07/03/style/keanu-reeves-movie-roles.html.

21. LeiLani Nishime, "Why Can't Keanu Act? Reading Race Back into Reeves," paper presented at the Association of Asian American Studies, April 2007.

22. "The New Face of America" (cover), *Time*, November 18, 1993, https://content.time.com/time/covers/0,16641,19931118,00.html.

23. Sim, *Subject of Film and Race*, 147.

24. Teresa Williams-León and Cynthia L. Nakashima, eds., "Reconfiguring Race, Rearticulating Ethnicity," introduction to *The Sum of Our Parts: Mixed-Heritage Asian Americans* (Philadelphia: Temple University Press, 2001), 3–10.

7. I Will Search for You to a Thousand Worlds and Ten Thousand Lifetimes: Keanu and Conceptualizing the Perfect Leading Man

1. Sarah El-Mahmoud, "Insanely Cute Clip of Keanu Reeves Telling Drew Barrymore She Can Be a Lover AND a Fighter Is Running Around on the Internet Again," CinemaBlend, August 27, 2022, https://www.cinemablend.com/movies/insanely-cute-clip-of-keanu-reeves-telling-drew-barrymore-she-can-be-a-lover-and-a-fighter-is-running-around-on-the-internet-again.

2. Stephanie Cram, "History, Humour and a Dash of Keanu Reeves: Women of the Fur Trade a Fun, Clever Look at Red River Resistance," CBC

News, February 28, 2020, https://www.cbc.ca/news/canada/manitoba/theatre-review-rmtc-women-of-the-fur-trade-1.5478175.

3. Bailey Richards, "Dolly Parton Reacts to Keanu Reeves Wearing Her *Playboy* Bunny Costume His Mom Designed: 'The Sweetest Guy,'" *People*, November 28, 2023, https://people.com/keanu-reeves-mom-designed-dolly-partons-playboy-bunny-outfit-8407467.

4. Caitlin O'Kane, "People Have Noticed That Keanu Reeves Keeps His Hands off Women in Photos," CBS News, June 13, 2019, https://www.cbsnews.com/news/people-have-noticed-that-keanu-reeves-respectfully-does-not-touch-women-in-photos/.

5. Kyle Buchanan, "Leading Men Age, but Their Love Interests Don't," *Slate*, May 26, 2015, https://slate.com/culture/2015/05/leading-men-age-but-their-love-interest-don-t.html.

6. "Study: How Much Older Are Male Leads in Romantic Films than Their Female Co-Stars?," Women and Hollywood, June 1, 2015, https://womenandhollywood.com/study-how-much-older-are-male-leads-in-romantic-films-than-their-female-co-stars-43ddef908f19/.

7. Cha, "'There Is No Spoon,'" http://www.jstor.org/stable/23416365.

8. "20 of Hollywood's Biggest Male Stars Have Never Worked with a Female Director," Women and Hollywood, February 25, 2016, https://womenandhollywood.com/20-of-hollywoods-biggest-male-stars-have-never-worked-with-a-female-director-f200097cc208/.

8. I Will Be Your Father Figure: Keanu Reeves's Most Triumphant (and Most Heinous) Parenting

1. Justin Vicari, *The Gus Van Sant Touch: A Thematic Study—"Drugstore Cowboy," "Milk" and Beyond* (Jefferson, NC: McFarland, 2012), 89.

2. Brian Lynch, "JOHN WICK is the dark timeline . . . ," Twitter/X, November 3, 2019, 7:20 PM, https://twitter.com/BrianLynch/status/1191072659779416064 (post deleted).

9. I'll See You In Hell, Johnny: Keanu Reeves and the Underworld

1. Naomi Fry, "Keanu Reeves Is Too Good for This World," *New Yorker*, June 3, 2019, https://www.newyorker.com/culture/culture-desk/keanu-reeves -is-too-good-for-this-world.

2. Ryan Netzley, ""Better to Reign in Hell than Serve in Heaven," Is That It?': Ethics, Apocalypticism, and Allusion in *The Devil's Advocate*," in *Milton in Popular Culture*, ed. Laura Lunger Knoppers and Gregory M. Colón Semenza (New York: Palgrave Macmillan, 2006), 113–124.

3. Regina M. Hansen, "Lucifer, Gabriel, and the Angelic Will in *The Prophecy* and *Constantine*," in *Giving the Devil His Due: Satan and Cinema*, ed. Jeffrey Andrew Weinstock and Regina M. Hansen (New York: Fordham University Press, 2021), 178–190.

4. David Hauka, "Advocating for Satan: The Parousia-Inspired Horror Genre," in *Giving the Devil His Due*, 191–206.

5. Jeffery A. Smith, "Hollywood Theology: The Commodification of Religion in Twentieth-Century Films," *Religion and American Culture: A Journal of Interpretation* 11, no. 2 (Summer 2001): 191–231, https://doi.org/10.1525 /rac.2001.11.2.191.

6. Andy Porter and Jessica A. Albrecht, "Nonviolent Utopias: Heroes Trans- gressing the Gender Binary in *The Matrix Resurrections*," *Feminist Media Studies*, October 10, 2023, https://doi.org/10.1080/14680777.2023.2266584.

7. William Sims Bainbridge, "Expanding the Use of the Internet in Religious Research." *Review of Religious Research* 49, no. 1 (2007): 11, http://www .jstor.org/stable/20447469.

8. Justin Kirkland, "Keanu Reeves Shares His List of the Movies Everyone Should Watch," *Esquire*, November 22, 2021, https://www.esquire.com/entertainment /movies/a38319312/keanu-reeves-movie-recommendations-list.

9. Tim Dickinson, "Gang Members Hold Positions at 'Highest Levels' of LA Sheriff's Department, Investigation Reveals," *Rolling Stone*, March 7, 2023, https://www.rollingstone.com/politics/politics-features/la-sheriff-department -gangs-alex-villanueva-1234691873/; see also Kevin Rector and Libor Jany, "The Foundation: Inside the LAPD's Secretive, Multimillion-Dollar Private Funding Arm," *Los Angeles Times*, January 4, 2023, https://www.latimes.com /california/story/2023-01-04/lapd-police-foundation-private-funding-arm.

10. Kirkland, "Keanu Reeves Shares His List," https://www.esquire.com /entertainment/movies/a38319312/keanu-reeves-movie-recommendations -list/.

11. *Random Acts of Flyness*, season 1, episode 5, "I tried to tell my therapist about my dreams / MARTIN HAD A DREEEEAAAAM," written and directed by Mariama Diallo, Darius Clark Monroe, Terence Nance, and Jamund Washington, aired August 31, 2018, on HBO.

12. Sezin Devi Koehler, "Who Gets to Be an Antihero: A Primer on White Devilry in Visual Media," *Black Girl Nerds*, August 17, 2022, https://blackgirlnerds.com /who-gets-to-be-an-antihero-a-primer-on-white-devilry-in-visual-media/.

13. "A Hamburger and a Bad Day," *Crisis*, March 25, 2021, https://naacp.org /articles/hamburger-and-bad-day.

14. Kelly Glass, *Looking at Privilege and Power* (New York: Enslow, 2019).

10. Men Were Deceivers Ever: Gender-Based and Sexual Violence as a Recurring Theme

1. JM McNab, "Trump Was Too Dumb to Realize 'The Devil's Advocate' Was Making Fun of Him," Cracked.com, October 17, 2022, https://www.cracked .com/article_35701_trump-was-too-dumb-to-realize-the-devils-advocate -was-making-fun-of-him.html.

2. Hauka, "Advocating for Satan."

3. "U.S. Teen Girls Experiencing Increased Sadness and Violence," Centers for Disease Control, press release, February 13, 2023, https://www.cdc.gov /media/releases/2023/p0213-yrbs.html.

4. "Missing and Murdered Indigenous Women (MMIW)," Native Hope, accessed June 3, 2024, https://www.nativehope.org/missing-and-murdered -indigenous-women-mmiw.

5. Alia Wong, "Native Hawaiian Women Too Often Go Missing and Face Violence. A New Federal Policy May Help," *USA Today*, December 30, 2022, https://www.usatoday.com/story/news/nation/2022/12/30/native-women -hawaii-face-high-violence-rates-new-policy-could-help/10966720002/.

6. Kelsey Turner, "A Native Hawaiian Call for Change," *Restoration Magazine* 18, no. 2 (June 2021), https://www.niwrc.org/restoration-magazine/june-2021 /native-hawaiian-call-change.

7. Mahealani Richardson, "Troubling Report Shines Spotlight on Missing, Murdered Native Hawaiian Women," Hawaii News Now, December 14, 2022, https://www.hawaiinewsnow.com/2022/12/15/report-highlights-missing-murdered-hawaiian-women-girls/.

8. Kirkland, "Keanu Reeves Shares His List," https://www.esquire.com/entertainment/movies/a38319312/keanu-reeves-movie-recommendations-list/.

9. Amy Zimmerman, "When Marlee Matlin Accused William Hurt of Sexual Assault," *Daily Beast*, March 18, 2022, https://www.thedailybeast.com/when-marlee-matlin-accused-william-hurt-of-rape.

10. Jasmine Payoute, "Gary Busey Accused of Sexually Assaulting Women During Photoshoot at Cherry Hill Convention," CBS News, August 22, 2022, https://www.cbsnews.com/philadelphia/news/gary-busey-sexual-assault-cherry-hill-monster-mania-convention/; Tyler Golsen, "Inside the Details of Anthony Kiedis' Troubling Sexual Assault History," *Far Out Magazine*, November 5, 2021, https://faroutmagazine.co.uk/anthony-kiedis-sexual-assault-history-details/.

11. Constance Grady, "Gary Oldman Just Won the Oscar for Best Actor. He's Also Been Accused of Domestic Violence," *Vox*, March 5, 2018, https://www.vox.com/culture/2018/3/2/17058230/gary-oldman-oscars-domestic-violence-accusation.

12. Anna North, "The Disturbing Story Behind the Rape Scene in Bernardo Bertolucci's Last Tango in Paris, Explained," *Vox*, November 26, 2018, https://www.vox.com/2018/11/26/18112531/bernardo-bertolucci-maria-schneider-last-tango-in-paris.

13. Jake Nevins, "Morgan Freeman Accused of Sexual Harassment by Eight Women," *Guardian*, May 24, 2018, https://www.theguardian.com/film/2018/may/24/morgan-freeman-sexual-harassment-accusations-claims-women.

14. Rebekah Clark, "Shia LaBeouf Expecting First Child with Mia Goth amid Sexual Assault Allegations," *Grazia*, February 1, 2022, https://graziamagazine.com/articles/shia-labeouf-mia-goth-pregnant/; Lindsay Kimble, "Shia LaBeouf Says 'I Would Have Killed Her' After Fight with Girlfriend Mia Goth in Newly Surfaced Video," *People*, July 27, 2015, https://people.com/movies/shia-labeouf-and-girlfriend-mia-goth-fight-captured-on-video/.

15. "'Game of Thrones' Star Jason Momoa Joked About Raping 'Beautiful Women' on Show," *Guardian*, October 13, 2017, https://www.theguardian.com/tv-and-radio/2017/oct/12/jason-momoa-game-of-thrones-raping-beautiful

-women; Mike Miller, "Jim Carrey's Ex-Girlfriend Claimed He Introduced Her to 'Cocaine, Prostitutes, Mental Abuse and Disease,'" *People*, September 29, 2017, https://people.com/movies/jim-carreys-ex-girlfriend-claimed-he -introduced-her-to-cocaine-prostitutes-mental-abuse-and-disease/.

16. Kyndall Cunningham, "'Beefs' Ali Wong and Steven Yeun Rally Around Self-Described 'Rapist' David Choe," *Daily Beast*, April 22, 2023, https://www.thedailybeast.com/beefs-ali-wong-and-steven-yeun-rally -around-david-choe-after-rape-uproar.

17. Katie Rife, "An Incomplete, Depressingly Long List of Celebrities' Sexual Assault and Harassment Stories," *AV Club*, last updated November 22, 2017, https://www.avclub.com/an-incomplete-depressingly-long -list-of-celebrities-se-1819628519.

18. Sara M. Moniuszko and Cara Kelly, "Harvey Weinstein Scandal: A Complete List of the 87 Accusers," *USA Today*, last updated June 1, 2018, https://www.usatoday.com/story/life/people/2017/10/27/weinstein-scandal -complete-list-accusers/804663001/.

19. Janelle Griffith, "Common Says He Was Molested by a Family Friend as a Child," NBC News, May 8, 2019, https://www.nbcnews.com/news/us-news /common-says-he-was-molested-family-friend-child-n1003466.

20. Gwilym Mumford, "Actor Terry Crews: I Was Sexually Assaulted by Hollywood Executive," *Guardian*, October 11, 2017, https://www .theguardian.com/film/2017/oct/11/actor-terry-crews-sexually-assaulted-by -hollywood-executive.

21. Laura Miller, "The Polanski Problem," *Slate*, April 18, 2023, https://slate.com /culture/2023/04/claire-dederer-monsters-book-roman-polanski-woody -allen.html; see also Claire Dederer, "What Do We Do with the Art of Monstrous Men?," *Paris Review*, November 20, 2017, https://www.theparisreview .org/blog/2017/11/20/art-monstrous-men/.

11. If We're Gonna Waste the Dude, We Oughta Get Paid for It: The American Dream Gone Wrong

1. Matthew Wills, "James Truslow Adams: Dreaming up the American Dream," *JSTOR Daily*, May 18, 2015, https://daily.jstor.org/james-truslow -adams-dreaming-american-dream/.

2. Jamila Osman, *Navigating Intersectionality: How Race, Class, and Gender Overlap* (New York: Enslow, 2019).

3. Jamie Ballard, "In 2020, Do People See the American Dream as Attainable?," YouGov, July 18, 2020, https://today.yougov.com/topics/politics /articles-reports/2020/07/18/american-dream-attainable-poll-survey-data.

4. John Larson, "The Big Problem with the American Dream," *Washington Post*, January 14, 2020, https://www.washingtonpost.com/outlook/2020/01/14 /big-problem-with-american-dream/.

5. CNN Newsource, "Couple Together for 57 Years Survives Infidelity, Murder Plot, and Prison Time," Local 12 WKRC-TV, February 17, 2023, https:// local12.com/news/offbeat/couple-together-57-years-survives-infidelity -murder-plot-prison-sentence-tony-frances-toto-i-love-you-to-death-movie -hollywood-film-tristar-pictures-homicide-kill-attempts-teenage-hit-men -affair-jail-relationship-allentown-pennsylvania.

12. The Desert of the Real: The Perils of Technology in Keanu Reeves's Cyber Cinema

1. "Parasocial Interaction," Oxford Reference, accessed June 18, 2024, https:// www.oxfordreference.com/display/10.1093/oi/authority.20110803100305809.

2. "Blue Brain Project," École Polytechnique Fédérale de Lausanne, accessed June 18, 2024, https://www.epfl.ch/research/domains/bluebrain/; David W. Kupferman, "Educational Futures and Postdigital Science," *Postdigital Science and Education* 4 (2022): 216–223, https://link.springer.com/content/pdf/10.1007 /s42438-021-00236-6.pdf.

3. Abbey White, "Keanu Reeves on Deepfakes and That Bruce Willis Russian Phone Commercial: 'You Lose Your Agency,'" *Hollywood Reporter*, February 14, 2023, https://www.hollywoodreporter.com/news/general-news /keanu-reeves-deepfake-bruce-willis-digital-twin-1235325500/.

4. Joe Hernandez, "A South Florida Man Shot at 2 Instacart Delivery Workers Who Went to the Wrong House," NPR, April 23, 2023, https:// www.npr.org/2023/04/23/1171507677/south-florida-shot-at-instacart -delivery-driver-wrong-address.

5. CNNWire, "Body Camera Video Released After 81-Year-Old Fatally Shoots Uber Driver He Believed Was a Scammer," ABC7 Los Angeles, April 19,

2024, https://abc7.com/uber-driver-shot-body-camera-video-released-after-ohio-man-fatally-shoots-he-thought-was-a-scammer/14694595/.

6. Dara Kerr, "The Sexual Assault Victims Suing Uber Notch a Legal Victory in Their Long Battle," NPR, October 11, 2023, https://www.npr.org/2023/10/11/1205135476/sexual-assault-victims-suing-uber-notch-a-legal-victory-in-long-battle; Josh Peck, "New Lawsuits Say Lyft Failed to Protect Its Users from Physical and Sexual Assault," NPR, September 1, 2022, https://www.npr.org/2022/09/01/1120391757/lyft-lawsuits-assault-allegations.

7. Kari Paul, "Is Uber Doing Enough to Protect Women from Drivers Who Stalk Them?," *Vice*, July 1, 2016, https://www.vice.com/en/article/mbqq7y/is-uber-doing-enough-to-protect-women-from-drivers-who-stalk-them.

8. Kerry Breen, "Woman Allegedly Kidnapped by Fake Uber Driver Rescued After Slipping Note to Gas Station Customer," CBS News, August 25, 2023, https://www.cbsnews.com/news/woman-allegedly-kidnapped-by-fake-uber-driver-rescued-after-slipping-note-to-gas-station-customer-arizona/.

9. Dennis Romero, "Passenger Shot and Killed Uber Driver She Believed Was Taking Her to Mexico, Police Say," NBC News, June 23, 2023, https://www.nbcnews.com/news/us-news/passenger-shot-killed-uber-driver-believed-was-taking-mexico-police-sa-rcna90901

10. Pierre Lemieux, "Why the Surveillance State Is Dangerous," Foundation for Economic Education, June 17, 2018, https://fee.org/articles/why-the-surveillance-state-is-dangerous/.

11. Patrick C. Toomey, "The Supreme Court Needs to Rein In the Surveillance State," *Nation*, February 23, 2023, https://www.thenation.com/article/society/wikimedia-nsa-government-surveillance/.

12. Andrew Atterbury, "Florida Must Clarify Parental Rights Law Under Settlement in 'Don't Say Gay' Lawsuit," *Politico*, March 11, 2024, https://www.politico.com/news/2024/03/11/desantis-lbgtq-groups-claim-victory-in-parental-rights-lawsuit-settlement-00146380.

13. Kate Moffat and Pietari Kääpä, "Taking the Green Pill? Keanu Reeves as 'Reluctant Eco-Celebrity,'" *Celebrity Studies* 13, no. 2 (2022), 200–213, https://doi.org/10.1080/19392397.2022.2063401.

14. Laura Simmons, "New Keanu Reeves Molecules Are Deadly Weapon in the Fight Against Fungi," IFLScience, February 7, 2023, https://www.iflscience

.com/new-keanu-reeves-molecules-a-deadly-weapon-in-the-fight-against-fungi-67424.

15. Zack Sharf, "Keanu Reeves Says Deepfakes Are 'Scary,' Confirms His Film Contracts Ban Digital Edits to His Acting: 'They Added a Tear to My Face! Huh?,'" *Variety*, February 15, 2023, https://variety.com/2023/film/news/keanu-reeves-slams-deepfakes-film-contract-prevents-digital-edits-1235523698/.

16. Heartwarming Moments, "Once Keanu Reeves left a post . . . ," Facebook, May 29, 2024, https://www.facebook.com/groups/fiftyshadesofkindness/posts/462221472950773.

17. Susan Devaney, "Keanu Reeves's Enduring Style Moments," *British Vogue*, May 7, 2020, https://www.vogue.co.uk/fashion/gallery/keanu-reeves-best-fashion.

18. Louis Wise, "Alexandra Grant on Finding Love with Keanu Reeves & Her Upcoming Marfa Invitational Exhibition," *British Vogue*, March 11, 2020, https://www.vogue.co.uk/arts-and-lifestyle/article/alexandra-grant-interview.

19. American Film Institute, "Keanu Reeves on *The Matrix*," YouTube, December 12, 2008, https://www.youtube.com/watch?v=MrXCHQBINUc.

20. White, "Keanu Reeves on Deepfakes," https://www.hollywoodreporter.com/news/general-news/keanu-reeves-deepfake-bruce-willis-digital-twin-1235325500/.

21. Jean Baudrillard, *Simulacra and Simulation*, trans. Sheila Faria Glaser (Ann Arbor: University of Michigan Press, 1994), 79.

22. Konstantin A. Pantserev "The Malicious Use of AI-Based Deepfake Technology as the New Threat to Psychological Security and Political Stability," in *Cyber Defence in the Age of AI, Smart Societies and Augmented Humanity*, ed. Hamid Jahankhani et al. (Cham, Switzerland: Springer, 2020), 37–55, https://doi.org/10.1007/978-3-030-35746-7_3.

13. A Role Model with a Nasty Habit: Keanu Reeves's On- and Off-Screen Smoking

1. "Reeves Desperate to Escape Smoking 'Prison,'" *Irish Examiner*, November 6, 2008, https://www.irishexaminer.com/lifestyle/arid-30385064.html.

2. Jennifer J. Tickle et al., "Favourite Movie Stars, Their Tobacco Use in Contemporary Movies, and Its Association with Adolescent Smoking," *Tobacco Control* 10, no. 1 (March 2001): 16–22. http://www.jstor.org/stable/20207860.

3. James D. Sargent, Susanne Tanski, and Mike Stoolmiller, "Influence of Motion Picture Rating on Adolescent Response to Movie Smoking," *Pediatrics* 130 (August 2012): 228–236, https://doi.org/10.1542/peds.2011-1787.

14. Painting the Sky with Rainbows: Keanu Reeves and Queer Representation

1. Shnayerson, "Young and Restless," https://archive.vanityfair.com/article /share/f2cd9db8-0d0a-4ee0-a5e1-deb619442a33.

2. Michael DeAngelis, *Gay Fandom and Crossover Stardom: James Dean, Mel Gibson, and Keanu Reeves* (Durham, NC: Duke University Press, 2001), 8.

3. Nishime, *Undercover Asian*, 21–40.

4. Kaylilani Minami, "Eh, You Māhū? An Analysis of American Cultural Imperialism in Hawai'i through the Lens of Gender and Sexuality" (senior thesis, Claremont McKenna College, 2017), https://scholarship.claremont.edu/cgi /viewcontent.cgi?referer=&httpsredir=1&article=2720&context=cmc_theses.

5. Daniel Herberg, "My Own Private Idaho (1991)," in *Screening American Independent Film*, ed. Justin Wyatt and W. D. Phillips (Milton Park, Abingdon, Oxon, UK: Routledge, 2023), chap. 32, digital ed.

6. "Straight Actors in Gay Roles: From River Phoenix to Michael Douglas (Photos)," *Hollywood Reporter*, accessed July 3, 2024, https://www.hollywood reporter.com/gallery/straight-actors-gay-roles-river-446610/.

7. Samuel Leighton-Dore, "A Young Keanu Reeves Starred in a 1984 Homoerotic Thriller Called 'Wolfboy,'" SBS, December 9, 2019, https://www .sbs.com.au/topics/pride/fast-lane/article/2019/12/09/young-keanu -reeves-starred-1984-homoerotic-thriller-called-wolfboy.

8. Theodore P. Mahne, "Passionate 'Wolfboy' Makes for an Intense Psychodrama at Mid-City Theatre," *Times-Picayune* (New Orleans, LA), April 23, 2013, https://www.nola.com/entertainment_life/arts/passionate-wolfboy -makes-for-an-intense-psycho-drama-at-mid-city-theatre/article _28788cc7-377c-5b03-96cd-2cf307851dee.html; Mark Shenton, "Musical Version of *Wolfboy* to Premiere at London's Trafalgar Studios with Rigby and Boys," *Playbill*, June 3, 2010, https://playbill.com/article/musical -version-of-wolfboy-to-premiere-at-londons-trafalgar-studios-with-rigby -and-boys-com-168926.

9. Cha, "'There Is No Spoon,'" http://www.jstor.org/stable/23416365.

10. Netflix: Behind the Streams, "Why The Matrix Is a Trans Story According to Lilly Wachowski," YouTube, August 4, 2020, https://www.youtube.com /watch?v=adXm2sDzGkQ.

11. Kevin Polowy, "Keanu Reeves Says He Didn't Know About 'Profound' Transgender Meaning Behind 'The Matrix,'" Yahoo Entertainment, August 17, 2020, https://www.yahoo.com/entertainment/keanu-reeves-the-matrix -transgender-allegory-lilly-wachowski-202620575.html.

12. See the documentary about trans representation *Disclosure*, directed by Sam Feder (Netflix, 2020).

13. Emily St. James, "How *The Matrix* Universalized a Trans Experience—and Helped Me Accept My Own," *Vox*, March 30, 2019, https://www.vox.com/culture /2019/3/30/18286436/the-matrix-wachowskis-trans-experience-redpill.

14. Connie Hanzhang Jin, "'I, Too, Was Living a Double Life': Why Trans Fans Connect to 'The Matrix,'" NPR, December 22, 2021, https://www.npr .org/2021/12/22/1066554369/the-matrix-original-trans-fans-resurrections.

15. Nick Duffy, "Keanu Reeves and Alex Winter Endorse Content Warning over Homophobic Slurs in Original Bill & Ted Films," PinkNews, September 29, 2020, https://www.thepinknews.com/2020/09/29/keanu-reeves-alex-winter -bill-ted-face-music-content-warning-homophobia/.

16. Anna Klassen, "How Keanu Reeves Inspired 'Keanu,'" Bustle, April 28, 2016, https://www.bustle.com/articles/157337-how-keanu-reeves-inspired-keanu -according-to-key-peele.

17. Lisa Johnson Mandell, "Hugh Laurie Admits to a Man Crush on Keanu Reeves," YouTube, April 9, 2008, https://www.youtube.com/watch?v=QjASLK25qyo.

18. Christine Tomlinson, "Gaming on Romance," *Contexts* 18, no. 4 (2019), https://doi.org/10.1177/1536504219883852.

19. See, for instance, Chris Barsanti, *What Would Keanu Do? Personal Philosophy and Awe-Inspiring Advice from the Patron Saint of Whoa* (New York: Media Lab, 2020).

20. Keanu Reeves, interview by Dennis Cooper, *Interview*, September 1990.

21. Angela Andaloro, "Dwyane Wade Says Family Is His Motivation for Having Left Florida: 'Would Not Be Accepted' (Exclusive)," *People*, April 26, 2023,

https://people.com/parents/dwyane-wade-family-motivation-having-left
-florida-exclusive/.

15. Period Pains: Keanu's Historic Fictions

1. Mullen, "Orientalist Commercializations," https://digitalcommons.unomaha
.edu/jrf/vol2/iss2/5.

2. Michael Parenti, "Friendly Feudalism: The Tibet Myth," *Swans*, July 7, 2003,
http://www.swans.com/library/art9/mparen01.html.

3. Sorrel Neuss, "What We Don't Hear About Tibet," https://www.theguard
ian.com/commentisfree/2009/feb/10/tibet-china-feudalism; Nico Hines,
"Inside Tibetan Buddhism's 'Rape' and Abuse Scandal," *Daily Beast*,
July 17, 2019, https://www.thedailybeast.com/inside-tibetan-buddhisms-rape
-and-abuse-scandal.

4. Mullen, "Orientalist Commercializations," https://digitalcommons.unomaha
.edu/jrf/vol2/iss2/5.

5. "Tibetan Buddhist Teacher Accused of Sexual Abuse Dies," BBC, August 28,
2019, https://www.bbc.com/news/world-asia-49505098.amp.

6. Amanda Dobbins, "Remembering the Other Great Movie Version of *Much
Ado About Nothing*," *Vulture*, June 7, 2013, https://www.vulture.com/2013/06
/remembering-branagh-much-ado-about-nothing.html.

7. Carina Johnson, "Native Americans in Europe," Oxford Bibliographies, September 30, 2013, https://www.oxfordbibliographies.com/display/document
/obo-9780199730414/obo-9780199730414-0203.xml.

8. "The Abduction of Pocahontas," Virginia Museum of History & Culture,
accessed July 25, 2024, https://virginiahistory.org/learn/abduction-poca
hontas; Jackie Mansky; "The True Story of Pocahontas Is More Complicated Than You Might Think," updated by Sonja Anderson, *Smithsonian
Magazine*, February 20, 2024, https://www.smithsonianmag.com/history
/true-story-pocahontas-180962649/.

9. "47 Rōnin," *Encyclopedia Britannica*, accessed October 1, 2024, https://www
.britannica.com/event/47-ronin.

10. Simon Abrams, review of *47 Ronin*, RogerEbert.com, December 25, 2013,
https://www.rogerebert.com/reviews/47-ronin-2013.

11. Toshi Nakamura, "Keanu Reeves Said His Lines in English and Japanese for *47 Ronin*," *Kotaku*, December 13, 2013, https://www.kotaku.com.au/2013/12 /for-47-ronin-keanu-reeves-said-his-lines-in-english-and-japanese/.

12. "47 Ronin (Comparison: International Version–Japanese Version)," Movie-Censorship.com, accessed October 1, 2024, https://www.movie-censorship .com/report.php?ID=122983.

13. "*Dangerous Liaisons* (1988)," AFI Catalog of Feature Films, accessed October 1, 2024, https://catalog.afi.com/Catalog/moviedetails/55748.

14. Kumiko Mendl, "Yellow Earth Theatre Explores Forgotten Stories of the British Chinese," Historic England, accessed July 22, 2024, https://historic england.org.uk/research/inclusive-heritage/another-england/your-stories /forgotten-stories-of-british-chinese/.

15. James Wood, "The Jesuit Who Met the King in 1687, the Circus Stars and the Sailors: New Book Reveals First Chinese Migrants to UK Who Were Welcomed as Curiosities Then Feared in Case They Debauched Local Women," *Daily Mail*, December 21, 2018, https://www.dailymail.co.uk /news/article-6519681/Stories-Chinese-migrants-Britain-arrived-300-years -ago-revealed-new-book.html.

16. James C. McNaughton, "Chinese-Americans in World War II," US Army Center of Military History, May 16, 2000, https://history.army.mil/html /topics/apam/chinese-americans.html.

17. "Why We Serve: Native Americans in the United States Armed Forces," National Museum of the American Indian, accessed July 22, 2024, https:// americanindian.si.edu/static/why-we-serve/topics/world-war-2/.

18. "The Robledo Story," Robledo Family Winery, accessed July 22, 2024, https:// www.robledofamilywinery.com/Our-Story.

19. Sarah Stierch, "6 Mexican-American Wines to Check Out from Sonoma and Napa," *Sonoma Magazine*, April 2017, https://www.sonomamag.com /mexican-american-wines-to-check-out-from-sonoma-and-napa/.

20. See, e.g., Stephen Holden, review of *The Last Time I Committed Suicide*, *New York Times*, June 20, 1997, https://archive.nytimes.com/www.nytimes .com/library/film/suicide-film-review.html; Dennis Harvey, review of *The Last Time I Committed Suicide*, *Variety*, January 26, 1997, https://variety .com/1997/film/reviews/the-last-time-i-committed-suicide-1200448290/.

21. Neal Cassady, "The Joan Anderson Letter," 1964, reprinted in *Sensitive Skin*, https://www.sensitiveskinmagazine.com/joan-anderson-letter-neal-cassady/.

22. "The Largest Mass Execution in US History," Death Penalty Information Center, accessed July 22, 2024, https://deathpenaltyinfo.org/stories /the-largest-mass-execution-in-us-history.

16. Embracing His Mediocre Nothingness: Keanu's Cinematic Stumbles According to Critics

1. Comicbookzookeeper, "All Keanu Reeves Movies Ranked," IMDb, accessed July 29, 2024, https://www.imdb.com/list/ls099063175/?sort=list _order,desc&st_dt=&mode=detail&page=1; "All Keanu Reeves Movies Ranked," Rotten Tomatoes, accessed July 29, 2024, https://editorial .rottentomatoes.com/guide/all-keanu-reeves-movies-ranked/; Tim Grierson and Will Leitch, "Every Keanu Reeves Movie Performance, Ranked," *Vulture*, March 27, 2023, https://www.vulture.com/article/best-keanu-reeves -movies-ranked.html; "Every Keanu Reeves Movie, Ranked," *GQ*, July 17, 2019, https://www.gq.com/story/every-keanu-reeves-movie-ranked; Kyle Wilson, "Every Keanu Reeves Movie Ranked from Worst to Best (Including The Matrix Resurrections)," *Screen Rant*, January 10, 2022, https:// screenrant.com/keanu-reeves-movies-ranked-worst-best/; Iana Murray, Jane Harkness, *Looper*, September 23, 2022, https://www.looper.com/221761 /best-and-worst-keanu-reeves-movies/.

2. Chuck Klosterman, "'Watcher' Doesn't Work," *Akron (OH) Beacon Journal*, September 8, 2000; Lisa Schwarzbaum, review of *The Watcher*, *Entertainment Weekly*, September 15, 2000, https://ew.com/article/2000/09/15 /movie-review-watcher-2/.

3. "Keanu: I Was Tricked into Making Film," *Guardian*, September 11, 2001, https://www.theguardian.com/film/2001/sep/11/news.

4. Drew Taylor, "Interview: 'John Wick' Star Keanu Reeves Talks Stunt Work, 'Side by Side' & the Possibility of Another 'Matrix' Movie," *IndieWire*, September 30, 2014, https://www.indiewire.com/features/general/interview-john-wick -star-keanu-reeves-talks-stunt-work-side-by-side-the-possibility-of-another -matrix-movie-271762/.

5. Grierson and Leitch, "Every Keanu Reeves Movie," https://www.vulture.com /article/best-keanu-reeves-movies-ranked.html.

6. "Replicas," Rotten Tomatoes, accessed August 8, 2024, https://www.rotten tomatoes.com/m/replicas_2019.

7. Steve Biodrowski, review of *Replicas, Hollywood Gothique*, January 12, 2019.

8. Emanuel Levy, review of *Feeling Minnesota, Variety*, September 16, 1996, https://variety.com/1996/film/reviews/feeling-minnesota-1200446860/.

9. Danielle C. Belton, "Exposed: How Keanu Reeves' Newest Film Got Whitewashed," *Root*, December 23, 2015, https://www.theroot.com /exposed-how-keanu-reeves-newest-film-got-whitewashed-1790862136.

10. Ignatiy Vishnevetsky, "*Exposed* Asks Whether It's Possible to Yawn for 102 Minutes Straight," *AV Club*, January 26, 2016, https://www.avclub.com /exposed-asks-whether-it-s-possible-to-yawn-for-102-minu-1798186350.

11. Robert Kojder, review of *Exposed, Flickering Myth*, March 10, 2016, https:// www.flickeringmyth.com/2016/03/movie-review-exposed-2016/.

12. Paula Young Lee, "The Price of Hollywood Whitewashing: How This Complex Drama About a Latina Woman Became Just Another Keanu Reeves Cop Movie," *Salon*, March 13, 2016, https://www.salon.com/2016/03/13/the _price_of_hollywood_whitewashing_how_this_complex_drama_about_a _latina_woman_became_just_another_keanu_reeves_cop_movie/.

13. "Generation Um . . . ," Rotten Tomatoes, accessed August 8, 2024, https:// www.rottentomatoes.com/m/generation_um.

14. Murray, "Every Keanu Reeves Movie," https://www.gq.com/story /every-keanu-reeves-movie-ranked.

15. "Siberia (2018)," Rotten Tomatoes, accessed July 29, 2024, https://www .rottentomatoes.com/m/siberia_2018.

16. "Johnny Mnemonic," Rotten Tomatoes, accessed August 9, 2024, https:// www.rottentomatoes.com/m/johnny_mnemonic; Roger Ebert, review of *Johnny Mnemonic*, RogerEbert.com, May 26, 1995, https://www.rogerebert .com/reviews/johnny-mnemonic-1995.

17. Verne Kopytoff, "Elon Musk's Futuristic Brain-Chip Startup Neuralink Gets FDA Approval for Human Testing That It Says 'Represents an Important First Step,'" *Fortune*, May 25, 2023, https://fortune.com/2023/05/25 /elon-musk-brain-chip-neuralink-fda-approval-human-testing/.

18. Petros Levounis, MD, MA, and James Sherer, MD, eds., *Technological Addictions* (Washington, DC: American Psychiatric Association, 2022).

19. Roxana Hadadi, "The Proto-'Matrix' 'Johnny Mnemonic' Never Tries to Be Anything but Itself," *Crooked Marquee*, May 26, 2020, https://crookedmarquee.com/the-proto-matrix-johnny-mnemonic-never-tries-to-be-anything-but-itself/.

20. Patrick Dahl, "Johnny Mnemonic in Black-and-White: Robert Longo Interview," *Screen Slate*, June 10, 2021, https://www.screenslate.com/articles/johnny-mnemonic-black-and-white-robert-longo-interview.

21. "Sweet November," Rotten Tomatoes, accessed July 29, 2024, https://www.rottentomatoes.com/m/1104841-sweet_november.

17. Yes, I CAN-ada: Keanu Reeves's Extraordinary Comedic Talent

1. John Morreall, "Philosophy of Humor," Stanford Encyclopedia of Philosophy, last updated August 20, 2020, https://plato.stanford.edu/entries/humor/.

2. Morreall, "Philosophy of Humor."

3. Dolf Zillmann and Joanne R. Cantor, "A Disposition Theory of Humour and Mirth," chapter 5 in *Humor and Laughter: Theory, Research, and Applications*, ed. Antony J. Chapman and Hugh C. Foot (New Brunswick NJ: Transaction, 2007; orig. publ. 1976)

4. Morreall, "Philosophy of Humor," https://plato.stanford.edu/entries/humor/.

18. Whoa. Yeah. Dude: Keanu Reeves's Art of the Monosyllable

1. Jason Hellerman, "Keanu Reeves Cut Down John Wick's Dialogue to Just 380 Words," No Film School, March 28, 2023, https://nofilmschool.com/wick-dialogue.

2. See, for instance, Alexander Kirschenbaum, "The Efficacy of Vacuity: Deciphering the Quiet Art of Keanu Reeves," *Film International*, June 26, 2017, https://filmint.nu/the-efficacy-of-vacuity-deciphering-the-quiet-art-of-keanu-reeves/.

3. Bastién, "Grace of Keanu Reeves," https://www.brightwalldarkroom.com/2016/04/21/the-grace-of-keanu-reeves/.

4. Gross and Altman, *They Shouldn't Have Killed His Dog*, 97.

5. Robert N. Kraft, PhD, "7 Reasons Why Brevity Fails Us," *Psychology Today*, July 1, 2020, https://www.psychologytoday.com/us/blog/defining-memories/202007/7-reasons-why-brevity-fails-us.

19. Chicks Dig Scars: Complicating Keanu Reeves's Underdog Sports Tales

1. Nadav Goldschmied, "The Underdog Effect: Definition, Limitations, and Motivations; Why Do We Support Those at a Competitive Disadvantage?" (master's thesis, University of South Florida, 2005), https://digitalcommons.usf.edu/etd/2899.

2. "Tua Tagovailoa," NFL official website, accessed August 28, 2024, https://www.nfl.com/players/tua-tagovailoa/.

3. Associated Press, "Ex-NHL Star Goldsworthy Dies of AIDS: Former North Star, 51, Had Cited Promiscuity," *Spokesman Review* (Spokane, WA), July 16, 2011, https://www.spokesman.com/stories/1996/mar/30/ex-nhl-star-goldsworthy-dies-of-aids-former-north/.

4. Meghan Gunn, "These Are the Real Dangers of the Sports Betting Boom for Young Men," *Newsweek*, March 22, 2023, https://www.newsweek.com/2023/04/07/sports-betting-boom-linked-rising-gambling-addiction-anxiety-suicide-1789055.html.

5. "Our Labor History Timeline," AFL-CIO official website, accessed June 25, 2023, https://aflcio.org/about-us/history (page discontinued).

6. Jeremy Greco, "The Replacements (2000)—Does It Hold Up?," *Royals Review*, January 23, 2021, https://www.royalsreview.com/2021/1/23/22245142/the-replacements-2000-does-it-hold-up.

7. Marina Fang, "'General Hospital' Is Now Using Scab Writers," *HuffPost*, July 26, 2023, https://www.huffpost.com/entry/general-hospital-scab-writers-writers-strike_n_64c16f49e4b09a9296950e2a.

8. Libby Torres, "5 Celebrities Who Openly Crossed Picket Lines or Were Vocally Unsupportive of the SAG-AFTRA and WGA Strikes," *Business Insider*, October 10, 2023, https://www.businessinsider.com/celebrities-who-crossed-picket-lines-sag-wga-strike-2023-10.

9. Jill von Büren, "4 Deaf NFL Players You Probably Didn't Know About," HearingLikeMe.com, February 5, 2016, https://www.hearinglikeme.com/4-deaf-nfl-players-you-probably-didnt-know-about/.

10. John Gunning, "Former Amateur Yokozuna Hidetora Hanada Shifts Gears Toward NFL Dream," *Japan Times*, March 9, 2022, https://www.japantimes.co.jp/sports/2022/03/09/sumo/hanada-xleague-combine/.

11. Daniel Chavkin, "Colorado State Awards Football Scholarship to Sumo Wrestler Hidetora Hanada," *Sports Illustrated*, December 16, 2023, https://www.si.com/college/2023/12/16/colorado-state-football -hidetora-hanada-sumo-wrestler-scholarship.

12. Callum Jacques, "Active NFL Players with UK Roots: Six Players Who Are Living the American Dream," *SportsByte Sunderland*, March 9, 2023, https://sportsbyte.sunderland.ac.uk/2023/03/09/active-nfl-players-with-uk-roots-six -players-who-are-living-the-american-dream/.

13. Spenser T. Harrison, "NFL: All-Time Felon Team," Bleacher Report, May 28, 2008, https://bleacherreport.com/articles/25919-nfl-all-time-felon-team.

14. Moline, "Keanu Reeves' Body as Battleground," https://doi.org/10.1080 /19392397.2022.2063399.

15. Carson Blackwelder, "'John Wick' Director Chad Stahelski Talks Friend-ship with 'Older Brother' Keanu Reeves," *Good Morning America* official website, March 24, 2023, https://www.goodmorningamerica.com/culture /story/john-wick-director-chad-stahelski-keanu-reeves-friendship -98078945.

16. Zack Sharf and Clayton Davis, "Oscar Stunt Category Being Discussed in the Academy, 'John Wick' Director Says Talks Are 'Incredibly Positive,'" *Variety*, June 21, 2023, https://variety.com/2023/film/news/oscars-stunt -category-discussed-academy-john-wick-director-1235650105/.

17. Zack Sharf, "Keanu Reeves Gifted 'John Wick 4' Stunt Crew T-Shirts That Listed the Number of Times They Died in the Movie," *Variety*, March 29, 2023, https://variety.com/2023/film/news/keanu-reeves-gifted -john-wick-4-stunt-crew-shirts-deaths-1235568260/.

18. Zachary Harper, "Keanu Reeves's Sweet and Generous Gift to Matrix Crew Members Revealed," *Hello!*, January 11, 2022, https://www.hel lomagazine.com/celebrities/20220111130582/keanu-reeves-generous -gift-crew-family-friends-matrix-premiere/.

20. Somewhere Between the Power Lines and Palm Trees: Keanu Reeves Transcending the Silver Screen

1. R. J. Sternberg and J. C. Kaufman, "Intelligence (as Related to Creativity)," in *Encyclopedia of Creativity*, 2nd ed., ed. Mark A. Runco and Steven R. Pritzker (London: Academic Press, 2011), 667–671.

2. Angela Watercutter, "Keanu Will Never Surrender to the Machines," *Wired*, February 14, 2023, https://www.wired.com/story/keanu-reeves -chad-stahelski-interview/.

3. Malene Arpe, "Keanu Reeves Talks Memes, Hockey and Licks Burgers During Reddit AMA," *Toronto Star*, October 22, 2013, https://www.thestar.com /entertainment/stargazing/keanu-reeves-talks-memes-hockey-and-licks -burgers-during-reddit-ama/article_0fbf851e-e561-53e4-bd93-6aec08a19389 .html.

4. Lyle Slack, "Keanu's Excellent Adventure," *Maclean's*, January 23, 1995; Alex Pappademas, "The Legend of Keanu Reeves," *GQ*, April 15, 2019, https:// www.gq.com/story/the-legend-of-keanu-reeves.

5. Logan Culwell-Block, "Keanu Reeves and Alex Winter Set Excellent Broadway Adventure with Jamie Lloyd-Helmed *Waiting for Godot*," *Playbill*, August 1, 2024, https://playbill.com/article/keanu-reeves-and-alex-winter-set-excellent -broadway-adventure-with-jamie-lloyd-helmed-waiting-for-godot.

6. Reeves, Mailhouse, and Domrose, interview by Hagendorf, https://www .youtube.com/watch?v=LaLpGTtbwlM.   https://www.youtube.com /watch?v=2q7t23hSnCU.

7. Basem Wasef, "First Drive: Arch's New Cafe Racer-Inspired Bike Is a Chortling Brute That's Light on Its Feet," *Robb Report*, March 19, 2023, https:// robbreport.com/motors/motorcycles/first-drive-arch-motorcycles -1234817978/.

8. Wesley Reyneke, "Review: Riding the (Frankly Bonkers) Arch KRGT-1," Bike EXIF, November 11, 2019, https://www.bikeexif.com/arch-motorcycle -review; Nic de Sena, "2023 Arch 1s Review: The $128,000 Question," *Ultimate Motorcycling*, February 3, 2023, https://ultimatemotorcycling .com/2023/02/03/2023-arch-1s-review-the-128000-question/.

9. "New Super Bowl Pitch by Keanu Reeves," RIDE-CT, January 29, 2018, https://ride-ct.com/new-super-bowl-pitch-by-keanu-reeves/.

10. Micah Toll, "Keanu Reeves's Motorcycle Company ARCH Floats Idea of Building an Electric Motorcycle," Electrek, March 18 2022, https://electrek .co/2022/03/18/keanu-reeves-motorcycle-company-arch-floats-idea-of -building-an-electric-motorcycle/.

11. *Ode to Happiness* item page, Amazon.com, accessed September 9, 2024, https://www.amazon.com/Ode-Happiness-Keanu-Reeves/dp/3869302097.

12. Genevieve Hassan, "Keanu Reeves' Ode to Happiness," BBC, June 22, 2011, https://www.bbc.com/news/entertainment-arts-13838742.

13. *Ode to Happiness* item page, https://www.amazon.com/Ode-Happiness-Keanu-Reeves/dp/3869302097.

14. *Shadows* item page, Printed Matter, accessed September 9, 2024, https://www.printedmatter.org/catalog/48791/lightbox?table_id=5315.

15. X Artists' Books official website, accessed September 6, 2024, https://www.xartistsbooks.com/.

16. Marios M. Giakalaras and Christos P. Tsongidis, "Posthuman: Avatars in Videogames" (conference paper, University of the Aegean, 2015), 143–153, https://www.researchgate.net/profile/Christos-Tsongidis/publication/312029291_Posthuman_Avatars_in_Videogames/links/586ab4b808ae8fce4918e5d5/Posthuman-Avatars-in-Videogames.pdf.

17. Michał Kłosiński, "Ghosts and Mirrors: Devourment by the Other in *Cyberpunk 2077*," *Journal of Gaming & Virtual Worlds* 14 (April 2022): 67–84, https://doi.org/10.1386/jgvw_00052_1; Alice Fox, "The (Possible) Future of Cyborg Healthcare: Depictions of Disability in *Cyberpunk 2077*," *Science as Culture* 30, no. 4 (2021): 591–597, https://doi.org/10.1080/09505431.2021.1956888.

18. Jordan Raup, "Watch: Sofia Coppola Directs Keanu Reeves in 100th Anniversary Celebration of Suntory Whisky," Film Stage, May 28, 2023, https://thefilmstage.com/watch-sofia-coppola-directs-keanu-reeves-in-100th-anniversary-celebration-of-suntory-whisky/.

19. Brad Japhe, "Keanu Reeves Talks Whisky, (John) Wick and What He Stocks on His Bar Cart," *Rolling Stone*, June 5, 2023, https://www.rollingstone.com/product-recommendations/lifestyle/keanu-reeves-suntory-whisky-1234747097/.

21. Dust in the Wind: The Imaginary Philosophies of Keanu Reeves

1. See, for instance, Irwin, ed., *Matrix and Philosophy*.

2. Hadley Freeman, "*To the Bone* Confirms There Are (Almost) No Good Movies About Anorexia," *Guardian*, July 12, 2017, https://www.theguardian.com/film/2017/jul/12/to-the-bone-confirms-there-are-almost-no-good-movies-about-anorexia.

3. Naomi Fry, "Keanu Reeves Is Too Good for This World," *New Yorker*, June 3, 2019, https://www.newyorker.com/culture/culture-desk/keanu-reeves -is-too-good-for-this-world.

22. Presenting a Unified Critical Reeves Theory: Keanu Is a Cinematic Treasure

1. David Miguel Gray, "What Critical Race Theory Is—and What It Isn't," *Yes!*, July 7, 2021 https://www.yesmagazine.org/social-justice/2021/07/07 /critical-race-theory-what-is-it.

2. Sezin Koehler, "Twin Peaks and Brechtian Sensibilities in Modern Visual Media," *Dilettante Army*, August 2017, https://dilettantearmy.com/articles /twin-peaks-brechtian-sensibilities-modern-visual-media.

3. Ella Kemp, "Party On: 'Bill & Ted Face the Music' Urges Fans to Record Videos to Appear in the New Movie," *NME*, May 6, 2020, https://www.nme.com /news/film/bill-and-ted-face-the-music-fans-video-entries-2660579.

INDEX